CASES IN ADVERTISING

CASES IN ADVERTISING

Philip Ward Burton
Professor, School of Journalism
Indiana University

Richard Sandhusen
Rider College

Grid Publishing, Inc., Columbus, Ohio

Printed in the United States

1   2   3   4   ☒   4   3   2   1

Library of Congress Cataloging in Publication Data

Burton, Philip Ward
    Cases in advertising.

    (The Grid series in advertising/journalism)
    1. Advertising—United States—Case studies.
I. Sandhusen, Richard, joint author. II. Title.
HF5813.U6B83   659.1′0973   79-21532
ISBN O-88244-206-6

CONTENTS

PREFACE

Marketing and advertising persons are fond of saying the real world is different from the classroom. True enough. Yet the case-study approach to marketing and advertising *brings* the real world to the classroom. Students are shown what has happened. They face the situations of real life and they are asked what they would do to resolve those situations.

Most casebooks of the past have presented cases that were mostly on a rather lofty level. Predominantly, they were concerned with decision-making by upper-management or middle-management executives in large corporations. Thus, while students were intrigued and often fascinated by these glimpses behind the scenes of some of America's largest corporations, they were often subject to a feeling of irrelevance. It is difficult for a college-age student who has never worked at a meaningful job to find solutions for problems that have vexed brainy corporation executives. Many students, understandably, simply cannot put themselves behind the corporate desks, as it were.

Still, the challenge is stimulating and students often meet the challenge admirably. In this book, however, we offer the student a mixture of cases. Some of them are on the lofty level described and involve some of the largest and most aggressive corporations. Others make no pretense to loftiness. One, for example, concerns a young man just starting out. He runs a maintenance service for swimming pools. His is the modest sort of enterprise that a student can relate to. Another case asks the readers of the book to assess the efforts of a college class to evolve a campaign to increase enrollment for a college. Another is concerned with the competitive problems of a local supermarket.

Categorizing cases offers some difficulties. Rarely does a case fall neatly into one category, such as only Copy Strategy or only Media Selection. Time after time a case will involve two or more categories.

Thus, it is necessary to cross-index in order that the user of the book can fully utilize the variety of categories. In many instances, it is impossible to say which category is more important. A case might, for example, call for a creative decision, but in order to carry out that decision it may be necessary to settle upon a suitable media mix.

Frequently, marketing decisions are as important as advertising decisions. The student may need to consider the product, pricing, or channels of distribution before proposing what to do about advertising. Positioning the product comes up frequently as a challenge in the cases. Likewise, analysis of research findings will be required of the student just as it is of the advertising or marketing person.

As in most advertising and marketing situations, there are few occasions when there is any totally right answer to the questions asked at the end of each case. In some instances, the questions are quite specific. Usually, if the question is very specific, there will be a possibility that the "right" answer is fairly clear-cut. Some end-of-case questions, however, are quite broad. The student may be asked to "assess" the possibility for success if the company follows a certain course of action. The student assessment may take several directions. All of these can be right, or all can be wrong. Likewise, if students are asked to propose a media or creative strategy, they will probably have broad choices just as they would in real life.

In addition to giving students an interesting and instructive glimpse of actual situations, the case approach provides them with many examples. Thus, when students leave the classroom for the business world they may have a sense of déjà vu when faced with parallel situations in real-life experience and business solutions without having been in business. Without the cases, everything would be *totally* new.

LIST OF CASES

CROSS-REFERENCE LIST
OF PRINCIPLES DEMONSTRATED

Case	Positioning	Media strategy and selection	Research	Marketing strategy	Promotional mix	Creative direction or strategy	Client-agency relations	Page
1. Amerchol				X		X		159
2. AMF, Inc.				X		X		169
3. Avon Products			X	X		X		45
4. Berger Chem. (A)				X	X	X		165
5. Berger Chem. (B)		X		X	X			259
6. Bermuda Dept. of Tourism		X	X	X		X		263
7. Blue Nun Wine		X		X		X		153
8. Bush Boake Allen		X			X	X		127
9. Contac Cold Med.	X		X	X		X		71
10. Jack Daniel's	X	X	X	X		X		237
11. Dannon Yogurt		X	X			X		113
12. DeBeers, Ltd.		X			X	X		215
13. Dr Pepper	X			X		X		147
14. Eastman Kodak				X		X		187
15. Eaton Corp.	X	X				X		17
16. Edsel Automobile				X	X	X		107
17. Five Campaigns	X			X		X		143
18. Fram Corporation		X		X		X		269
19. Goodbuy Market	X		X	X	X			5
20. Gourm-egg	X	X		X				39
21. ITT Company			X	X		X		287
22. Irving Trust	X			X		X		197
23. Johnson Controls, Inc.	X	X	X	X		X		297
24. Kean College	X	X		X		X		57
25. King's Beer	X		X	X		X		25
26. Knox Gelatine	X	X	X	X				11
27. Marine Supply				X	X			139
28. Matson Trust							X	327
29. Meter-Rite Co.				X	X			137
30. Mobil Oil (A)						X		309
31. Mobil Oil (B)		X				X		313
32. The Money Store		X		X		X		221
33. The Natural Bank		X		X		X		65
34. N.Y. Times		X				X		251
35. Ourbank	X		X					31
36. Perdue Chickens		X	X	X		X		51
37. Preakness Shopping Mall	X			X	X			75
38. Prudential Ins.		X	X			X		227
39. Rapidata				X	X			89
40. Red Rose Tea	X	X	X	X		X		175
41. Rit Household Dyes				X	X			101
42. Rustic Acres		X		X	X		X	97
43. SCORE Hair Cream (A)	X	X		X	X	X		247
44. SCORE Hair Cream (B)			X		X			279
45. Sherman Toyota		X				X		201
46. ShopRite		X		X	X	X		119
47. St. Regis Paper Company			X			X		283
48. Slater & Associates		X				X		255
49. Solna Corp.		X			X			83
50. Thru-Mov		X		X		X		243
51. Trancol	X			X		X		191
52. Tru-Copy, Inc.		X				X	X	319
53. Union Carbide (Prestone)				X		X		183
54. United Airlines		X		X		X		209
55. Utilco Corp.			X		X			133
56. Vulcan Company		X				X		293

INTRODUCTION

The purpose of this casebook is to present a series of reasonably short cases that can serve as a focus for textbook concepts or real-life experiences to help students develop—

1) a realistic understanding of the options and approaches available to contemporary advertisers and their agencies in creating, implementing, and appraising advertising campaigns;
2) the critical insights required to recognize situations where the wrong option or approach might have been applied, or the right one misapplied.

Campaigns—some successful, some unsuccessful—which cover a broad range of products and services are presented. These include a friendly airline, an unhappy automobile, happy chickens, elongated eggs, a second-fiddle shopping center, a misunderstood soft drink, a furious oil company, a frustrated computer, a natural bank, and a potent cup of tea. These campaigns also cover a broad range of markets, from small, highly specialized segments of industrial and institutional markets to all-encompassing consumer mass markets. The size of the advertisers covered in these cases ranges from a one-man swimming-pool-servicing operation to multi-billion-dollar multinationals.

Regardless of size, scope, or product-market characteristics, however, the basic assumption is that there is a logical sequence of steps followed in planning advertising campaign strategy. This underlies all the cases in the seven sections of this casebook. The sequence of steps, which serves as the scheme for organizing these cases, encompasses the following activities: (1) positioning the product, (2) determining marketing-mix emphasis, (3) determining promotion-mix emphasis, (4) devising the appeal, (5) devising media mix, and (6) controlling campaign effectiveness. (The seventh section of the casebook covers agency-client relations.)

A brief introduction preceding each of these sections discusses the nature, purpose, and characteristics of the particular campaign-planning step, and how the featured cases pertain to this step.

This introduction, therefore, will discuss only in general terms the campaign-planning process, and will present the cases which illustrate this process.

CAMPAIGN PLANNING: LOGICAL, ORDERLY

As a starting point, it should be noted that the campaign-planning process is logical and orderly, in the sense that each step is a necessary prerequisite for the steps that follow it. Thus, for example, an understanding of how a product is (or should be) *positioned* is a necessary prerequisite for an understanding of the relative emphasis each element of the *marketing mix*—product, price, place, promotion—should receive in the campaign.

In turn, this understanding of the relative importance of each element of the marketing mix is necessary for an understanding of how much emphasis each element of the *promotion mix*—advertising, personal selling, publicity, sales promotion—should receive, and how the elements of both mixes can be integrated for strong persuasive impact.

Finally, this focus on the purpose and relative importance of each element of the promotion mix leads, logically, to a determination of (1) the *appeal* that best furthers the campaign's persuasive purpose, (2) the *media mix* that most efficiently conveys this appeal to target audiences, and (3) the standards against which performance can be measured in *appraising* campaign effectiveness.

One case from this book—the Goodbuy Supermarket case—illustrates, as well as any, the logic behind these campaign-planning steps. Essentially, this case (page 5) centers on campaign-planning decisions made by a large midwestern supermarket chain in opening a single outlet. Before undertaking any of these decisions pertaining to marketing/promotion mixes and creative/media/control strategies, however, Goodbuy's marketing management first performed a deep, detailed study to define its position both externally, among competing supermarkets, and internally, in the minds of potential patrons. This study included analyses of (1) the location, size, and sales volume of other competitors in the proposed Goodbuy outlet's trading area; (2) ethnic, racial, and economic characteristics of groups situated in various zones of the proposed trading area; and (3) attitudes and perceptions held by these groups toward potential Goodbuy competitors.

Only at this point, when sufficient information had been generated to identify and define a strong position for its services, did Goodbuy marketing people turn to the other steps in the campaign-planning process, including:

1) *Determining the marketing mix that would most effectively differentiate this outlet from competitive outlets and relate to the demographic/psychographic characteristics of its trading area constituency.* In Goodbuy's case, these marketing-mix considerations resulted, for example, in decisions to include a pharmacy, bakery, and liquor department in the new outlet, and to maintain price levels lower than the competitive average price.

2) *Determining the promotion mix best calculated to persuasively highlight the components of the marketing mix.* These promotion-mix decisions pertained to such diverse areas as how the "Grand Opening" ceremonies would be handled, what products (at what prices) would be featured during the first month, how radio and print media would announce the new outlet, and how publicity and couponing would contribute to the campaign's success.

3) *Determining creative and media strategies. What* to say in its promotion campaign, *how* to say it, and which media to use in delivering its campaign appeals were other decisions that could now be made based on information gathered, and decisions made, during the previous steps of the campaign-planning process. Additionally, realistic campaign objectives could be set, as well as procedures for measuring performance against standards (one standard that was easily achieved was the first week's sales, which exceeded the $300,000 expectation by $89,000).

HOW CASES ILLUSTRATE CAMPAIGNS

In illustrating the steps of the campaign-planning process, there is, as might be expected, considerable overlapping of content among the cases in the seven sections of this casebook. Indeed, many of these cases describe entire campaigns, from initial research to identify viable positions, to post-campaign research to measure campaign effectiveness in entrenching products in these positions.

For this reason, each of these illustrative cases has been slotted into its category on the basis of the planning *emphasis* each exhibits, not under the assumption that the case just focuses on one step of the process.

Thus, in part I of this casebook, "The Positioning Decision," you will read about research undertaken on behalf of Knox Gelatine to find both a product and a position in the competition-cluttered chocolate drink market and on behalf of a brewery to carve out positions favorable to the young, liberated female market. Other cases in this first section focus on research undertaken to position new products in existing markets (Goodbuy), or existing products in new markets (Eaton and Ourbank).

In part II, "Building The Marketing Mix," you will read about marketing-mix decisions, based on positioning research, designed to attract new markets (Gourm-egg, Avon, Kean College), promote new products (Natural Bank, Contac), or overcome negative attitudes (Perdue, Preakness).

Part III narrows the focus to the promotion-mix component of the marketing mix, examining cases where advertising works closest with the direct selling (Solna, Rustic Acres), or with publicity (Rit, Edsel), practically by itself (Shoprite, Dannon Yogurt), or with practically all the other elements of the promotion mix (Rapidata, Bush Boake Allen).

The cases in part IV, "Creating The Appeal," illustrate how different appeals tie in with different positioning strategies and relate to differing marketing and promotion mixes. Thus, for firms pioneering products in new markets (Dr Pepper, Red Rose), or attempting to increase market share in existing markets (Amerchol, Irving Trust, Sherman Toyota), the emphasis is on the differential. Other products, assured a leadership position in their fields (Prestone, Eastman Kodak), de-emphasize differentials in appeals of a reminder nature; while still others (Trancol, AMF) craft appeals to cover a broad family of products.

Part V cases examine the thinking behind costly decisions involved in selecting the most effective media mix for carrying the appeal to target markets, and making reach-frequency-continuity tradeoffs to assure the most productive use of this mix. As with decisions in the "appeal" area, these media decisions are strongly dependent on product-market-promotion decisions made earlier in the campaign-planning process. For example, "unsought" products sold in mass markets (Prudential, The Money Store) tend to emphasize reach and continuity, while short, one-shot campaigns aimed at such markets ("SportsMonday") stress reach and frequency. Other campaigns tailor media decisions to audience demographics—for example, male-oriented media to carry male-oriented appeals for Fram, SCORE, and Jack Daniel's. Still other media decisions are based largely on regional decisions (Slater and Associates, Thru-Mov) or seasonal decisions (DeBeers, Bermuda).

In part VI, the case emphasis is on tools and techniques for appraising the effectiveness of entire campaigns, or specific components of such campaigns, such as the appeal or the media mix. With these cases, the campaign-planning process, which started with research to identify and define strong positions, comes full circle with research to identify and define strengths and weaknesses in campaigns designed to entrench these positions. Mostly, this research involves tests and more tests. St. Regis, for example, undertakes a number of tests to measure the impact of four creative concepts; SCORE hair cream undertakes tests to measure an entire promotion mix; ITT tests the effectiveness of a broad-based advertising campaign designed to "counter an antagonistic drift in public opinion"; and, in a lively controversy, Mobil Oil fails the test of acceptability of two television networks and, in turn, fails one of these networks on its own standards of "fair play."

Finally, in part VII, two cases examine the advertiser-agency relations which are so vital to the effective functioning of the campaign-planning process. In the first case, Tru-Copy, the problem is deciding whether or not to take on a client; in the second case, Matson Trust, the problem is deciding whether or not to resign an account. In the process of analyzing these problems, both cases offer insights into what a productive client-agency relationship should be, but too frequently isn't.

In preparing this textbook, the authors are especially indebted to the many advertisers and advertising agencies who not only made these cases available, but also took the time and effort to proofread them and made useful suggestions for improving their interest and usefulness in the education process.

PART I
THE POSITIONING
DECISION

Logically, the campaign-planning process begins with an understanding of the product being sold, whether it is a vacation, or a chicken, or a controversial idea. With equal logic, it follows that this understanding extends well beyond the dimensions of this product itself. For example, in creating a persuasive appeal, or piecing together an efficient media schedule, it would certainly help to know something about the nature and needs of the people who could use this product, and their attitudes and perceptions toward other products they could use in its stead—in short, the "position" the product occupies in markets and minds.

OLD CLICHÉ, NEW MEANING

This, then, is what this first group of cases is all about: "positioning" the product so that the right product is delivered at the right price and place to the right group of prospective customers. Additionally, the promotion for this product—whether delivered by a salesman, the mailman, a television announcer, or a newspaper—will be saying the right things about this product so as to effectively differentiate it from other products while stimulating interest and perhaps even buying action on the part of these prospects.

The key word, though, is "positioning," an advertising cliche that has been around for a long time but has recently been taking on a new meaning, or at least a new emphasis.

EXTERNAL vs. INTERNAL POSITIONING

Specifically, where once the emphasis was on the position the product occupied *in the marketplace* with respect to competitive products, more recently the emphasis has shifted to the position the product occupies in *people's minds*, again in relation to other products which also occupy niches in these collective crania.

Two cases from this casebook illustrate the significant differences between *external* positioning, with its emphasis on share of market, and *internal* positioning, with its emphasis on share of mind.

The first case, on the Edsel automobile advertising campaign (page 107), illustrates the essential characteristics of external positioning. Here, a decision was made to position a new automobile among competitive automobiles in order to plug a gaping hole through which a significant portion of Ford's market was dropping.

Here's how a spokesman for Ford's agency at the time, Foote, Cone & Belding, explains the rationale behind this decision:

> Actually the Edsel was positioned as a medium priced car. In the early 50's, the market was divided into three fairly well defined segments, low priced cars, medium priced cars, and high priced luxury cars. By 1955 the medium priced cars had grown to approximately 36% of the units sold. Approximately 80 percent of the people who had stepped up from a Chevrolet to a higher priced car stayed within the General Motors family via a purchase of an Oldsmobile, Pontiac, Buick or even the higher priced Cadillac. . . . In contrast, the Ford Motor Company held on to only 25% of the people who stepped up from a Ford car, with only one medium priced car, the Mercury, versus three medium priced cars for General Motors. Hence, the basic reason for introducing the Edsel was to "create another stall in the marketplace."

One interpretation frequently offered for the demise of the Edsel was that it didn't have the same well-conceived position in people's minds that it had in the marketplace. As this case brings out, most attitudes toward the Edsel were either ambiguous or downright negative.

The second case, on Menley & James' anti-cold medication Contac (page 71), dramatically illustrates the opportunities and problems attendant on an internal positioning strategy. Interestingly, the share-of-mind position that this product occupied in relation to its major competitors (Dristan and Coricidin) was not at all what the campaign planners originally had in mind. Yet this position was so powerful that Contac seized the lion's share of market within a year of its introduction. Then, ironically, this internally positioned image of the product became a barrier to further growth, and the agency undertook to *re*position the product internally so its image was consistent with external realities.

WHAT *IS* EFFECTIVE POSITIONING?

Understanding the nature of, and differences between, internal and external positioning strategies provides a conceptual framework for both understanding and critically appraising the cases in this first section, which basically focus on research undertaken to identify and define viable internal and external positions.

Thus, while all the research undertaken in these cases is concerned, to some extent, with both internal and external positions, the emphasis shifts sharply from case to case.

For example, in the Goodbuy and Knox Gelatine cases, the primary research emphasis is on identifying and defining strong positions in external markets—in the Goodbuy case, among more than 50 other large and small competitive supermarkets, and in the Knox case, among a dozen or so producers in the keenly competitive chocolate milk products market. The implicit reasoning behind this research is that if no viable external position exists, why even bother searching for a viable internal position? (A question that, in turn, might be questioned by the reader.)

At the other extreme, the research focus of another case—Eaton—is on identifying strong internal positions for its products. In the Eaton case, a number of strong external positions occupied by "highly rated" quality products did not have an equally solid internal counterpart: at best, people had only the fuzziest concept of what the Eaton Corporation was and did. Here, the research aim was to define an approach for sharpening Eaton's image as a "modern, dynamic corporation."

Two other cases in this section illustrate research approaches designed to accomplish the often fruitless task of internally *repositioning* products by changing long-held, deeply entrenched attitudes and perceptions. *King's Beer*, for example, undertakes research to transform beer into a women's drink, and *Ourbank* undertakes research to make itself a lot less sedate and stodgy in the perceptions of its publics. (Later in the casebook, the Natural Bank case illustrates the extent to which research of this sort can reposition a bank.)

1

GOODBUY SUPERMARKET

The Goodbuy supermarket in Oakdale, Michigan, occupies 42,000 square feet of the total of 79,000 square feet available in its shopping center locale. Store hours are from 8 a.m. to 11 p.m., seven days a week (township statutes prohibit 24-hour operation).

Approximately a year before the Oakdale Goodbuy supermarket opened, however, a research team from the Grand Markets Corporation (Goodbuy's parent company) was gathering information on economic, demographic, social, and competitive characteristics of the area in order to answer questions such as these:

1) In terms of area ethnic composition, what facilities (such as a delicatessen or liquor store) and product lines should be represented in the new Goodbuy outlet?
2) In terms of the geographic distribution of various ethnic and economic groups, what media should be used to promote these facilities and product lines?
3) Based on an understanding of facilities offered and products carried by competitive stores in the new outlet's trading area, and consumer attitudes toward these competitive outlets, how might Goodbuy's marketing mix (i.e., products stocked, services offered, prices charged, promotional appeals, etc.) be planned to fill competitive gaps?
4) Based on all of the foregoing considerations, how much business could the new store expect to do in an average week?
5) What effect would the sales volume generated by this new outlet have on the sales volume of other Goodbuy outlets in the area?

Following are some of the key findings of this research effort, all of which affected, directly or indirectly, the advertising planning effort.

POPULATION TRENDS

According to census figures, more than 150,000 people live within eight minutes of the proposed Oakdale Goodbuy, with practically no population growth shown during the previous five years.

In terms of distances that these people would have to travel to get to the proposed Goodbuy, the population breakdown was as follows:

Minutes from Proposed Goodbuy	Population	Population, Cumulative
0-2	8,200	
2-4	36,500	44,700
4-6	61,100	105,800
6-8	52,000	157,800

ETHNIC COMPOSITION

The ethnic breakdown of the population located within eight minutes' travel time of the proposed new outlet was as follows: black, 20 percent; Italian, 16 percent; Spanish, 10 percent; Jewish, 8 percent; Polish, 7 percent; other, 39 percent.

However, when this ethnic breakdown was considered in terms of traveling distances from the proposed new Goodbuy, a different picture emerged:

1) Forty-seven percent of the population residing within four minutes of the new Goodbuy outlet were of Italian descent.

2) Of the 38,500 blacks residing within the overall eight-minute traveling area, 35,700 lived between four and eight minutes from the proposed new outlet and accounted for roughly one-third of the total population in this zone.

3) Of the 16,000 people of Spanish descent living within the overall eight-minute area, nearly 75 percent, or 12,000, resided in the four-to-eight minute zone and accounted for 10 percent of the total population in that zone.

4) While only 13,800 (8 percent) of the total population of the eight-minute zone were Jewish, 80 percent of this total lived within four minutes of the proposed new outlet.

INCOME

The research team also discovered that the median family income in the overall eight-minute zone—$13,500—was slightly above the norm for the entire state. However, because of sharp variations among different groups within this area, income was examined in depth on a town-by-town basis. Following are some of the more significant results of this study.

Royal Park (predominantly Spanish descent)	$ 8,900
Harpur Village (predominantly black)	12,200

East Rapids (predominantly Italian)   17,600
Oakdale Hills (predominantly Jewish)   18,800

COMPETITIVE FACTORS

This investigation focused on both qualitative considerations (i.e., consumers' perceptions of various competitors) and quantitative considerations (sales volume, share of market of various competitors). Among the key findings:

Sales volume

Following is a summary of sales volume totals among the higher-volume supermarkets in the proposed Goodbuy's eight-minute primary trading zone.

Store	Sales Volume (Weekly)
Oakdale A&P	$250—275,000
Fernwood Shopwell	200—250,000
Grubtown	175—200,000
Harpur Village A&P	130—150,000
Royal Park Shopwell	125,000
Foodfair	100,000

Among these six competitors, the closest to the proposed Goodbuy location (one minute) was the Oakdale A&P. The other five stores on this list were located in outlying areas of the proposed Goodbuy trading area, between six and eight minutes away. And since these five large stores were located in the same two-minute time band, the researchers concluded that there was a strong likelihood that they would act as trading area "cut-offs," shortstopping Goodbuy's customers from beyond the six-minute circumference. Thus, while the typical Goodbuy outlet got between 20 and 30 percent of its business from the area beyond the eight-minute circumference, it was felt that the Oakdale Goodbuy was likely to get in the neighborhood of only 10 percent.

In addition to the above-mentioned "Big Six" competitors, the research team also developed the following information on 48 smaller competitors in the eight-minute area.

Store name and location
Weekly sales
Sales/square feet
Number of cash registers
Type of meat trays (foam vs. clear)
Produce (pre-pack vs. loose)
Deli (service vs. self-service)
Seafood (fresh or frozen)

Bakery (in-store vs. vendor)
Sunday—open or closed
General appearance
Liquor department
Pharmacy

Among these 48 smaller competitors, the researchers took note of DiFranco's in East Rapids, approximately two minutes away from the proposed Goodbuy. With only 6,000 square feet of selling space, the store was doing between $74,000 and $90,000 per week. Also, according to the research findings, DiFranco's had built up a loyal clientele among middle- and upper-income groups, and had attained and maintained an excellent reputation for quality and service. As compared to customers at other outlets (including the nearby Oakdale A&P, which presented a generally "seedy" appearance), the DiFranco customer would probably be least likely to transfer to the new Goodbuy. Neither the DiFranco nor the Oakdale A&P outlet featured in-store baked goods or an in-store pharmacy, and the DiFranco outlet had no liquor department—all planned for the new Goodbuy.

SALES VOLUME PROJECTIONS

Based on the above research findings, plus historical data on the experience of other Goodbuy outlets, the research team projected the following figures pertaining to potential sales at the new Goodbuy outlet, and the impact these sales would have on other Goodbuy outlets within, or just beyond, the eight-minute trading zone.

Oakdale Goodbuy

At the end of its first year's operation, the Oakdale outlet should be doing approximately $300,000 per week in sales, more than any of their competitors in the eight-minute primary trading zone.

Impact on Area Goodbuys

The researchers estimated that the new Goodbuy would drain the following sales volumes from other Goodbuy outlets in its general trading area: (1) Harpur Village Goodbuy—between $5,000 and $10,000 per week, (2) Smoky Rapids Goodbuy—between $15,000 and $20,000 per week, (3) Unity Goodbuy—between $5,000 and $8,000 per week. On the average, this sales volume loss represented about 8 percent of the total volume generated by each of these outlets.

For all of these Goodbuy outlets, however, the researchers concluded that a significant portion of the lost business could be regained with aggressive promotion programs. This was especially true in the case of the Smoky Rapids outlet, which was situated in the center of a densely populated area.

Figure 1-1.

Prices effective Sunday, October 10 thru Saturday, October 16
So that we may serve all our customers, we reserve the right to limit sales of any item. Items offered for sale not available in case lots. Certain items not available where prohibited by law. Items and prices valid only at Pathmark Supermarkets. Not responsible for typographical errors. Some pictures shown in this circular are for design purposes and do not necessarily represent items on sale.

☑ **Hormel Imported Polish Cooked Ham**
Freshly sliced
59¢
¼-lb.

☑ **Hebrew National Griddle Franks**
Kosher
$1.49 lb.

☑ **Hillshire Farm Polska Kielbasa**
$1.49 lb.

Cold Cuts
☑ Pastrami Lean (By the Chunk) (Sliced on Request) lb. $1.49
☑ Corned Beef Chef Mark Cooked (Freshly Sliced) ¼-lb. 65¢
☑ Hard Salami Hormel Burgermeister (Freshly Sliced) ¼-lb. 59¢
☑ Chicken Roll ¼-lb. $1.09
☐ Wunderbar Wide Bologna (Freshly Sliced) Artificial Casing ¼-lb. 59¢

Cheese & Salads
☑ Fresh Salad Potato Salad, Macaroni Salad or Cole Slaw lb. 49¢
☑ Kraft Swiss Casino Domestic ¼-lb. 99¢
☑ Wine Cheddar Cheese ¼-lb. 89¢
☑ Dak Danish Havarti Cheese ¼-lb. 99¢
☑ Provolone Domestic Cheese ¼-lb. 89¢

Seafood (Fresh Fish Available Wed. thru Friday)
☑ Fresh Cod Fillet lb. $1.59
☑ Fresh Whiting Pan Ready lb. 99¢
☑ Clams Casino or Stuffed Clams Crystal Bay - Frozen 1½-oz. pkg. 89¢
☐ Frozen Smelts Highliner Eviscerated 1-lb. pkg. 79¢
☐ Sea Trout Fresh Pan Ready ¼-lb. $1.39

Advertisement with ethnic slant.

QUESTIONS

1. Should Goodbuy open the proposed store in view of the heavy competition it faced?
2. Should the ethnic composition of the area be a factor to consider in the marketing and advertising planning? If not, why not? If yes, which ethnic groups should receive the most attention in Goodbuy's planning?
3. If you were planning the character of the promotional approach to be used by the proposed Goodbuy store, should it be—
   a. highly competitive in prices, or middle-of-the-road?
   b. concentrated simply on offering low prices, or should it draw as well on sales promotion techniques such as coupons, games, trading stamps, cents-off deals, and the like?
   c. slanted toward ethnic groups, or should the marketing area be treated as a homogenous entity?
   d. dignified and reflective of a quality image, or should it be unsubtle and concerned with price more than quality?

2

THOMAS J. LIPTON, INC. "KNOX GELATINE"

As the leader in the unflavored gelatine field for more years than most people could remember, there seemed to be no compelling reason for the Knox Gelatine Company of Johnstown, New York, to undertake a program of product line diversification. After all, reasoned Knox's management, why risk confusing customers by burying Knox's hard-won image as "the original" unflavored gelatine under a plethora of "me too" products?

On the other hand, the fickle, unpredictable future has a way of knocking the props out from under even the sturdiest product leaders, and simple business prudence also suggested to Knox management a policy of at least exploring alternate product possibilities.

That, then, was the decision: that Knox marketing management, working closely with its advertising agency, D'Arcy, MacManus and Masius, would undertake to identify new product possibilities (if such existed) which would be consistent with the following policy guidelines laid down by Knox management.

1) Any new product investigation must be restricted to the food field.
2) Any new product investigation should be restricted to an area not competitive with Knox's basic "unflavored gelatine" field.
3) Any new product investigation should be restricted to an area that would make effective use of Knox's mass production facilities, and would produce profits within two years after entry into the market.
4) Initially, at least, all new product research and development activities should focus on one product at a time.

Within the context of this policy mandate, one field that seemed to represent an attractive opportunity was the $200 million chocolate drink market, and it was in this area that the Knox-D'Arcy team decided to initiate their investigation into new product possibilities.

Working together, the team dug up the following facts and figures relating to the five submarkets (i.e., chocolate sodas, shake mixes, instant breakfasts, syrups, and sweetened cocoas) comprising this large market.

Chocolate Sodas

Target Market. Primarily youth market (8 to 18 years old) and blue collar workers.

Total market size. Approximately $30 million.

Geographic distribution pattern. More than 90 percent of total sales are restricted to eleven East Coast states, with 50 percent of this total restricted to the New York metropolitan area.

Competition. For practical planning purposes, the only real competitive influence in this submarket is the "Yoo Hoo" company, whose chocolate soda totally dominates the East Coast territory. All other chocolate sodas are local or regional brands.

Advertising. Total advertising expenditures by all firms in this submarket totalled a minuscule $312,000 with more than 90 percent of this total representing the "Yoo Hoo" company's budget.

Shake Mixes

Mixed with milk, these powders produce drinks that manufacturers claim are similar to soda-fountain milk shakes.

Target market. The largest user segment is the 18-or-under "youth" segment, which accounts for 40 percent of the total population of the country.

Total market size. Roughly the same as the "chocolate soda" market—$30 million.

Geographic distribution pattern. Unlike the chocolate soda market, this market is national rather than regional in scope.

Competition. Also unlike the chocolate soda market, which is dominated by a single brand ("Yoo Hoo"), with a number of regional and local brands trailing far behind, the competitive situation in this submarket features a number of strong national brands locked in lively competition. Also contrasting sharply with the chocolate soda market are the uniformly high promotional expenditures characterizing brands in this field.

The following table shows the relationships between advertising expenditures and market share among the five national brands that comprise this entire submarket.

Brand	Market Share	Advertising Expenditures
Great Shakes	40 percent	$ 2.2 million
Quick Shakes	20 percent	1 million
Frosted Shakes	20 percent	2.3 million
Moo Juice	15 percent	353 thousand
Shakes Ala Mode	5 percent	146 thousand

Media Mix. The four largest competitors in this submarket all emphasize national television, with special emphasis on Saturday morning "youth" programs. Advertising expenditures in magazine and newspaper advertising among these leaders are negligible. A "Moo Juice" radio campaign proved ineffective.

The fifth competitor, "Shakes Ala Mode," limits its advertising expenditures to newspapers and women's "homemaker" magazines, with an advertising appeal geared to the concerns of mothers who will presumably be purchasing the shake mixes for their youth-market offspring.

Instant Breakfasts

These powder mixes are quite similar in composition and use to the shake mixes, except that they don't thicken quite as much when mixed with milk, and contain a number of nutritional elements said to include upwards of one-fourth of the minimum adult requirement for vitamins and minerals.

Target market. Unlike the orientation of the shake mix market toward the youth "junk food" segment, the thrust among the instants is toward families with incomes of more than $15,000 a year. These families have children in the 5-to-15 age bracket. Within these families, the market thrust is focused on mothers who decide what family members will eat and drink (this segment, incidentally, is practically identical with the "heavy users of cereals" segment).

Market size. About $40 million.

Geographic distribution patterns. An interesting combination of the situations characterizing the "soda" and the "mix" markets: like the "soda" market, it is dominated by a single brand—Carnation—which accounts for about 75 percent of total sales and is the only brand marketed nationally. However, like the "mix" market, it also includes a number of strong competitors that compete head-on with the leader and are eager to attain national distribution status.

Advertising. Here is how the advertising expenditures of the four leaders in this field compare to the share-of-market of each:

Brand	Market Share	Advertising Expenditures
Carnation	70 percent	$3.4 million
Pillsbury	10 percent	2 million
Foremost	5 percent	326 thousand
Mead Johnson	5 percent	280 thousand

One of the reasons for the high advertising expenditures among competitors in this submarket is that, with a 75 percent annual growth rate over a five-year period, it is the fastest growing of all the chocolate drink submarkets.

Media Mix. The only two competitors using national TV, and using it exclusively of all other media, are Carnation and Pillsbury. All the other competitors rely primarily on local TV.

Syrups

In general, this product combines the characteristics of the two previous products: like the mixes, they are milk additives; like the instants, they are generally promoted for their nutritional value.

Target market. Almost totally made up of the "younger child" segment (i.e., under ten years of age), which comprises approximately 25 percent of the population of the country.

Market size. The largest of all the chocolate drink submarkets, with more than $50 million in annual sales.

Geographic distribution patterns. The two brands that dominate this market—Bosco and Clanky—are also the only two brands that have achieved national distribution. Competition from regional and local brands is a negligible factor.

Competition. A single product, Bosco, dominates the market with a 72 percent share. The other major competitor, Clanky, runs a sickly second with a 22 percent market share. Packaging of both these products reflects the composition of the "younger child" market: Clanky comes garbed in a plastic robot suit, and Bosco in both a clown costume and a standard plastic jar.

Media mix. This also reflects the makeup of the market, or, more precisely, the limited vocabulary of the "younger child" segment (one-third of whom can't read). Thus, TV is the only medium used by either, with commercials limited exclusively to the Saturday morning children's "ghetto."

Sweetened Cocoas

This is perhaps the most competitive of all the chocolate drink submarkets, with four national manufacturers—Hershey, Nestle, Borden, and National Sugar—accounting, collectively, for about 95 percent of the $40 million market, but with no clearly dominant leader among the four.

Target market. The nature of the largest market segment for these cocoas—children between 5 and 14 years of age—is reflected in the lively, colorful packaging of these products.

Advertising. One of the unusual aspects of this submarket is that two of the competitors—Hershey (the leader) with 38 percent of the market and Borden with 20 percent—do no advertising at all; while National Sugar, with 10 percent of the $40 million market, spends only $193,000 in advertising (all on local TV).

Nestle, the runner-up, with 32 percent of the total market, is the only really big spender in the group, investing $1 million in TV, practically all for programs of interest to children and teenagers.

Because these four companies dominate both national markets and distribution channels, the national market is generally considered too difficult and costly to penetrate successfully.

Growth trends. For a number of years, this had been the fastest growing of all the submarkets, with annual increases averaging 21 percent. However, in recent years, this growth rate has diminished to less than 10 percent.

WHAT THE AGENCY RECOMMENDED

Taking all of the above marketing facts and figures into consideration, and processing them through both human and electronic craniums, the research agency came up with the following summarized recommendations.

1) Regardless of which submarket (if any) Knox planned to enter, it should plan to invest at least one million dollars in advertising and sales promotion alone during the first two years.
2) Although all the markets seemed to represent a sizable entry risk, the sweetened cocoa market, nearing saturation, represented probably the largest risk of all.
3) To somewhat mitigate this risk element, Knox should plan to

introduce the new product entry on a regional basis first, ideally in the New England region because of its density of population, its proximity to Knox's manufacturing operations, and the fact that cold weather would tend to keep members of target markets glued to their TV sets during a longer portion of the year.

4) Probably the least risky submarket to enter would be the chocolate soda market, although Knox would somehow have to contrive to avoid the mistakes made by an earlier entry by the Pepsi Cola company called Devil Shake, which failed abjectly.

5) If it was decided to enter this submarket, media emphasis should be on local TV, with the majority of advertising between 3:00 p.m. and 6:00 p.m. to catch the youth and blue-collar-worker markets.

QUESTIONS

1. Although all the submarkets represent some entry risk, which one seems to be the most risky? Which one appears to be the least risky?
2. What media strategy should be used if the least risky entry is introduced?
3. Should the new product be introduced nationally, or regionally? If regionally, what region should be used? Why?

EATON CORPORATION

What is the Eaton Corporation, what does it manufacture, how big is it, and what is its mission in life?

Among other things, it is a well-diversified Midwestern capital goods producer that ranks number 110 on the *Fortune 500*. In a typical year, it produces $1.75 billion in sales. It used to be called Eaton, Yale and Towne before it changed its name. Those who know the company well usually rate it highly, especially in the quality of products and management.

As an audit of corporate reputation made painfully clear, however, very few people knew the company well, or at all.

To quote Dennis Ritzel, Eaton's manager of national advertising:

The results surprised and disappointed us. We were even more lost in the corporate jungle than we thought.

We found that ... a great many among our key publics—including members of the business and financial communities and prospective shareholders—had little awareness of Eaton Corporation, or were confused as to what we did.

Particularly bruising to the corporate ego was the fact that many, even among those who were aware of us, estimated our annual sales to be less than a third of what they were.

Many people who should have been better acquainted with us saw us simply as an automotive parts manufacturer, or as a lockmaker or supplier of fork lift trucks, and those who knew just a little about us were inclined to give us low marks ... our research and development capabilities went largely unnoticed, and we were not perceived as a modern, dynamic corporation, although our growth rivalled that of any major company.

PERFORMANCE NO LONGER ENOUGH

Even granting that Eaton had a fuzzy image, why did Eaton's management feel it was worth a multi-million-dollar advertising and sales promotion effort to clear it up?

In answer, Ritzel notes, first, that—

Time was when a business like the old and much smaller Eaton could mind its own affairs and stay quietly in business. "Concentrate on performance, and reputation will take care of itself" was a standard saying.

But performance is no longer enough. People today demand that pursuit of profits and accountability to society go hand in hand.

We believed then, and believe even more now, that with the increasing difficulty in raising capital it becomes imperative that a corporation communicate broadly all facets of its stewardship.

So we had to bridge the awareness gap between what Eaton is and what it was perceived to be, and it was clear that we had to do it in as little time as possible.

CCD SHAPES A CAMPAIGN

To help determine how to bridge this awareness gap, Eaton's management turned to the Corporate Communications Division (CCD) of its advertising agency, J. Walter Thompson. Together they shaped a corporate image campaign which featured a number of communications tools directed to selected target audiences ("everything from corporate print campaigns to a magazine for truckers"), but which centered on a $1.5 million annual TV budget.

Here is how Ritzel—and CCD—rationalize this emphasis on television:

It may not be the right corporate medium for every company, but for the company that wants to make a significant impact and do it as quickly as possible, television's power is unsurpassed.

It's an ideal umbrella under which other programs can be synchronized. Employees take great pride in the sponsorship of good programming, in a way that doesn't happen in any other medium. And, finally, it is the medium of greatest social magnitude because of its extraordinary reach.

So our reasoning justifying our TV schedule went something like this:

First, we really wanted to reach a broad spectrum of publics with our corporate communications program, and advertising would play a leading role in this program.

Second, instant celebrity, or target public awareness in the shortest possible time, had high priority.

E·A·T·N

Figure 3-1.

60-SECOND TV COMMERCIAL- "CENTER PIVOT IRRIGATION" QEAD 7066

Here's a perfect place to grow corn.

It rains every day-- and just the right amount.

This is why. It's called center pivot irrigation. It sweeps around in a circle, half a mile across. Regular as clockwork.

That calls for steady, reliable power at every wheel-- and a lot of companies are competing to supply it.

This is Eaton's solution. Lightweight hydraulic motors.

Dirt and moisture don't bother them.

They just keep running and running and running:

Reliability. At Eaton we build it into everything we make.

Like our hydrostatic transmissions, which provide smooth, precise control on everything from combines to earthmovers.

Or our materials handling equipment...

truck and automobile components...

appliance controls...

industrial drives. If we want to keep growing, we have to keep building things to last.

In American business that's the way it is.

Because if we don't, our competitors will.
In American business, that's the way it is.

Figs. 3-1, 3-2, 3-3, and 3-4 are photoboards of Eaton Corporation television commercials that give some idea of the variety of important products made by the company. The corporation's problem, as this case points out, was how to obtain greater recognition as the maker of products. Reprinted with permission from Eaton Corporation.

Figure 3-2.

EAT·N

60-SECOND TV COMMERCIAL — "FORK-LIFT TRUCKS" QEAD 7056

The cost of just about everything keeps going up.

But there is one thing that's helping to hold it down . . .

we're finding better ways to move things. Competition makes that inevitable.

New equipment . . . like this Yale lift truck from Eaton Corporation . . . has to be more reliable, and more efficient.

Because businessmen don't buy lift trucks for fun.

They buy them to increase productivity and cut handling costs.

And that's what Eaton equipment does . . . with the broadest line in the business . . .

with more new lift truck models than anybody else . . .

And with everything from hoists to automated warehouses . . .

to Timberjack log skidders.

It's the same with most of the things Eaton makes. Components for trucks . . .

And for agricultural equipment . . . appliance controls . . .

industrial drives. We're selling to businessmen, and they're the toughest customers of all.

In American business that's the way it is.

So only the toughest competitors survive. In American business, that's the way it is.

EAT·N

Reprinted with permission from Eaton Corporation.

Figure 3-3.

EAT•N

60 SECOND TV COMMERCIAL — "VINTAGE TRUCK" REVISED QEAD 6056

In 1911, this kind of thing used to happen all the time.

So Joe Eaton and Viggo Torbensen started building axles specially designed for trucks. That was a breakthrough.

But in American business, one breakthrough is never enough.

You always have competitors trying to catch up. Your customers demand more . . .

Bigger payloads — higher speeds. And you do it — or someone else will.

So trucks have come a long way . . . a lot of it on Eaton axles.

And with Eaton brakes, air conditioning, and transmissions.

Today, Eaton has expanded into many other businesses.

But the same principle applies.

We have to keep topping our own improvements or our competitors will.

In American business, that's the way it is.

Reprinted with permission from Eaton Corporation.

Figure 3-4.

E·T·N

60-SECOND TV COMMERCIAL- "PLANNED OBSOLESCENCE REV." QEAD 7076

Eaton Proving Ground
Marshall, Michigan

Eaton Proving Ground
Marshall, Michigan

SPOKESMAN: Some people say American business designs things to wear out fast. "Planned obsolescence."

I'm not sure you get away with that in any business for long....

E.M. de Windt
Chairman, Eaton Corporation

you lay yourself wide open to the first competitor whose product holds up... and I know it won't work in the businesses we're into at Eaton.

Take the axles and transmission we built for this truck.

We expect them to go hundreds of thousands of miles before an overhaul, and so do our customers.

And when we build the clutches for a tugboat that pushes around

loads like this, they'd better be able to take it.

(SFX) The same goes for our Yale lift trucks.

At Eaton we're proud of the way our products hold up. But pride isn't the only reason we build them this way. We've got lots of competition.

In American business that's the way it is.

So if our products didn't last, neither would we. In American business, that's the way it is.

E·T·N

Next, social responsibility was also high on our list of corporate objectives.

In short, we wanted to establish a corporate personality that embodied excitement, warmth, and modernity, and the expense of television was within our spending power, with money also available for other elements of our corporate image campaign.

WHAT KIND OF PROGRAMMING?

When the decision had been made to use television programming as the centerpiece of Eaton's corporate image campaign, the logical question followed: What *kind* of television programming?

QUESTION

If you were the Corporate Communications Division of the J. Walter Thompson advertising agency, what kind of programming would you recommend for the Eaton company? Be specific. Explain your reasoning.

4

KING'S BEER COMPANY

What kind of an appeal (or appeals) would be most appropriate for an advertising campaign designed to persuade women to drink beer (or, if they were already beer-drinkers, to drink *more* beer)?

This was the challenging query that preoccupied marketing management at King's Beer Company when the company first introduced its new "light" beer. Their reasoning was that, with only half the calories of standard beers, light beer was a natural for different segments of the diet-conscious female market. However, preliminary research indicated that women had rarely, if ever, been on the receiving end of campaigns promoting beer. It just wasn't the type of advertising one associated with the *Ladies' Home Journal* or *Good Housekeeping*, for example. Indeed, at the time King's was planning its light beer advertising, practically the only association between beer and women occurred when women appeared as window dressing in advertising campaigns aimed at various segments of the beer-drinking male market.

HOW TO APPEAL TO WOMEN

In order to answer questions as to how, what, and where a persuasive appeal for light beer could be created and aimed at the female market, King's first undertook a broad-based research study to pin down the needs, perceptions, and habits of women as they applied to the consumption of beer.

The most important aspect of this study was an extensive survey of women, which featured personal interviews from a structured questionnaire. Three hundred women from all parts of the country participated in this survey, with two-thirds of them either attending college or working full-time in business firms with between 100 and 500 employees. The remaining one-third were married, and of these half were employed on a part-time basis, usually in secretarial or lower management positions.

As a supplement to these personal interviews, another 2,000 questionnaires were mailed; telephone follow-ups were made to non-respondents. The total response from this mail-phone effort was just over 1,000.

WHAT THE SURVEY SHOWED

After questionnaire and interview responses were tabulated and analyzed, the following key findings emerged regarding the "average" American woman.

1) She viewed herself as intelligent, humorous, outgoing, and straightforward.
2) Most single women watched TV rarely, with total viewing hours of between three and five hours per week being the maximum in about half the cases.
3) Married women with children (about one-sixth of those interviewed) watched, on the average, between 10 and 20 hours of TV per week.
4) Almost all women interviewed read some form of printed media every day, primarily newspapers, with women's magazines a somewhat distant second.
5) When questioned on buying habits, almost all respondents agreed they shopped around for bargains and specials; however, they rarely purchased unknown brands just to save money.
6) On the subject of alcoholic beverage consumption, two-thirds of the single women stated they drank, on the average, once a day, while the remaining one-third drank two to three times per week. Most of the married women related their drinking frequencies to their husbands' drinking habits. The drinks most preferred were, in order: vodka, table wines, blended whiskeys, scotch whiskeys, beers, and ales.
7) Of the total number of women interviewed, only one in eight had never drunk beer. The other seven usually drank beer in group activities, such as picnics, card games, or relaxed social situations. In general, women beer-drinkers were from middle-class and upper-middle-class economic groups.
8) Of the seven-in-eight women who drank beer with varying degrees of regularity, more than half stated that they resented much beer advertising and did not purchase brands whose advertising they felt was "chauvinistic." Miller beer (showing men relaxing after heavy physical activity), Schaefer (showing men engaging in sports contests), and Schlitz (showing men in adventurous settings) were three brands cited by this sizable "sensitive" group as falling into this category.

9) Aside from these chauvinistic considerations, however, brands of beer were relatively unimportant to the surveyed women, and few had a single brand preference as men tended to have.

10) Among women beer-drinkers, the most frequently cited reason for drinking beer was that it could be consumed without causing intoxication. Other reasons included the "smooth taste," and the way it permitted them to "open up" more at parties and other social gatherings. Most women did not drink beer to quench their thirst as men often did.

11) Among beer-drinking women, more than three-quarters of all respondents stated that they didn't drink beer as often as they might because of concern over beer's caloric content. This was often cited as the reason for a preference for wine, in that a single glass of wine contained only one-half the calories of a glass of beer.

USING YANKELOVICH

In addition to the information resulting from the primary data obtained from its survey of women, King's marketing team also made use of secondary data on life-style trends prepared by the Yankelovich research organization. This study, covering a number of key trends and developments in American society, would, team members agreed, help them prepare a campaign for women that would have a more "modern" look and would relate better to current ideas and attitudes among Americans in general and American women in particular.

The specific trends uncovered by the Yankelovich study that were considered to be most pertinent in designing creative and media strategies for the proposed new light beer campaign were the following:

Trends relating to the "psychology of affluence." These life-style trends manifested themselves in a de-emphasis on money and possessions, and an emphasis on more meaningful work and an expression of "self" through products.

Trends reflecting a quest for "excitement and meaning" beyond life's routines. Examples: the search for "change" and "adventure" in life, an emphasis on "sensuousness" (through "touching and feeling") and mysticism (through new kinds of spiritual experiences).

Trends reflecting reactions against the complexity of modern life. Included in this area were "back to nature" life-styles, strong ethnic identification, a rejection of artificiality and "bigness."

Trends reflecting new values pushing out traditional values. Examples: pleasure "for its own sake," "living for today," a blurring of sex roles, and more liberal attitudes toward sex.

Trends reflecting the personal orientations of those now in the teens and twenties. Included in this category were trends toward the tolerance of disorder (including a rejection of fixed plans and schedules), and the rejection of hypocrisy, affecting attitudes toward exaggeration in communications and female careers away from traditional home/marriage satisfactions.

PULLING THE RESEARCH TOGETHER

Based largely on the foregoing primary and secondary research, the following recommendations were offered for an advertising campaign designed, primarily, to persuade women to switch from other drinks (alcoholic or otherwise) to King's light beer.

1) The main objective of this for-women-only campaign would be to position King's light beer against other drinks (including non-beers) in terms of King's low calorie-content.
2) The campaign should be geared to middle- and upper-middle-class women, with advertisements featuring situations with which women could identify. Examples of such situations might include (1) social occasions with men and women mixing but with the emphasis on women drinking nonfattening beer and (2) situations showing women enjoying a King's light beer while engaged in housekeeping chores. The implication would be that she *can* enjoy a beer break, and doesn't have to feel guilty about it.
3) Any scenes featuring food, such as picnics, should be de-emphasized in the advertising as inconsistent with the basic low-calorie message of the campaign.
4) A variety of life-styles should be portrayed in the advertising, including, and perhaps emphasizing, life-styles not typically associated with stereotyped female roles. For example, the advertising might portray women in competitive situations with men, with the implicit suggestion that women can do a lot of things as well as men, including drinking beer.
5) Emphasize that beer is a natural, simple, refreshing drink, which can be suggested in advertisements featuring a simpler, back-to-nature life-style (such as a man and women drinking beer in a log-cabin setting).

THE CAMPAIGN EMERGES

Advertisements were prepared to appeal to both married and single women. Figure 4-1 shows sections of the Yankelovich questionnaire and one of two "young singles" proposed advertisements.

Figure 4-1.

The "young singles" advertisements focused on the differential between King's light beer and other beers ("You can have two glasses of ours for the same number of calories as one glass of theirs"), and also appealed to women as a subtle dig against male chauvinism ("You can match him one for one with King's light beer with only half the calories").

QUESTIONS

1. Do you think that King's beer can position itself in advertising as a beverage to drink instead of non-beers?
2. Assess the proposed approach in which women would be shown drinking King's beer while engaged in household work.
3. Should the "young singles" advertisements be accepted, or rejected?

5

OURBANK

Ourbank, located near a big Midwestern city, dissatisfied with the volume of business it was obtaining, undertook a research study to identify the strengths and weaknesses in its marketing mix. This strong commercial bank hoped that the findings, properly organized, analyzed, and interpreted, would provide the bank's advertising and sales promotion manager with material for a recommendation to be presented to top management.

The manager found that some of the findings were repetitive, some irrelevant, and some significant only when combined with other findings. Furthermore, he found data gaps which forced him to fill in with his own assumptions. Overall, however, some useful information was uncovered by the research study.

FINDINGS

1) Although only 25 percent of Ourbank's checking accounts are businessmen, they contribute 75 percent of its demand deposits.
2) Ourbank is not competitive in obtaining customers for time savings (i.e., C.D.'s and savings accounts requiring notification of withdrawal). Not only does Ourbank fail to draw outside dollars, it is generally unable to sell time savings even to its own customers.
3) Ourbank has more women customers than any of its competitors, but even for *them* the majority of their dealings are with women.
4) Ourbank has done a generally poor job of getting the business of families who have moved into its area in the last two years. Most increases in its business come from families who have lived in the area for more than five years.

5) Ourbank used to be #1 in auto loans but has slipped to third place in this category (see table 5-1).

	Ourbank	Competitor "A"	Competitor "B"
Checking Accounts	41	25	16
Regular Savings Accounts	34	24	14
Time Savings	10	14	5
Bank Credit Cards	34	6	10
Auto Loans	15	20	27
Personal Loans	37	27	12
Trust Services	17	33	7
Mortgage Loans	30	20	30

Table 5-1. Ourbank vs. its two key commercial bank competitors

6) In general, time savings accounts have the greatest appeal to people 60 years of age and over, although such accounts should be a logical component of the total financial picture in families in other age categories.

7) Among Ourbank's customers, 55 percent of those who have either a checking or a regular savings account have both. No competitive bank exceeds the 50 percent crossover level.

8) Ourbank is perceived as offering a great variety of banking services—much more so than its two major competitors.

9) Noncustomers tend to think of Ourbank's personnel as "distant" and "unfriendly" to a much greater degree than personnel at competitive banks. Interestingly, just the opposite attitude prevails among existing customers, who view Ourbank people as "friendly" and "cooperative."

10) Among customers and noncustomers surveyed, the following proposed new services were felt to be the most worthwhile additions to the bank's offerings: (1) computerized income tax preparation, (2) family financial counselling, (3) direct billing of bank accounts by major creditors.

11) Women are strongly influential, but not usually decisive, in choosing banks and bank services.

12) Although Ourbank's credit card is the most widely circulated, its usage is not nearly as high as it should be for borrowing cash or making purchases in local stores.

13) Unaided awareness of bank advertising is highest for Ourbank (60 percent of respondents volunteered some mention of Ourbank vs. 35 percent for the nearest competitor).

14) Due largely to media exposure from savings banks, people in the area are coming more and more to categorize and stigmatize commercial banks as oriented away from people and toward businesses.

15) Thirty percent of Ourbank customers feel that teller services should be faster—a higher percentage than for any competing bank.

16) Most of Ourbank trust business comes from middle-income families not able to produce profitable trusts instead of from high-income families ($40,000+). Heads of these high-income households generally have a low opinion of naming a bank as an executor of a will.

17) Ourbank has been relatively successful at gaining multiple-service customers due to good selling at the promotional level and the existence of a customer group inclined to use multiple services. However, platform officers do a poor job of cross-selling—they don't question prospects about additional services needed or attempt to sell them on these services.

18) Ourbank is perceived by customers as the bank that offers a free checking account. However, few noncustomers realize the advantages of free checking, and even fewer remember anything about these accounts from Ourbank's advertising.

19) While Ourbank advertising has a high degree of awareness, all bank advertising, including its own, was found to be generally ineffective in selling specific services.

QUESTIONS

1. At what target market (or markets) should Ourbank's campaign be directed?
2. What type (or types) of advertising should comprise this campaign? For example: Advertising that builds a favorable image? Promotes specific services? Reminds people of the bank's leadership position? Other directions?
3. What creative theme (or themes) will best summarize and dramatize the campaign messages?
4. What media mix will best carry the campaign messages?

PART II
BUILDING THE
MARKETING MIX

The cases in this section assume that exploratory research of the sort illustrated in part I has produced information on products and markets required to identify and define strong external positions (among competitive products) and strong internal positions (in the minds of prospective customers) for the advertised product.

Using this information as a point of departure, cases in this section focus on the second phase of the campaign-planning process—building marketing mixes that will help to entrench these products in these positions.

For our purposes, a marketing mix will be broadly defined as that combination of product, price, place, and promotion utilities best calculated to attract one or more segments of a market to the product. Since part III illustrates the "promotion" component of the marketing mix, the emphasis in this section will be on the other three components—particularly the "product" component.

To illustrate the process of building appealing marketing mixes, consider the Gourm-egg case in this section (page 39).

An extruded, salami-shaped product that duplicated the center slices of perfectly hard-cooked eggs, Gourm-egg faced a positioning problem that was essentially external in nature. Specifically, the segment of the market in which it was originally positioned—picturesquely referred to as the "tablecloth restaurant" segment—simply didn't have a sufficient number of uses for the product to justify profitable, large-scale production, and the producer, Ralston Purina, was seriously considering discontinuing production.

This decision never materialized, however, because informal research indicated the existence of a large, expanding market segment that *would* support profitable, large-scale production—the noncommercial segment of the institutional market (such as the people laboriously manufacturing a mountain of egg salad for the students in the Irving, Texas, school system).

PRODUCT, PRICE, PLACE DECISIONS

At this point in the advertising process—roughly the point reached by the firms in part I cases—the problem facing Ralston Purina and its advertising agency was essentially a marketing problem. Well before advertising campaign decisions were made pertaining to points such as promotion mixes and creative platforms and media strategies, other decisions first had to be made pertaining to the product-price-place elements of the marketing mix.

1) What should the *product* be and do and look like in order to prove attractive to this segment of the market?
2) What *price* will be most appealing to members of this segment?
3) What distribution channels will most quickly and economically get this product in the right *place* for distribution to this market?

It was only after decisions were made in these first three "P" elements of the marketing mix that the fourth "P", promotion, could be wheeled into place, with emphasis on the "advertising" component of this mix. Then, with product-price-place features and benefits matched to segment needs and perceptions, persuasive appeals could be created to attract both users and distributors of Gourm-egg, media decisions implemented for carrying this appeal to these customer groups, and controls established to measure campaign performance against standards in achieving campaign objectives.

POST-POSITION, PRE-PROMOTION DECISIONS

In *this* section, however, case emphasis is on what advertisers and their agencies do *after* positioning decisions have been arrived at, and *before* decisions pertaining to the promotion mix are undertaken. (Part III cases will examine promotion mix decisions.)

As a frame of reference for organizing, understanding, and critically appraising the cases in this section, it should be noted that the relative emphasis placed on each marketing mix component is a function of the product being promoted, the market in which it is promoted, and the nature of the competition in this market.

For example, both the Gourm-egg and Avon cases discuss unique *new* products being promoted in *new* markets, in which strong competitive influences have not yet coalesced. In Avon's relatively affluent Venezuelan consumer market, however, the emphasis is much more on the unique features of the product than it is in Gourm-egg's noncommercial institutional market, where product benefits are stressed. Both advertisers, however, are concerned with product distribution (the "place" component) and price economies.

On the other hand, the Perdue, Kean College, and Natural Bank cases illustrate marketing mix problems facing advertisers hoping to attract new customers in a fierce competitive environment in which too few differentials exist among these competitors (banks are banks, colleges colleges, chickens chickens). In this environment, the focus is on somehow changing the product in such a way that it is clearly differentiated from its amorphous competition and can be dramatized when the promotion mix is pieced together. The apparent assumption behind this product change strategy is that if it succeeds, "price" and "place" problems will solve themselves.

While generally similar to the three previous cases, the Contac and Preakness cases differ in at least one significant respect. Specifically, each of these advertisers is searching for a marketing mix that will change people's attitudes toward the product without actually changing the product itself. Thus, these cases really illustrate marketing-mix strategies appropriate to efforts to internally reposition products (respectively, a cold remedy and a shopping center). Intrinsically, however, there is really nothing new about the product or about the market in which it is sold.

6

THE GOURM-EGG

In the early '70s, the Ralston Purina Company, a large agribusiness, developed an extruded egg product that duplicated the center slices of perfectly hard-boiled eggs. Except for the addition of a small amount of starch to the yolk, the product was pure egg white on the outside, yolk in the center. The presence of starch gave the yolk a stability and resistance to crumbling not unlike the white, but quite unlike ordinary yolks of hard-boiled eggs.

The product was felt to be of potential value in foodservice industries and, it was decided, would be extruded to a 13-inch length, frozen, and packed in a clear, cryovac-type plastic, with two-color printing of the product name, ingredients, and usage instructions. The package design would also visualize the egglike nature of the product and emphasize that approximately "75 Center-Cut Slices" could be produced from one roll. Each roll weighed 1 lb. 1 oz. The product was named Gourm-egg, a play on *gourmet*.

THE FIRST MARKETING PLAN

Ralston Purina added Gourm-egg to its line of foodservice products in 1974. This line included the well-known Chicken-of-the-Sea tuna, Ralston cereals, desserts, juices, and a line of frozen entrees.

The pricing on Gourm-egg was about $1.25 per roll, each equivalent in volume and weight to a dozen medium-sized eggs but yielding more center-cut slices than 17 conventional medium-sized eggs. Eggs at that time were selling at about 60 to 70 cents a dozen, so by weight one paid a 50 percent premium for a roll of Gourm-egg, although this premium decreased to 35 percent when measured in terms of center-cut slices.

Offsetting this premium, however, were labor savings involved in boiling, cooling, and peeling the 17 eggs equivalent to one Gourm-egg roll. Additionally, a Gourm-egg slicer was made available, at a cost of under $20, which cut perfect-sized 5/32-inch slices.

Implementing the Marketing Plan

With no sales tools except product data sheets and samples, Ralston salesmen and brokers began selling Gourm-egg. Their primary calls were on "tablecloth restaurants," where Gourm-egg was sold as an alternative to hard-boiled eggs. The integrity of each slice, its ability to hold up without breaking, and its perfect appearance were felt to be strong selling points.

A number of restaurant operators purchased Gourm-egg rolls, but usually in low-volume quantities of a case or less at a time. Storage was a factor in their purchase levels, as well as the fact that the product was primarily a garnish, so not much was used at any one time. Along with initial sales, the rate of repeat sales was also sluggish, and hardly equal to the sales time and dollars spent. In general, most customers considered the product to be something of a novelty, and distributors were not happy about carrying Gourm-egg unless they were already distributors of other Ralston frozen foods.

Distribution reached a level of about 100 foodservice distributors out of a universe of 3,000, and the optimum for any foodservice manufacturer was considered to be 600 to 800.

Because of the low sales volume and novelty "image" of Gourm-egg, the company considered dropping the product or possibly selling off the rights and equipment to a company that might be in a better position to market such a specialty. Considerable marketing expense had already been incurred with no prospect of a payback after two years.

Enter Mandabach & Simms—At this time, the newly formed New York office of Mandabach & Simms Inc. was retained by Ralston Purina as an advertising-marketing agency. The agency's New York director, Ron Plummer, was given the assignment of researching three alternatives.

1) Ralston would continue to manufacture and sell the product.
2) A buyer would be found for the Gourm-egg process.
3) A new marketing plan would be recommended for building sales and distribution to a level that would generate a profitable picture for Gourm-egg.

THE SECOND MARKETING PLAN

Ron Plummer, by virtue of his contacts in the foodservice field, began sounding out a number of manufacturers about taking on Gourm-egg. Most felt that the product had a limited appeal because it seemed to be a gourmet specialty that only a few operators might use. In general the market seemed limited to hard-to-reach independent restaurants and chains with salad bars that would be interested in perfectly-sliced eggs. Otherwise, the cost seemed too high to justify using the product chopped up in salads or as a garnish. At about this time, egg prices moved up some 20 percent and so did the cost of Gourm-egg, making the product even less attractive.

Also at about this time, Plummer was giving a merchandising seminar program for the National Restaurant Association in Irving, Texas, during which he paid a reacquaintance call on Melbagene Ryan, foodservice director of the Irving independent school district. On a tour of her operation, Plummer noticed two women preparing an egg salad for an upcoming meal. It was their job to hard-boil 8,000 eggs, cool and peel them, then chop and mix them into a mountainous egg salad—a process that required 12 hours just to reach the stage where the eggs were ready to be chopped.

Plummer commented on the labor intensity of this task and promised to supply some Gourm-egg for trial. Ryan said that she didn't think she could afford a Gourm-egg product because of the cost, but that she would be happy to test the product for Plummer's client.

New Market, New Opportunities

As a result of this test, Plummer concluded that the real potential for Gourm-egg lay not in the white-tablecloth (and theme) restaurant market, but in the noncommercial segment of the institutional market, where large volumes of the product could be used. For example, more than 100 cases of Gourm-egg were used each time egg salad was prepared for the Irving school system, and the cost was more than competitive if the 12 hours spent boiling, peeling, and cooling were taken into account.

Unfortunately, selling into the school market usually requires approval from the U.S. Department of Agriculture, which Ralston did not have. However, if a product was already used by one school foodservice system, others could use it too.

Plummer therefore sent his public relations writer to the Irving schools to prepare a story with pictures, which was sent to *School Foodservice Journal* (fig. 6-1). The *Journal* printed it, because Mrs. Ryan was considered an innovative operator in her field.

Some 5,000 reprints were prepared and given to all Ralston salesmen and brokers. In addition, a new marketing strategy was devised, based on these tactics:

1) Sell the product to large-volume operators, especially in the noncommercial segments of the institutional market.
2) Stress the fact that Gourm-egg pays for itself in labor savings and is always ready without preparation.
3) Begin calls on schools, branch into hospitals, nursing homes, cafeterias, colleges, and in-plant feeding, using the *Foodservice Journal* story as a leave-behind.

Figure 6-1.

School Foodservice Journal

UNIQUE HARD BOILED EGG PRODUCT OFFERS UNLIMITED SAVINGS TO ANY TYPE OF FOODSERVICE OPERATION

The attached article, which appeared recently in SCHOOL FOODSERVICE JOURNAL, is applicable to you, whatever your operation. This article dramatically illustrates how a foodservice operator, with cost and labor problems similar to yours, used the new Gourm-egg® hard boiled egg product to help solve many of these problems. We are sure that your operation would also like to have more time available to do many things such as, more merchandising of your food, better utilization of your employees' time, and saving money.

If you find this success story of interest to you, please contact your nearest Checkerboard Foodservice Distributor for more product information or contact me at: (314) 982-3801

David B. Smart
Director, Food and Specialty Products
Ralston Purina Company
835 South 8th Street
Checkerboard Square
St. Louis, Missouri 63188

"Reprinted with permission, SCHOOL FOODSERVICE JOURNAL, copyrighted November/December, 1973."

Story about Gourm-egg that appeared in *School Foodservice Journal.* This was prepared by the advertising agency public relations writer. Reprinted with permission from Mandabach & Sims.

4) Gain distributors who can sell to the comparatively low-volume commercial component of the institutional market, generally not considered worth a direct selling effort by Ralston Purina salespeople.

Other marketing communications support efforts began in the following order:

1) A product data sheet was prepared to hand out on sales calls.
2) When calling on distributors who did not carry other Ralston products, the Ralston salesman or broker typically brought with him or her an order resulting from a missionary call on a prospective customer.
3) The *Foodservice Journal* story was mailed to other foodservice operators with a trial offer for a supply of Gourm-egg rolls. Respondents were called on by the broker.
4) Small-space advertisements (one column by 10 inches) were started in magazines serving the noncommercial market, stressing Gourm-egg's labor-saving qualities.
5) Full-color advertising was delayed two years, when four-color advertisements began in commercial and noncommercial publications. By this time, distribution for Gourm-egg had grown to some 500 distributors.
6) Full-color advertisements continue to the present, supported by continuing public relations work. The latter consists of cue-ing in with food editorials in foodservice trade magazines to make sure that Gourm-egg recipes are used in food stories. Color shots are taken as needed.
7) Currently, a dozen recipes have been printed with serving and garnishing ideas. In addition to the publicity use of these recipes, they are also given by salesmen to operators.

QUESTION

Do you think that the new positioning of Gourm-egg offers Ralston Purina any more promise of success than the product experienced when it was introduced to the "tablecloth restaurant" industry? Explain.

7

AVON

Avon Products Inc. is one of the few companies in the world to rely solely on door-to-door sales representatives to sell their products. Typically, these representatives are housewives calling on friends and neighbors to earn extra money. In managing this highly personalized marketing approach, Avon continually faces two interrelated challenges: motivating the seller to sell Avon products, and motivating the buyer to buy Avon products. (One index of the success of this effort is Avon's status as the world's largest manufacturer and distributor of cosmetics, toiletries, and costume jewelry.)

A key element in the success of Avon's marketing effort is its lively, colorful sales brochure, which supplements the personalized sales presentation of Avon's representatives in arousing interest and buying action among consumers. In deciding which products will be presented in this brochure, Avon marketing people face a number of considerations, ranging from the nature and needs of the market in which the brochure will be shown, to the high aesthetic standards governing fashion advertising in general.

PLANNING THE "SWISS MOUSE" CAMPAIGN

To illustrate this planning process, here are some of the considerations involved in the decision to include a single entry in an Avon brochure designed for the Venezuelan market, one of Avon's oldest Latin-American subsidiaries. The product, in this case, was a cologne decanter called the "Swiss Mouse," which had originally appeared in an Avon brochure prepared for the U.S. market (fig. 7-1). The decision to include this decanter as a key new product in Avon's Venezuelan brochure was based on the following considerations:

Figure 7-1.

Cover for Avon brochure. This version appeared in the promotion in the U.S. market.
Reprinted with permission from Avon Products, Inc.

1) In Venezuela, Avon would have thousands of representatives selling in a relatively stabilized market with a low inflation rate and little governmental interference with international firms.
2) The third-quarter period in which this brochure would be utilized encompassed the last half of summer vacations, the back-to-school period, and the beginning of fall—in general, a period offering few gift-giving occasions.
3) During most of this period, many customers and Avon representatives would be away on vacations, affecting the depth and scope of territorial coverage.
4) Due largely to this lack of gift-giving occasions, and the vacation and back-to-school expenses usually associated with this period, low-priced products would be especially effective as motivators and door-openers.

For this particular third-quarter promotion, the Avon marketing team was looking for products that fit summer/early-fall fashions and life-styles, as well as low-priced gifts that a woman might purchase for herself.

The Swiss Mouse cologne decanter seemed to fit nicely into this latter category: it was a cute, "gimmicky" item with a planned limited life through Christmas, and such novelty products had done well in the past. In the Venezuelan market, furthermore, more than 50 percent of the population is under 25 years of age, and marketing team members felt that this type of product would have a strong appeal to this group.

NEXT STEP: CREATE A CAMPAIGN

In preparing campaign brochures a typical Avon subsidiary, being closer to the market, is delegated considerable authority, responsibility, and flexibility in deciding how the products will be featured.

As for the treatment of the Swiss Mouse entry, the Venezuelan Avon subsidiary had three options: (1) use the treatment employed in the earlier Swiss Mouse entry in the U.S. brochure, (2) modify this original brochure, or (3) create an entirely new promotion for the product.

In the case of this Venezuelan campaign, the marketing team decided on the third option, for these reasons:

1) The original campaign in the United States had not been especially successful, and the brochure promotion might have had something to do with that result.
2) In the U.S. campaign, the Swiss Mouse decanter had been competing against more than a dozen other new products; in the more constricted Venezuelan market, however, it would be the main product in the campaign, a fact which would influence its location in the brochure as well as the amount of space allocated to it and the basic appeal supporting it.
3) Venezuela has its own unique set of customs and tastes which would require a unique promotional thrust.

Implementing this decision, the team prepared a preliminary layout (fig. 7-2), which was sent to the New York headquarters for approval. Avon's New York office sent back the following statement, along with a suggested replacement layout (fig. 7-3).

Figure 7-2.

Preliminary layout for brochure to be used in the Venezuelan market (Version 1). Reprinted with permission from Avon Products, Inc.

Given the decision not to utilize the U.S. format we realize the challenge was not easy to create something apropos for the introduction of the new decanter, for dealing with mice can be very touchy if not treated with delicacy, humor, and charm. It was felt, therefore, that the visual effect of your layout would not inspire the customer to buy the product. Showing the product in this kind of setting with a mouse trap and relating it to the somewhat musty smells of an attic represents it in a rather unattractive and unfeminine way. In addition, although you have indicated the background to be out of focus, it nevertheless appears that the size relationship of the product to the props is incorrect. Also keep in mind when using props not to use too many, thereby taking away from the product.

The following instructions accompanied the replacement layout.

An 8×10 transparency of the carton art is being sent in addition to a film of the product (which is to be silhouetted). Please strip the product film into the enlarged art of the carton, positioning both as layout indicates. The art is taken from the front, left, and right panels of the carton. Please note that silhouetting of the leaves is necessary where it meets the bottom of the product film (this will help the product to stand out against

Figure 7-3.

NUEVO
Ratoncito Suizo

ESPECIAL Bs 29⁰⁰

Replacement layout for brochure to be used in the Venezuelan market (Version 2).
Reprinted with permission from Avon Products, Inc.

Figure 7-4.

Once upon a time there was a cute little mouse who loved to play in the field.

One day much to his surprise, he found a beautifully fragrant piece of cheese which he immediately took to his fiancée.

She liked it so much that the very next day they both went back to the field to search for more pieces of the fragrant cheese.

Now you can have or give this whimsical little mousey the piece of cheese... in 3 fine fragrances.

New Swiss Mouse with Splash Cologne. The little golden mouse sits atop the frosted glass cheese. Choose from Moonwind, Charisma and Roses Roses.
3 oz. size normal

Copy for Version 2. This is the handwritten copy as produced by the copywriter.
Reprinted with permission from Avon Products, Inc.

the background). Also delete the butterfly. Following the layout, please create border art to look like an old piece of paper with 2 curled corners and a few small tear marks on the edges. (Note, bottom right corner is torn as if the mouse took a bite out of it.) The art of this border should print P-95 with the inside pure white. The story art is 50% reduction of the carton art.

Please have a photo taken of the carton with a small pink bow.

Body copy pertaining to the product description sets in 9 pt. Bookman. The story [fig. 7-4] sets in 11 pt. Bookman with swash initials to the size indicated in layout. Remainder of display type sets in Bookman Bold to size indicated.

Please use rainbow circle (with correct copy). Type inside drops out white. "Nuevo" prints E-111. All other type prints black.

QUESTIONS

1. What possible negative can you see in the Swiss Mouse theme for use in the U.S. market?
2. Do you feel version 1 or version 2 (for the Venezuelan market) was to be preferred? Why?

8

PERDUE CHICKENS

Is it possible to take a basic commodity food product and, by effectively manipulating the elements of the promotion mix (especially the "appeal"), create both a high demand *and* a high price for this product?

The economics of the situation seem to say *no*. Take, for example, chickens. From the viewpoint of the consumer, there are dozens of substitutes for chickens, from frankfurters to filet mignon. Thus, if the price of any one of these substitutes falls to the point where this substitute becomes a "better buy" than chicken, then that is likely to be what will end up on the family table. In the words of the economist, the "marginal utility" of, say, hamburger, with its dropped price, is now higher than that of the chicken. Thus, demand shifts from chicken to hamburger.

GIVING CHICKENS APPEAL

Does demand necessarily *have* to shift from chicken to hamburger, in spite of this price differential? That, more or less, was the question that Frank Perdue, president of Perdue Farms, Inc., of Salisbury, Maryland, wanted answered, and he was willing to sit through 47 advertising agency presentations in seven months to get his answers.

The agency presentation that finally sold Perdue (and, eventually, his chickens) was prepared by Scali, McCabe and Sloves. This winning advertising agency recommended an "image" campaign. Actually, there were two images involved—of Frank Perdue and of Frank Perdue's chickens. Both were projected by the same thematic appeal. Here are the steps used in building this appeal:

First, basic research was undertaken to uncover a "differential" that

Figure 8-1.

SCALI, McCABE, SLOVES, INC.
CLIENT: PERDUE FARMS
PRODUCT: PERDUE CHICKENS

TITLE: "UNKNOWN ANCESTRY"
LENGTH: 30 SECONDS
COMM'L. NO.: TV-PD-3b

1. FRANK PERDUE: Most chicken parts are of unknown ancestry.

2. Where do you suppose these came from?

3. The fact is when you buy most chicken parts you have no way of knowing.

4. Unless they're my chicken parts.

5. Perdue Pedigreed Parts.

6. They're the only ones that come from tender young Perdue Chickens.

7. And the only ones identified with a name tag

8. and my money-back quality guarantee.

9. I don't know about you, but when I was a little boy

10. my father told me never to take chicken from a stranger.

11. (SILENT)

would so distinguish Perdue chickens from other chickens (or hamburgers or pork and beans or any other competitive staple food) that these chickens would be, at least in the minds of the consumers, in a no-substitute class.

Much of this research was carried on by agency personnel who learned at Perdue's Maryland chicken farm facility what is required to raise chickens, and what made Perdue's chickens better than, and different from, other chickens.

Based on this on-site research, interviews with Perdue and his people, and a study of competitive products and promotions, agency creative personnel devised a creative story and a rationale to support this story. Basically, it was a story about a man who strongly believed in his product and stood strongly behind it.

Among the competitive advantages that the advertising agency personnel thought should be incorporated in the campaign for Perdue were the following:

1) Perdue's chickens not only eat better than other chickens; they eat better than most people (pure yellow corn, soybean meal, expensive imported marigold petals, and clear water from deep wells, all of which combine to give them "a healthy, yellow color").
2) Perdue's chickens even *lived* better than other chickens and most people, in spacious, well-ventilated houses, some with intercoms installed so Mr. Perdue could listen from time to time "to make sure they were happy."
3) Perdue's quality control standards were so high that his inspectors rejected about 30 percent of the chickens that had been passed by government inspectors.

TOUGH, NOT FOOLISH

Knowing, now, what they wanted to say, the advertising agency account people needed somebody to say it. Ed McCabe, vice president and copy director for the agency, felt that nobody in the world could communicate this message better than Frank Perdue himself.

"He is a product believer with a special commitment to quality," said McCabe. "This alone gives him great believability. On top of that, he has unique and individual characteristics which come across to the public in a strong, honest, straightforward manner."

However, persuading Perdue to do his own commercials was another matter. Another agency, in making an earlier presentation, had wanted to use Mr. Perdue in his own commercials, but he refused because he felt the commercials made him and his business look "foolish," and chickens, to Perdue, were a serious business indeed.

It was this tough-minded commitment to his business that was largely responsible for sparking, in McCabe's mind, the idea for the Perdue campaign's creative appeal:

Figure 8-2.

SCALI, McCABE, SLOVES, INC.
CLIENT: PERDUE
PRODUCT: PERDUE CHICKEN

TITLE: "TWIST ARMS"
LENGTH: 30 SECONDS
COMM'L. NO.: TV-PD-30

1 FRANK PERDUE: Everybody knows how tough it is

2 to get kids to eat what's good for them.

3. But you don't have to twist their arms.

4. Just give them one of my legs.

5 It's a perfect children's portion.

6. One Perdue drumstick and thigh has more protein value

7. than a hamburger, a hot dog, or some other things kids eat.

8. (SILENT)

9. And kids love it.

10. Look. It's even got its own handle.

11. (SILENT)

"IT TAKES A TOUGH MAN TO MAKE
A TENDER CHICKEN."

McCabe saw this appeal as projecting the kind of image that fit both Frank Perdue, with his high standards, and the quality product resulting from these standards. The appeal also appealed to Perdue, who agreed to do the commercials.

TOUGH THINKING BEHIND THE TOUGH MAN

As discussed in an article appearing in the *New York Times* magazine section,* the Perdue campaign is typical of a whole new wave of "tough, sardonic," highly competitive advertisements. According to this article, advertisers and agencies feel that the emergence of this kind of advertising "has to do with perceiving the 70's as a decade of lost illusions and tight money . . . they have come to the conclusion that the consumer, like an insect that builds up resistance to DDT, is getting harder to fool. They have pioneered the era of dog-eat-dog advertising, in which the rival brand is the enemy and the marketplace is no-man's land."

THE PAYOFF

Frank Perdue currently spends about $1.5 million in advertising his chickens each year, or roughly three times as much as when he first decided on SM&S as his agency, but only about one percent of his current $150-million-plus sales volume. And this is not a national account: because Perdue refuses to freeze his chickens for transit to distant points, his business is restricted to the mid-Atlantic states.

Television was the primary medium for Perdue, with radio as a secondary medium. In support were poster displays in stores prepared by the agency. Only occasionally were advertisements scheduled in newspapers and magazines.

QUESTIONS

1. Discuss the selection of television advertising as the chief medium used by Perdue.
2. Comment on the use of Mr. Perdue as a television spokesman for the company's television commercials.
3. List the pros and cons of Perdue's viewing 47 advertising agency presentations in order to select an advertising agency.

---

* "New! Improved! Advertising!" *The New York Times*, January 25, 1976.

9

KEAN COLLEGE – Development Of A Marketing Communications Program

THE RESEARCH BASE

During the late 1970s, the state college system of New Jersey (along with other higher education systems in the United States) faced a predictable crisis: a shortage of students for many of its programs. Among the reasons for this crisis were wrong projections about baby booms. Also, student priorities underwent a change. Student shortages were likely to cause the same troubles in the educational field that a shortage of customers would cause a business.

To cope with this crisis, Dr. Nathan Weiss, president of Kean State College of New Jersey, decided to utilize the creative energies of students and faculty members to supplement the efforts of college administrators. One result of this decision: the formation of a team-taught marketing communications workshop. In this were honor students from a number of disciplines, including management science, fine arts, and speech-theater-media. All participants had a common career interest in market-related fields.

THE RATIONALE: LEARN BY DOING

Behind the formation of the workshop was the educational rationale that it would provide students a learn-by-doing opportunity to apply and test textbook concepts in an on-the-job situation. The workshop was structured to fulfill this role by functioning as *the* advertising agency for Kean College. Groups of students would be assigned to such agency departments as media, research, copy, and art. Because the state legislature in the previous year's budget cut had eliminated advertising and public relations departments in the state college system, the workshop was literally the only source of advertising for the college.

The task given the workshop was to develop a complete marketing communications program to attract many more students to Kean College from existing and new market segments. This program would be based on research into the needs of members of the two segments. The research would ascertain the strengths and weaknesses of Kean College and competitive colleges and would discover, it was hoped, the most effective media and appeals to reach potential students.

FIRST STEP: RESEARCH THE MARKET

During pre-course planning meetings of the four professors who would conduct the course, certain key decisions were made pertaining to priorities, procedures, standards, and controls. In general, it was agreed that—

1) Although the workshop was structured by specialized interest groups, there would be cooperative interaction among the groups. All class members, accordingly, would participate to some extent in the formulation and implementation of all phases of the overall marketing program.

2) Students would be given much freedom and flexibility in devising and implementing marketing plans and strategies. The four professors would support, coordinate, and direct student efforts.

3) Major criteria for appraising student performance would be the marketing plan and the extent to which individual students contributed. The guiding professors agreed that they would shun any actions that would subordinate the "real-world" environment of the workshop. Such actions were taking attendance, giving quizzes, assigning grades, and even holding regular class sessions. This real-world orientation was carried to the point of viewing participants as employees, and workshop sessions as business meetings. During such business meetings, information and ideas were shared, new plans and priorities were established, and the overall Kean College marketing plan was shaped.

An important decision made by the professors during pre-course planning sessions was that "image" studies should be undertaken by workshop participants. These studies would determine what groups of prospective students expected from a college education, and how Kean College and its competitors met these expectations. This research base would then support the recommendations for the marketing communications program which emerged from the workshop.

Illustrative of this type of "image" study undertaken by workshop participants is the conceptual map shown in figure 9-1. This was based on answers to preference-perception questions provided by juniors and seniors in the management science department of Kean College.

Figure 9-1.

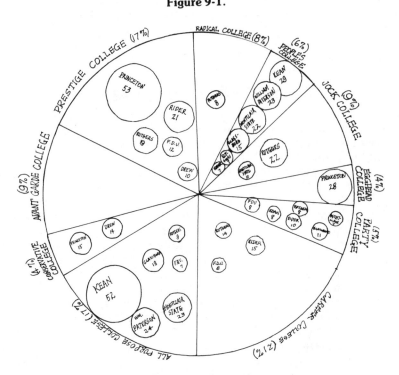

Largest "Preference" Categories: "Career" (21%), "Prestige" (17%), "All Purpose" (17%)

Most Desirable Preference/Perception Ratios: "Career" 21%/37, "Avant Garde" 9%/0, "Radical" 8%/8

Lowest Profile Colleges: Drew (24), Farleigh Dickinson University (FDU) (35)

Highest Profile Colleges: Princeton (96), Kean (89), Rutgers (87)

The questions in the "preference" portion of this study asked students to indicate, from among ten choices, which *type* of college they would attend if they had the choice and funds. The results of this portion of the study appear as "pie slices" in figure 9-1, with larger slices indicating that a larger percentage of students preferred this option.

The "perception" portion of the study asked students to indicate how each perceived colleges in New Jersey (including Kean) in terms of the same choices listed in the preference portion of the study. The results of this portion of the study appear as labeled circles in the figure 9-1 pie slices, with larger circles indicating that more students perceived this college as falling into this category.

By way of illustrative example, note that the largest number of students (21 percent) indicated that they would prefer to attend a "career" college, but most students placed Kean in "all purpose" and "people's college" categories along with a number of other state colleges in New Jersey.

The second section of this case describes and discusses the marketing communications program that emerged from the research base.

THE COMMUNICATIONS CAMPAIGN

The first section of this case described an approach adopted by Kean State College of New Jersey to help solve the accelerating problem of declining student enrollments. In substance, this approach teamed students and faculty members with members of the college administration in developing a broad-based marketing communications campaign for Kean College that would prepare and direct advertising and public relations messages toward internal and external segments of Kean's student market. The main device for creating this campaign was a team-taught Marketing Communications Workshop, which functioned (1) as a course of study for honors students interested in marketing careers and (2) as the advertising agency for Kean College.

The first part of this case described a "conceptual map" research study undertaken to give participants a starting point for building the entire campaign. This final section of the case shows highlights from the scripted slide presentation that summarized and illustrated the entire marketing communications campaign deriving from this research. When the slide presentation was shown to Kean College's Board of Trustees, it was approved. The Board also approved the entire program for further implementation.

The presentation shown to Kean College trustees and other interested observers included more than 140 slides. Some of the slides from the presentation are shown in figure 9-2 to illustrate the essence of the workshop recommendations. The scripted portion of this presentation has also been reduced to this essence.

The Kean College Marketing Communications Workshop is an experimental course set up as a practicing advertising agency. It is composed of students and faculty from management science, fine arts, and speech-theatre-media who function as specialists in the three major functions of an agency—research, design, and copy.

The members of the Kean College community have recognized the need for improved communication on a variety of levels—in clarifying our identity, improving our programs, and promoting ourselves to our target markets.

We have no full-time public relations department at the college. As a result, our promotional strategy lacks clarity and strength, our advertising lacks unity, and the bulk of our college publications are in no way distinguishable, or indicative of a quality institution.

Where do we begin? We must start by looking at our strengths:

Figure 9-2.

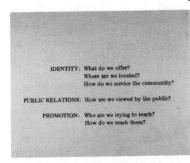

IDENTITY: What do we offer?
Where are we located?
How do we service the community?

PUBLIC RELATIONS: How are we viewed by the public?

PROMOTION: Who are we trying to reach?
How do we reach them?

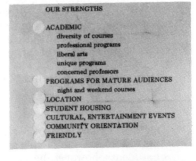

OUR STRENGTHS

ACADEMIC
diversity of courses
professional programs
liberal arts
unique programs
concerned professors
PROGRAMS FOR MATURE AUDIENCES
night and weekend courses
LOCATION
STUDENT HOUSING
CULTURAL, ENTERTAINMENT EVENTS
COMMUNITY ORIENTATION
FRIENDLY

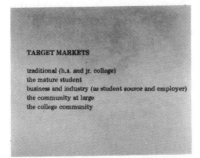

TARGET MARKETS

traditional (h.s. and jr. college)
the mature student
business and industry (as student source and employer)
the community at large
the college community

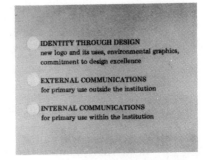

IDENTITY THROUGH DESIGN
new logo and its uses, environmental graphics,
commitment to design excellence

EXTERNAL COMMUNICATIONS
for primary use outside the institution

INTERNAL COMMUNICATIONS
for primary use within the institution

Slides pointing up Kean College campaign elements and strategies.

1) We have a variety of programs that the public doesn't know about.
2) We have an excellent, concerned faculty.
3) We offer special night and weekend courses for mature students.
4) We offer apartments on campus for student housing.
5) We have a variety of cultural and entertainment events.

However, what we are and how we are perceived are two different things. Our research shows that the community is misinformed, or unaware of the facts.

Our target markets can be divided into five groups, (1) the traditional high school and junior college graduates representing our largest source of students; however, because of shortages in these traditional markets, other potential sources are becoming more attractive, including (2) the mature student segment, and (3) the business and industry segment. In addition to directing our appeals to these groups, we must also project our image to (4) the college community and (5) the surrounding community.

We propose to get through to these groups in three ways:

1) An institutional identity campaign featuring a new theme and a new logo.
2) An external communications campaign.
3) An internal communications campaign.

THE INSTITUTIONAL IDENTITY CAMPAIGN
A theme is a unifying element to provide a clear tie-in to all applications for our message. Our proposed theme is:

Quality Education with . . .

The first part of this theme was based on research as to what students want in a college—quality education. The second part of this theme would be flexible, to change with the changing needs of different segments. For example:

Quality Education with Professional Programs
Quality Education in a Friendly Atmosphere
Quality Education in Suburban Surroundings

A logo is a company's or an institution's signature, which reflects its personality and usually provides a subtle, indirect message to the public. Here is the proposed new logo for Kean College, which would be used on the school flag, the college diploma, notebooks, and parking stickers, to name only a few applications.

Environmental graphics are important in reflecting our image. The outside appearance of the grounds and buildings all reflect Kean's personality. Some proposals along these lines include:

1) Signs identifying campus buildings which are consistent with our image and use our logo.
2) Campus map signs at all entrances.

3) Bulletin boards and color-coded parking lot signs.
4) Graphics, designed by students, for such areas as the gym, science labs, and the pool area.

EXTERNAL COMMUNICATIONS

External communication concentrates on the communication flow outside the institution to our key target markets. Vehicles used to carry these messages would include advertising, public relations, television productions, and publications.

All our advertising would carry our "quality education" theme and would be designed to appeal to such groups as high school students and the mature student, including housewives and businessmen.

Radio is a pervasive medium to promote the Kean College story. People use radios at home, in cars, in offices, at the beach. Here is an example of a radio commercial that we might use.

SONG: Oh, it's time to start living
Time to take a little from this world we're given
Time to take time for spring will turn to fall
In just no time at all.

(Music fades out)

It's time to start living! At Kean College of New Jersey we offer interesting courses in pleasant surroundings. At Kean College you can take a few courses or join us full time. Kean College. Where you can learn by day or learn by night. Our courses are tailored to fit your busy schedule. Kean College in Union. Quality education for a more interesting you. Start living!

(Music up and out)

There are many external publications that reflect our image, including the college catalog, the admissions booklet, and department brochures.

Here are some examples of new graphic designs that we have developed to reflect a more current image of Kean College.

1) An attention-getting poster for high school counselors shows a four-year calendar and reads: "It may just be the best four years of your life—come spend it with us."
2) This poster includes a pop-out map of Kean College which will allow for cutting out and assembling of a three-dimensional map of the campus.
3) Department literature could be designed with a common format and could be combined with literature from other departments in folders containing all department offerings. These folders, containing information on teachers, courses, and special programs, could be part of a recruitment program through high school guidance counselors and our own offices.

4) Other components of this recruitment program could include slide shows on specific programs, and display set-ups at Kean and visited high schools.

Public service announcements can be used to promote campus events and activities. All radio stations provide this service free to nonprofit institutions. Also, feature stories can be submitted to newspapers for free publicity.

Effective use can be made of student-power in our public relations campaigns. For instance, photography students in the fine arts department can be used regularly for covering news events, and writers from speech-theatre-media can write news releases.

Kean on television! We have developed ideas for two types of regular television productions to be broadcast on cable TV and other New Jersey television stations. Cable TV liked the idea so much that their news director has already requested an outline and a firm commitment that we send him a tape every week.

QUESTIONS

1. To what extent does the projected institutional campaign for Kean College reflect the research findings?
2. Should Kean College use an "image" campaign, or would it be better for the college to use a promotional campaign that emphasized specific course offerings?
3. Kean College's promotional program had access to local cable television, as well as many television stations in New Jersey. Existing production facilities would be adequate for production of such shows as Kean College might devise. The only additional cost would be for a professional production specialist to coordinate the ventures.

   Suggest some ways television might be used for promoting Kean College. Consider the school's objectives. Then supply specific program ideas that might help attain the objectives and project the desired image for Kean College.

10

THE NATURAL BANK

During the late '70s, following a generation of intensive promotional activity targeted toward ever-diminishing market segments, banks, and bank advertising, began to run out of competitive steam. Essentially, it was a problem of disappearing differentials. There were just so many services banks could offer customers—only so much interest that could be paid legally on deposits; so many hours in the day (or night) when customers could be served; so many gifts that could be offered as deposit incentives during branch-opening ceremonies.

As these "product" differentials became more trivial and imaginary, new differentials were sought in the promotion mix, including innovative advertising, and direct-mail campaigns, and media strategies (one bank in Pennsylvania, for example, had both its president and board chairman participate in singing commercials on pop music shows).

As was generally the situation of its competitors in the suburban Los Angeles area, the Getaway bank found itself caught up in the "disappearing differentials" mudslide. Like other banks', its approach was characterized by a murky sameness in marketing mix offerings and occasional frantic efforts to break out from the rut.

That these efforts were generally unsuccessful for the Getaway bank was amply evidenced by feedback appraisals of its promotion, which included advertising specialties; direct mail; and TV, radio, newspaper, and magazine advertising. After one three-month-long media blitz campaign, for example, research feedback showed that, while awareness of the bank's existence had improved appreciably, the degree of understanding of the bank's offerings hardly budged and the number of depositors actually decreased. Apparently, the net result of this all-out promotional effort was to project an image of "just another bank," indistinguishable from its competitors.

CALL IN THE IMAGE DOCTOR

Among the many suggestions made by bank staff members during the brainstorming sessions convened to help solve Getaway's image problem was one that ultimately caught the fancy of A.W. Hobler, Getaway's board chairman and chief decision maker. According to this suggestion, the solution to Getaway's image problem was a completely new, unbanklike image, and the best person to tool this new image was Jeff Wright, the "image doctor." An ex-art director at a large local advertising agency, Wright, along with two associates, had opened a small research-creative boutique which specialized in image change problems of the sort facing Getaway. After two interviews, Wright and his associates were retained by Getaway.

Following are excerpts, and exhibits, from the report submitted by Wright's firm after six weeks of deep research and creative ferment.

. . . In trying to define the bank's distinctive characteristics, our group undertook research designed to identify real, differentiating elements not being emphasized by other banks. Following are significant research findings which contributed to this identification effort.

1) All banks, of course, offer security and safekeeping for deposits, so this is hardly a differentiating characteristic. Nor are interest rates, which are similar from bank to bank, although our research indicated these rates are overstressed in advertising.
2) Of all the features offered by banks and desired by depositors, "service" ranks first—fast, accurate, streamlined service, to be precise.
3) One of the major reasons Getaway's deposits have remained at a relatively stable level over the past five years is because it is situated in a neighborhood-in-transition, and most original depositors have either moved out or passed away.
4) Replacing these original depositors is a much more youthful group of males and females between the ages of 20 and 30 in the upper-middle socioeconomic class. Members of this group tend to be less inhibited in attitudes and actions, and evidence a strong concern for creature comforts and the surrounding environment (especially those who live in the city, where there is a lack of trees and streams, etc.).
5) In attempting to define this youthful new target market for Getaway's banking services, two nationwide lifestyle trends identified by a recent Yankelovich study were examined: the trend toward "a quest for excitement" and the trend toward "reactions against life's complexities."

. . . Based largely upon our research findings, we recommend that the client discard its former corporate signature, "The Getaway Bank," and replace it with a new signature, "The NATURAL BANK." We also recommend that a new, simplified system for handling customer transactions be developed and stressed in the bank's promotional campaigns.

Following is the rationale behind these recommendations.

Figure 10-1.

Video	Audio
1. CU trees and plants in bank. SFX birds chirping, soft breezes blowing.	Ann: This is not a tropical jungle.
2. MCU same scene, and background SFX.	It's not even an island paradise.
3. MS of bank interior, and SFX.	It's a bank. Not just any bank-- it's the Natural Bank, a different sort of bank designed to make you more comfortable and...
4. CU depositor walking about the bank, admiring the natural look.	...not only more comfortable but also...
5. CU depositor at teller's window. Hands slip to teller.	...easier.
6. Teller hands money to depositor.	That's because our new simplified system, as we call it...
7. Depositor walking toward door.	...gets you through the transactions in a hurry.
8. Depositor stops. Looks around. Sits in a comfortable sofa.	Of course, if you'd like to relax for a few minutes...
9. CU depositor talking to a smiling official.	...be our guest. Enjoy the scenery. It's...
10. Camera picks up natural beauty of interior.	...real.
11. ECU of one leaf. Logotype dropped out.	The Natural Bank. Branches throughout Los Angeles and suburbs.
12. MS bank exterior. Come to CU of sign with words: Natural Bank.	We're different because you are.

The purpose of this television commercial is to make the target audience aware that the Natural Bank exists. Two additional goals are sought: (1) to show in color the striking appearance of the bank; (2) to make banking seem easy because of the bank's "simplified system." There is an absence of high pressure in keeping with the unhurried, "natural" concept.

1) The "natural bank" is an entirely new concept in banking, emphasizing a natural environment in both the exterior and interior of the bank. This new corporate image departs dramatically from traditional marble floors and tables toward a naturalistic setting where the customer can feel more comfortable—maybe even *enjoy* his visit to the bank.

2) This "natural bank" image has a number of strong advantages from a promotional viewpoint, in addition to its advantage as a unique differential. For one thing, it lends itself to colorful, dramatic, compelling visual interpretation, as the attached layouts attest. For

Figure 10-2.

Figure 10-3.

Headline   At last! A bank that dares

to be <u>different</u>

Copy   Here's a new idea in banking--the <u>Natural</u> Bank.

When you look around our lush interior you might think

you're in an exotic tropical jungle, or a relaxing island

paradise.

The way we have it figured, a bank doesn't <u>have</u> to be

made of marble to be a bank. In the past, it's been that

way but the <u>Natural</u> Bank has made a big change, a real break

with the past. You'll see what we mean the instant you step

into the lobby and see the <u>Natural</u> Bank's natural environment

that makes your banking a time for enjoying yourself, not a

chore-time.

In addition to the fascinating surroundings, we've developed

a new technique (called our "Simplified System") to make banking

easier for you--no more hassles no matter <u>what</u> kind of transaction

you put through.

Be sure to step in soon to take a good look around. We

guarantee you're going to like the <u>Natural</u> Bank.

Slogan: We're different because <u>you</u> are.

Logotype: <u>Natural</u> Bank

This newspaper advertisement takes its cue from the television commercial (fig. 10-1) in copy and layout.

another, the concept of simple, natural surroundings emphasizes the simple new banking system which will serve customers' wants, needs, and interests more efficiently.

3) Perhaps the strongest promotional advantage of this "natural bank" image is that it reflects the concerns and values of our youthful new target-market clientele. Thus, in reflecting the quest-for-excitement trend, the natural bank emphasizes feelings, an exotic environment,

back-to-nature romance. In reflecting the trend toward the reaction against life's complexities, the natural bank emphasizes a simple, natural lifestyle, unencumbered with artificiality.

. . . A uniform and well-designed visual communications program, encompassing electronic and print-media advertising, wall graphics, and outdoor signs, is strongly recommended to relay this new "natural" look to the public. Television is thought to be the most important component of this campaign because the *visual* image will play a vital role in communicating the new "look" of the bank and its new simplified banking system. Because of this emphasis on the visual, radio broadcasting will not be of use, at least initially, in this campaign.

Magazine and newspaper advertising are also recommended in this campaign, primarily because of the selectivity and continuity of impression offered by these media and not offered by television.

Also included with Wright's presentation were a sample television commercial (fig. 10-1) and sample newspaper advertising copy and layout (figs. 10-2 and 10-3).

QUESTIONS

1. Comment on the basic concept (pro and con) of the "natural" bank.
2. What is your opinion of the bank's media selection? Explain.

11

CONTAC COLD MEDICINE

When the Foote, Cone & Belding advertising agency was assigned to help develop a broad-based marketing mix for a new anti-cold medication about to be introduced by its client, the Menley & James pharmaceutical company, the firm first undertook a number of research studies to guide these efforts.

The new product was a successor to the Menley & James product Ornade—an anti-cold medication requiring a doctor's prescription. Removal of the prescription ingredients resulted in an over-the-counter anti-cold medication which, tests showed, was extremely effective in combating cold symptoms. The two major competitors of this new over-the-counter drug were Dristan and Coricidin. At the time this new Menley & James product was introduced, Dristan controlled approximately 60 percent of the market, and Coricidin about 30 percent.

WHAT THE RESEARCH SHOWED

Here are some of the pertinent findings resulting from the Foote, Cone & Belding research studies.

1) There are few, if any, significant differences among over-the-counter cold medicines because practically all the ingredients are mandated by federal regulations.
2) People who claimed that over-the-counter cold medicines (or *any* cold medicines) actually cured colds were probably wrong. Essentially, what these medicines did was to attack the allergic symptoms of a cold, such as coughing and sneezing.

3) The fact that cold medicines didn't actually cure colds was essentially irrelevant in light of the fact that, as with most drugs, users considered the *relief* of symptoms to be the most important benefit.
4) In general, users of Dristan felt that this medicine was highly effective in relieving cold symptoms, although some complained about upset stomachs resulting from aspirin in the drug.
5) Coricidin was generally recommended by doctors and, hence, had a more respectable image than other cold medicines. It was frequently taken to ward off cold symptoms as well as to relieve these symptoms.

THE CREATIVE-MARKETING MIX

Based on these research findings, as well as past experience in introducing new products into the pharmaceutical market, a team consisting of Foote, Cone & Belding and Menley & James marketing people set about building a creative marketing mix designed to capture a large share of the market from the competition.

Following are some of the important components of this marketing mix.

Product. The product itself would be in capsule rather than tablet form, because people tended to associate capsules with doctor's prescriptions. Each capsule would contain a number of "tiny time pills," multi-colored to create the impression that each contained a different ingredient that would be released in succession, over a period of time, to ward off or fight cold symptoms.

Package. A flat "sleeve" package design for the tablets was decided on for two reasons: (1) the elongated surface would provide a space on which to write the name of the product and (2) this design would lend itself to a preferential shelf position, whereas a bottle could easily get lost behind other bottles. (An early mistake was printing the name of the product on the bottom of the package, which was often hidden by the lip of the shelf.) The red and white package color was selected to give an impression of "power and cleanliness."

Brand name. The name *Contac* was selected as an acronym for "continuous action," the major product benefit the creative mix was designed to dramatize.

Appeal. The creative appeal the agency creative team came up with flowed logically from the product's major "continuous action" benefit. Specifically, to dramatically communicate this benefit, the product's basic selling proposition was that it had to be taken only once every 12 hours.

GRABBING THE MARKET SHARE

The impact of the creative-marketing mix proved successful beyond even the most optimistic expectations. For example, within 12 months of the introduction of Contac, it had captured 42 percent of the cold remedy market, primarily from Dristan, whose share of market eventually dropped from 60 to 16 percent.

Interestingly, the main reason for this successful product launch seemed to be based on an interpretation of the product's creative appeal that had never occurred to the creative team when they first decided on the "once every 12 hours" appeal.

Specifically, while the creative team had intended to promote the idea of "continuous action," Nielsen and other feedback reports showed that people associated Contac with strength; i.e., they assumed that any product that could effectively relieve cold symptoms for up to 12 hours must be more potent than medicines that had to be taken once every 4 hours. Therefore, they associated "strength" and "immediate relief" with the product, *not* "continuous action," and further research showed these associations were strengthened by the "tiny time pills" concept. Also, because Contac didn't contain aspirin, most of the product switching was away from Dristan, which did. (Actually, except for the aspirin component, the ingredients of both Contac and Dristan were identical, and distribution rights for these ingredients were held by Coricidin.)

THE SECOND CAMPAIGN

Ironically, the major reason for the success of Contac's first campaign—the fact that consumers interpreted "continuous action" to mean "more powerful"—eventually proved to be a brake on the campaign's effectiveness in further building Contac's market share over its two largest competitors.

More specifically, post-campaign research showed that, primarily because of Contac's "more powerful" associations, a significant number of consumers purchased and used Contac on the second or third day after cold symptoms appeared, assuming that it was the only medication powerful enough to relieve those symptoms. These associations made it especially difficult to penetrate Coricidin's market, since people thought of Coricidin as being endorsed by doctors and hence somehow safer and more "respectable." Thus, they tended to purchase Coricidin as a cold preventive, even before cold symptoms emerged.

The result of these post-campaign research findings was a decision to reposition Contac using a follow-up campaign featuring the appeal "Get ahead of your cold before it gets ahold of your head."

During the campaign, the following points were emphasized in support of this appeal:

Figure 11-1.

Up here, you don't fool around. You take Contac for early cold symptom control.

Contac moves in on your head cold symptoms fast. In cold country that's important.

Contac is not like a cold tablet. Instead, "600 tiny time pills" in each capsule contain medicines that help clear up your nasal passages, your runny nose and your sneezing for up to 12 full hours. That's three times longer than cold tablets.

That's what early cold symptom control is all about. Take Contac. Take it early. Feel better.

CONTAC

The head cold medicine.

Advertisement that stresses speedy action. Reprinted with permission from Menley & James Laboratories.

1) If Contac is taken when symptoms first appear, it will prevent the ensuing cold from spreading to other parts of the body, or to other people.
2) Contac can also be taken for allergic reactions not necessarily associated with colds.
3) Taken for whatever reason, Contac is as safe as any other cold remedy.

As a result of this second campaign, Contac bit off a large piece of Coricidin's market share, while maintaining its market share advantage against Dristan. Toward the end of this campaign, Contac's share increased from 42 percent to 60 percent of the total cold remedy market.

QUESTIONS

1. What three important generalizations stem from this case? Back up each generalization with a discussion-rationale.
2. Contac's "tiny time pills" were multi-colored. Because of this, users thought that each color represented a different ingredient. Should any ethical question be raised about the erroneous impression thus created? Are there any other ethical questions raised by this case?

12

THE PREAKNESS
SHOPPING MALL

When the Preakness Shopping Mall of Wayne, New Jersey, retained the Carelli, Glynn & Ward (CGW) advertising agency to handle its advertising and sales promotion campaigns, the mall's management had two objectives: (1) to change consumer attitudes toward the shopping center and (2) to increase traffic into and through the center.

To understand why these objectives were paramount in the center's marketing plans requires, first, an understanding of its competitive situation, which could almost be summed up in a word: *Willowbrook*.

The Willowbrook mall, Preakness's close neighbor, was more than just huge—it was one of the biggest shopping malls in the country.

Thus, Preakness's position in the minds of prospective customers was definitely one of second, perhaps even third, fiddle. It was the shopping center people went to if they didn't have the time to go to Willowbrook—or if Willowbrook didn't have an item in stock. This attitude largely restricted Preakness's trading area to prospects located within a half-mile radius, although Preakness could handle a much larger sales volume. Furthermore, average total purchases of Preakness shoppers were significantly smaller than average purchases of Willowbrook shoppers.

THE PREAKNESS POSITIONING STRATEGY

In attempting to change this "poor sister" position, Preakness management, working with CGW personnel, devised a positioning strategy designed to portray Preakness as giant Willowbrook's pert, vivacious, attractive competitor, with much to offer and an ever-so-eager-to-please attitude. As a first step in developing a campaign to implement this strategy, the client-agency marketing team agreed upon the following campaign goals:

1) Increase *awareness* of the Preakness mall among prospective customers in the five-mile-radius area Preakness considered its potential trading area—ideally, make "Preakness Shopping Mall" a household word.
2) Enhance *understanding* among prospective customers of the broad range of products and services offered by the mall.
3) Change *attitudes* toward Preakness as being different from Willowbrook in significant ways.
4) Increase sales and profits by increasing both overall mall traffic and average purchase size.

Creative Question: What can PM Offer?

In the context of these objectives, the first problem the CGW creative team faced was devising a creative theme for its new image-projecting campaign. And since at that time New Jersey, along with the rest of the country, was sliding into a period of inflationary recession when money was not only getting tighter but was also losing its value, the creative question became:

What can the Preakness Shopping Mall offer consumers that will (a) encourage them to spend their hard-to-come-by dollars at Preakness, (b) enhance the mall's image in a dramatically different way so as to profoundly affect understanding and attitudes.

One of CGW's answers: "Dollar-Stretcher Seminars" during which professional people in various fields, as well as representatives of Preakness retail outlets and wholesale and manufacturers' suppliers, would conduct short courses specifically designed, as the campaign slogan put it, to help people "Live and live it up during the recession."

"Save money, save health, and have a good time doing it," said the announcements promoting the seminars, which were held either at a sponsoring merchant's establishment or, if the store size wouldn't permit, at a nearby theater.

The seminars were held during May—typically a relatively warm, dry month, with two busy holidays to spur retail sales: Mother's Day and Memorial Day. Also, they were held toward the end of the week, when traffic was usually heaviest, with women's interests represented on Thursdays and Fridays, and men's interests on Saturdays. Products demonstrated during these seminars were all available at Preakness outlets. To increase traffic and live up to the "value" promise, sales of various demonstrated items were timed to coincide with the seminars.

Seminar Ideas

Here, from portions of the marketing plan prepared by CGW, are some aspects of the "value" campaign:

ANNOUNCEMENT OF DOLLAR-STRETCHER SEMINARS:
SAVING MONEY
AT PREAKNESS
MEANS *MORE* THAN A SALE

Recession is forcing everyone to do without, tighten belts, and realign lifestyles. It's tough, to say the least. Most merchants offer sales as their only answer to recession. Preakness Shopping Mall is offering sales, great everyday low prices, and one thing more—"DOLLAR-STRETCHER SEMINARS." As a part of our Community Involvement Program, we've invited professionals in many fields to teach you how to live—and live it up—during recession. They'll show you how to save money, save your health, and have a good time doing it yourself. Watch our circular for the times and places of "DOLLAR-STRETCHER SEMINARS" at Preakness. At Preakness Shopping Mall we're doing a little MORE about recession.

PREAKNESS SHOWS YOU
HOW TO LIVE AND LIVE-IT-UP DURING RECESSION!

PREAKNESS PRESENTS:
DOLLAR-STRETCHER SEMINARS

Preakness is doing MORE against recession with a series of "Dollar-Stretcher Seminars"—Professional demonstrations for you on everything from the IMAGE OF YOURSELF to YOUR HEALTH, HOME IMPROVEMENT to HOME ENTERTAINING, JOB HUNTING to VACATION HUNTING and back again. These are fabulous ideas on how to do it yourself, make your dollar go farther, and have FUN in the bargain!

... JUST ONE MORE WAY PREAKNESS IS HELPING YOU WIN THE BATTLE OF THE BUDGET.

PROMOTION:
DOLLAR-STRETCHER SEMINARS—Professionals in various fields give demonstrations on ways to save money by doing it yourself using Preakness's products.

GOALS:
A) To show that Preakness is working extra hard against recession.

B) To boost the Preakness image as a friendly shopping center that offers real service as well as good prices.

C) To help insure that money people DO spend will be spent at Preakness.

DETAILS:
PROFESSIONALS—By professionals, we mean either product representatives from a national manufacturer, or people who do this particular thing for a living. (This would include, of course, merchants who would like to participate.)

EXAMPLES—
"Gourmet Cooking on a Budget"
"Sew and Save"
"Vacation Bargains"

Where?
We could have these demonstrations in the sponsoring store, if the store is big enough. If impossible, we could do them in the theatre, or outside.

When?
A warm-weather month, probably May, during a sale. The demos would run Thursday, Friday, and Saturday, with more women's interest features on the first two days.

How does a store tie in?
No matter where the demo is held, there would be a mention of where the products can be found, or, if you want, a sign. The individual merchant would provide some of the materials* for the demonstration and, if he desires, the talent.

*Includes any free literature or samples available on the subject.

Additional Seminar Ideas Accepted by Preakness

A NEW YOU
JUMPING BACK INTO THE JOB POOL—Tips for the woman who wants to go back to work after raising a family. (This is one demo with no specific store tie-in, but it leads to others that DO tie in.)

MAKING UP—National cosmetic product representatives, contacted through STERN'S, KRESGE'S.

FASHION SHOW—Look well dressed for less. Show specifically how a few pieces of clothing can coordinate to make a number of outfits. Also show how basic clothing can be accessorized to change its whole look, from casual to formal. STERN'S, CORBO'S, RAINBOW SHOPS, BAGATELLE, AMENTO'S, AND NATIONAL SHOES.

EXERCISE DEMO—GET-A-WAY SPORTS STORE. This would not, you understand, involve an expensive piece of equipment. Maybe those little dumbbells—something fairly cheap.

GOING TO YOUR HEAD—Demonstration on the difference a new hairstyle makes. Rep. from PATERNO'S HOUSE OF BEAUTY could cut and blow-dry and style the hair of one volunteer from the audience.

HIDDEN TALENTS
HOME SEWING—Product representative from large pattern company to be sponsored by KRESGE'S, STERN'S, or PREAKNESS FABRICS.

GOING GOURMET ON A BUDGET—Chef with some credentials (or cookbook writer who could plug her book) could give a demo sponsored by PREAKNESS GOURMET AND GARDEN STATE FARMS.

DRINK THE BEST FOR LESS—Demo on how to pick a nice, inexpensive wine. Sponsored by ARNIE'S TAVERN.

HOME DECORATING—Sponsored by SEELA'S PAINT AND WALLPAPER and PREAKNESS CURTAINS.

MS. FIXIT—Sponsored by RICKEL'S. Clever things women can learn to do in terms of home maintenance and improvement.

BELLY DANCING FOR FUN AND RELAXATION—Naval Academy, Teaneck. Well, why not? Wouldn't you enjoy it?

LOOKING TO SUMMER
HOME IMPROVEMENT—Sponsored by RICKEL'S. Summer projects, primarily oriented to men. Also, the pro would field *any* home-improvement questions asked after the demo.

THE BEST VACATION BARGAINS—SOME'S WORLD OF TRAVEL.

FAIR EXCHANGE—Demo on exchange rates by FIRST NATIONAL BANK.

SAVE DOLLARS AND YOUR HEART—BIKE!—GET-A-WAY SPORTS CENTER.

GET THE RIGHT PICTURE THE FIRST TIME—Seminar on taking good vacation pictures with a rep. from a local photography club or GAF, or Kodak. Sponsored by WAYNE CAMERA.

HOW TO GROOM YOUR PETS—Sponsored by SCUFFY PETS.

Any Ideas? Tips? Suggestions? We'd love to hear them!

QUESTION

What promotional ideas can you suggest that will help Preakness achieve the positioning it wants?
a. Suggest a promotional idea in full detail that would involve the entire shopping center.
b. Suggest three ideas (in detail) suitable for individual stores in the center. Select any three from the stores named under the subheading "Additional Seminar Ideas Accepted By Preakness." NOTE: *Your* promotional ideas should *not* be related to the Dollar-Stretcher Seminars.

PART III
THE PROMOTIONAL
MIX

In this section, the focus narrows from broad positioning and marketing mix decisions illustrated in the first two sections of this casebook, to a single element of the marketing mix—the "promotion" component—and to the components of this component.

Broadly defined, the promotional mix includes all those activities and devices which *directly* or *indirectly* assist in promoting the sale of the product. Typically, direct promotional activities include the face-to-face selling of the product, i.e., salesmanship, while indirect promotional activities, such as advertising, sales promotion, and publicity, support these direct, face-to-face selling activities.

Within the context of this definition, a broad range of promotional mix possibilities present themselves, from virtually total emphasis on a single element (such as direct mail or personal salesmanship) to a balanced reliance on all the elements of the mix.

The specific elements included in any single promotional mix are usually contingent on marketing mix decisions of the sort illustrated in part II, which, you will recall, were themselves contingent on the nature of the product sold, and the competitors and prospective customers in the market for the product.

EMPHASIZE SALESMANSHIP

For example, in the Solna and Rapidata cases, the products being sold are complex and expensive, and the prospective customers sharp, selective, and numerically small. Hence, the direct selling function is the key element of the promotional mix of these firms, under the assumption that this is the most effective and economical way to get the message to the market. However, each firm selects different indirect promotional elements to support this direct selling effort.

Direct selling is also stressed in the Rustic Acres case, in which a long, detailed, highly persuasive pitch is needed to persuade people to part with considerable sums of money in purchasing campsites. However, because this direct selling pitch is delivered in the consumer market, the supportive promotional mix elements chosen differ from those selected by Solna and Rapidata, selling in industrial markets.

EMPHASIZE PUBLICITY

Other cases in this section illustrate an emphasis on various indirect selling components of the promotion mix. Rit and Edsel, for example, believed that the unusual nature of their product-market situation dictated an initial emphasis *solely* on publicity and public relations, by way of creating a path for other direct and indirect elements of the mix. Dannon Yogurt, on the other hand, decided on paid advertising as the most effective way to carry its unusual message to a large, if somewhat cautious and conservative, market.

Two other cases, Shoprite and Bush Boake Allen, pulled out all the stops by including all the elements of the promotional mix in their campaigns, and, finally, three cases—Utilco, Meter-Rite, and Marine Supply—simply didn't know *which* elements to include in their mixes.

Perhaps you can help them out.

13

SOLNA CORPORATION'S "TOOLS" CAMPAIGN

The Solna Corporation, U.S., is a branch of a Swedish parent company engaged in making, selling, and servicing offset printing presses in competition with such large, promotionally aggressive firms as Multilith, Royal Zenith, Rotaprint, Harris, and Crabtree-Vickers.

Although its territory encompasses the entire United States, Solna's field sales force numbers only 17; thus, advertising and promotional campaigns play an important role in the firm's overall marketing program.

WHAT THE SURVEY SHOWED

As part of an effort to obtain the Solna account, Mandabach & Simms advertising agency of Chicago conducted a mail survey of more than 550 printing firms, 20 percent of which were Solna users. One hundred eighty-five firms responded to this mailing. The summarized findings were presented to Solna's marketing committee by Sheldon Kahn, vice president of Mandabach & Simms, and Rod Grieg, the account executive, and ultimately became part of a broad-based advertising and sales promotion campaign for Solna. (Partly as a result of this mail survey, and campaign recommendations deriving from it, M&S did obtain the Solna account and handled the campaign planning and implementation described in this case.)

A CREATIVE STRATEGY EMERGES

Of particular interest to M&S account people in developing Solna's advertising strategy for the year were the answers to questions 3 and 4 on this questionnaire, pertaining, respectively, to "most important" factors considered by graphic arts executives (Solna's largest target market) in purchasing a new offset press, and the impressions among these executives of salesmen from Solna and competing firms. As applied to the campaign, this input would help M&S put together a creative strategy to emphasize Solna strengths over competitive weaknesses, and upgrade the image of Solna salesmen among prospective customers.

Another important input into the campaign-planning process was the reluctance among printers at that time to invest in new equipment due to the problem of maintaining productivity and profitability in the face of a highly uncertain economy.

THE CAMPAIGN

Taking these considerations into account, M&S recommended a campaign which would feature a number of promotional "tools" designed to generate requests for reports to help customers and prospects solve problems relating to productivity and profitability. Among these tools were the following reports, in booklet form.

1) For the commercial sheet-fed printer: "10 Point Guide to Pressroom Profitability"

Figure 13-1.

NAME

TITLE TEL. NO.

INSTITUTION

ADDRESS

CITY STATE ZIP

FOR FREE INFORMATION CIRCLE:

1	2	3	4	5	6	7	8	9	10	11	12	13	14	15	16
17	18	19	20	21	22	23	24	25	26	27	28	29	30	31	32
33	34	35	36	37	38	39	40	41	42	43	44	45	46	47	48
49	50	51	52	53	54	55	56	57	58	59	60	61	62	63	64
65	66	67	68	69	70	71	72	73	74	75	76	77	78	79	80
81	82	83	84	85	86	87	88	89	90	91	92	93	94	95	96
97	98	99	100	101	102	103	104	105	106	107	108	109	110	111	112
113	114	115	116	117	118	119	120	121	122	123	124	125	126	127	128
129	130	131	132	133	134	135	136	137	138	139	140	141	142	143	144
145	146	147	148	149	150	151	152	153	154	155	156	157	158	159	160
161	162	163	164	165	166	167	168	169	170	171	172	173	174	175	176
177	178	179	180	181	182	183	184	185	186	187	188	189	190	191	192
193	194	195	196	197	198	199	200	201	202	203	204	205	206	207	208

FOR CONVENIENCE . . . CIRCLE GENERAL PRODUCT CATEGORIES:

801 Medical and Surgical Equipment	805 Administrative Services
802 Medical and Surgical Supplies	806 Food Service Supplies and Equipment
803 Housekeeping and Maintenance Products	807 Construction Products
804 Administrative Supplies and Equipment	808 General Furnishings

PLEASE CHECK THE FOLLOWING QUESTIONS FOR YOUR IDENTIFICATION

1. SERVICE DESIRED
A ☐ Immediate Purchase
B ☐ Future Purchase

2. JOB FUNCTION
C ☐ Administration
D ☐ Purchasing
E ☐ Nursing Service
F ☐ Pharmacy
G ☐ Food Service
H ☐ Housekeeping
I ☐ Plant Operations
J ☐ Other

3. TYPE OF SERVICE
K ☐ Short-term care
L ☐ Long-term care
M ☐ Extended care
N ☐ Clinic
O ☐ Architect-Consultant
P ☐ Business Industry

4. INSTITUTION SIZE
Q ☐ 300 beds and over
R ☐ 200-299 beds
S ☐ 100-199 beds
T ☐ Under 100 beds

5. PURCHASING DECISION
U ☐ Full Responsibility
V ☐ Recommend
W ☐ Specify
X ☐ Information Only

Reader service card. Reprinted with permission from Solna Corporation.

Figure 13-2.

Reprinted with permission from Solna Corporation.

86

Figure 13-3.

PUBLICATION	JUNE	JULY	AUGUST	SEPTEMBER	OCTOBER	NOVEMBER	DECEMBER	JANUARY	FEBRUARY	MARCH	APRIL	MAY
GRAPHIC ARTS MONTHLY 1p b/w 3x @ $1385 2p b/w 3x @ $2770 $12,465		2 pages 2770			2 pages 2770		1 page 1385		2 pages 2770		1 page 1385	
PRINTING IMPRESSIONS Tab pg.b/w 3x @ $2220 7x10 VIP 2x @ $1030 7x10 F/R 1x @ $1415 $10,135			7x10 F/R 1415	Tab page 2050		7x10 VIP (Web) 1030		Tab page F/R 2050		7x10 VIP (Web) 1030		Tab page F/R 2050
INLAND PRINTER 1p F/R 3x @$1370 1p Demo 3x @ $1030 $7200		1 page Demo (Web) 1030			1 page F/R 1370	1 page F/R 1370		1 page Demo 1030	1 page F/R 1370		1 page Demo 1030	
REPRODUCTIONS REVIEW 1p b/w 6x @ $1280 $7680	1 page 1280			1 page 1280		1 page 1280		1 page 1280		1 page 1280		1 page 1280
PRINTING TRADES BLUE BOOK 2 pjs. Southeastern Ed. 2 pjs.New York Ed. $860.			2 pages (Southeastern) 430						2 pages (N.Y. Ed.) 430			
TOTALS $38,340	1280	3800	1845	4885	4140	3680	1385	4530	4570	2310	2415	3500

Reprinted with permission from Solna Corporation.

2) For the in-plant market and the small commercial sheet-fed printer: "Solna 25 Format Guide"

3) For the large web-fed printer: "The Profitability Side of Web Offset"

M&S felt that these tools were highly promotable in trade magazine advertisements as well as by direct mail, in publicity releases, and in direct sales calls. Account personnel felt that this approach was superior to merely offering press literature, as had been done in the past, and would produce many more inquiries for Solna salesmen to follow up (an important consideration because of the vast size of Solna's territory and the limited number of salesmen). M&S also felt that the tools would help to upgrade the company image as a corporation interested in the welfare of the entire industry as well as its own customers. Also, it was hoped that the campaign would enhance the image of the Solna salesmen among prospective customers.

SELLING THE TOOLS

To promote the use of these tools among customers and prospects, M&S relied primarily on publicity releases and advertisements offering bingo cards (fig. 13-1) appearing in the following graphic arts trade magazines: *Graphic Arts Monthly* (fig. 13-2), *Printing Impressions*, *Inland Printer*, and *Reproductions Review*. A copy of the advertising schedule for the year is also shown (fig. 13-3).

QUESTIONS

1. Discuss the "tools" campaign—pro and con—as utilized by the Solna Corporation.
2. What are the "bingo" cards referred to in the case? How important are they?
3. Comment on the coupon used in the magazine advertisement,
4. What are "buying influences"? Explain their relative importance in the consumer and business fields.

14

RAPIDATA'S RAPIDTEN®

How can all the elements of the promotional mix—including advertising, sales promotion, publicity, and direct sales—be effectively integrated in support of a new product sales campaign?

That's the problem that Richard Bergman, a product manager for Rapidata, Inc., faced when sales and profit projections for a new product assigned to him failed to materialize.

Actually, this "product" was a service, a fourth-generation time-sharing computer service, called "Rapidten®," which had just been integrated into the firm's nationwide telecommunications network. Through this network, Rapidata provided a broad range of remote-access computer services to a diverse group of customers, including 300 industrial corporations (most listed among *Fortune*'s 500) and 175 financial institutions.

For a typical client, Rapidata collected and analyzed data pertaining to functions such as sales analysis, inventory control, and financial controls. The company programmed and maintained customized client applications and provided numerous supportive media and consulting services.

DEVELOPING THE "BENEFITS" STORY

It did not seem reasonable that Bergman's product, Rapidten, should be in the sales and profit doldrums, when it offered customers a larger core memory, faster processing of data, and a broader range of computer-language programs than the system it was designed to replace. From the customer's viewpoint, this meant a greatly improved cost/performance ratio, i.e., much more data could be processed much more quickly for each cost dollar. Indeed, studies showed that the new Rapidten system would be 50 percent more cost-effective than its predecessor on large programs, 25 percent more effective on smaller ones.

From Rapidata's viewpoint, the Rapidten system meant a strong competitive edge in a highly competitive field, as well as an opportunity to greatly expand its capabilities and services in future years.

PLUGGING THE PROFIT DRAIN

Few of these profitable possibilities were likely to emerge if Rapidata did not sell its new Rapidten service; and, unfortunately, sales were unsatisfactory. During the first few months following its introduction, the Rapidten system was costing an average of $50,000 per month to operate while returning average monthly revenues of only $16,000. Ironically, while the Rapidten system, equipped to handle large programs, was virtually sitting idle, the system it was designed to replace was greatly overworked, straining at its electronic seams.

As a first step in solving this under-utilization problem, Bergman consulted with the people most directly responsible for persuading people to utilize Rapidten—Rapidata's sales managers and salesmen. From these conferences, he arrived at the following conclusions:

1) In general, Rapidata's salesmen had only a cursory understanding of Rapidten's features and competitive benefits. In addition, many of the salesmen had distinctly negative attitudes toward the new system, labeling it, among other things, as "unreliable" and "noncompetitive."

2) Even when Rapidata's salesmen did understand Rapidten's competitive features and benefits, many were still reluctant to "push" the system, because this could have an adverse effect on their monthly sales quotas. Time and effort required to sell the new system, they felt, would cut into more productive selling time for older, proved Rapidata systems, on which quotas were based.

SIZING UP THE COMPETITION

By way of coping with the problem of salesmen's lack of understanding of Rapidten's features and benefits, Bergman initiated a series of studies comparing Rapidten with three major competitors, in order to identify and document Rapidten's competitive edge. These findings were presented in a report that compared, feature for feature, Rapidten and competitive systems, and showed salesmen how the market for Rapidten might be most effectively segmented and penetrated. For example, certain industries—such as utilities and banking—would most profit from Rapidten's quicker response time, while others would find its reduced storage costs, or its larger program capacity, most helpful.

In substance, this report not only documented Rapidten's reliability, flexibility, and cost-effectiveness over competing systems, but also showed salesmen and support personnel where and how these benefits could be most effectively promoted. In addition, this report also made the point that any decline in sales on other Rapidata services resulting from a Rapidten push would shortly be picked up as its superiority became apparent and large orders started to roll in.

PROVIDING SALES INCENTIVES

In addition to showing and telling salesmen about Rapidten's competitive benefits, as well as where and how to sell these benefits, Bergman, with the help of advertising manager Arden Knudsen, devised a contest to provide salesmen with incentives to put this information to productive use in their territories.

Called STREAK (Start-Talking-Rapidten-Economy-and-"K"apability), the contest's objective was to provide incentives for Rapidata's salesmen and technical support people to increase Rapidten sales among three categories of customers: (1) new users of time-sharing computer services, (2) existing users of competitive time-sharing computer services, and (3) existing users of Rapidata's computer services that Rapidten was largely designed to replace.

The contest was planned to last three months. In this time salesmen and support personnel would compete for points awarded on the basis of the size and number of new Rapidten contracts. These points, in turn, would qualify salesmen for individual monthly awards and a grand prize at year's end. Accompanying the contest were these supplementary incentives:

1) A special pricing option, which salesmen could make available to new users of Rapidten, that allowed a 30 percent reduction for night use and a 60 percent reduction for weekend use.
2) Supplementary promotional paraphernalia, including campaign STREAK buttons and STREAK posters to be distributed to customers by salesmen and support personnel.

SUPPORTING THE SALES EFFORT

Having provided information and incentives to support the direct selling effort, Bergman's planning now focused on the indirect aspects of the Rapidten push—(1) designing the external and internal communications campaigns used to presell prospects on Rapidten benefits and (2) informing Rapidata sales and support personnel of their progress in the STREAK campaign.

The brunt of this communications effort was handled by Arden Knudsen, Rapidata's advertising and sales promotion manager, who prepared the following indirect selling materials:

Figure 14-1.

Dear Customer:

On November 9 a letter was sent announcing our new RAPIDTEN service. Much has happened since that time.

With this letter we are proud to announce release 2 of RAPIDTEN service. Release 2 incorporates the power and flexibility of the DEC 1070 with the ease of use of the Rapidata command language environment.

Perhaps the most dramatic announcement we have at this time is that we have implemented a greatly improved, <u>extremely cost effective</u> version of RAPIDTAB compatible with the 400 version. This new version has an increased capacity of 7000 elements and up to 17 digits of precision. In addition, a new RAPIDTAB utility has been developed which will accept run-time, terminal input. Large reports may yield savings up to 50% on CPU usage; smaller reports average 25% savings.

The improved cost effectiveness of RAPIDTAB, coupled with the RAPIDTEN pricing option (30% reduction in CPU cost for night usage, 60% reduction in CPU cost for weekend usage) makes very large RAPIDTAB systems extremely viable. A company-wide monthly report from several locations with an accompanying consolidation which previously cost $1000 per month may be reduced to only $300 by taking advantage of RAPIDTEN's economies.

In the area of language development, we have released Version 2 FORTRAN which features more cost effective performance and many additional language features. It has been tested extensively for the last six months and has now been made available for general use. In this regard, we have two new utility programs of importance to FORTRAN users:

1. We have installed a more cost effective version of NEWFOR*UTL, a utility to reformat free form codes, resequence FORMAT statement numbers and resequence statement references, transforming messy code into readable standard format code.

2. A 400 FORTRAN translator is now available which will perform most of the conversion from 400 FORTRAN to RAPIDTEN FORTRAN. Areas that cannot be directly converted are flagged and warning messages are printed (i.e., wordsize dependent code).

Improvements have also been made to BASIC and COBOL and, for those of you who are ASSEMBLY Language buffs, MACRO-10 is now available on a limited support basis using system MAC.

Most User Numbers are already valid on RAPIDTEN, so why not begin taking advantage of these economies now. It is our intent to continue to supply you with the finest remote computing capabilities available.

For more information, call your nearest sales office or call our Corporate Headquarters and ask for Rich Bergman at 201-227-0035.

Sincerely,

Louis R. Lambiase
Vice President Marketing

LRL/ch

Customer letter. Reprinted with permission from Rapidata.

Figure 14-2.

```
FOR:   RAPIDATA, INC.  (OTC)

FROM:  Ronald F. Hengen
       Bejan and Hengen, Inc.
       One New York Plaza
       New York, New York 10004
       (212)  425-0940
```

FOR IMMEDIATE RELEASE

RAPIDATA REPORTS RELEASE 2 OF RAPIDTEN SERVICE

FAIRFIELD, NEW JERSEY, March 29 -- Rapidata, Inc., a remote access computer service company, today has announced Release 2 of their RAPIDTEN service. Major strides have been taken to improve its capabilities and performance. Release 2 incorporates the power and flexibility of the DEC 1070 with the ease of use of the Rapidata command language environment.

Perhaps the most dramatic announcement at this time is the availability of a greatly improved version of RAPIDTAB, a tabular financial report generator. This new version has an increased capacity of 7,000 elements and up to 17 digits of precision. In addition, there is a new RAPIDTAB utility which accepts run-time input. Large reports may yield savings of up to 50% on CPU costs, with smaller reports averaging 25% savings.

The improved cost effectiveness of RAPIDTAB, coupled with the RAPIDTEN pricing option (30% reduction in CPU cost for night usage, 60% reduction in CPU cost for weekend usage), makes very large RAPIDTAB systems extremely viable. According to L. R. Lambiase, Vice President of Marketing, "Company-wide reports including consolidations which previously cost $1,000 per month may be reduced to only $300 by taking advantage of RAPIDTEN'S economics."

In the area of language development, a new version of FORTRAN has been released which includes optimized code, and provides improved cost effectiveness with many extended language features. In this regard, two new FORTRAN utilities of importance to FORTRAN users are now available:

1. An extremely cost effective version of NEWFOR*UTL has been released. NEWFOR provides the capability to reformat free format code, to resequence FORMAT statement references, transforming free format code into readable, standard format code.

2. A FORTRAN translator is now available which will perform most of the conversion from 400 FORTRAN to RAPIDTEN FORTRAN. Areas that cannot be directly converted (i.e., word size dependent code) are flagged and warning messages are printed.

Further enhancements have also been made to BASIC and COBOL with particular emphasis on file handling, and because of customers' requests, MACRO-10 Assembler is being made available on a limited support basis.

For more information, call Rapidata Headquarters at (201) 227-0035.

Press release. Reprinted with permission from Rapidata.

Figure 14-3.

Mr. & Mrs. Carl R. Jon
200 South Road
Ramshead Way, New Jersey 08012

Dear Carl and Enid:

    Rapidata is pleased to announce a CONTEST to accelerate sales
of our RAPIDTEN service. All sales and support personnel qualify
for BONUSES and PRIZES.

    From April 1st through June 30th there will be three prizes
awarded each month to the deserving sales or support personnel.
During this period, a 7.5 percent BONUS will be paid on all RAPIDTEN
revenue growth. In addition, everyone has a chance to win an all
expense paid vacation for two to Puerto Rico, Bermuda, Nassau (East
Coast), Acapulco or Puerto Vallarta (West Coast).

    RAPIDTEN has been developed as the ultimate follow-on to our
present Honeywell hardware. It is the key to our future revenue
growth.

Your performance can help the Company meet its objectives while
earning you BONUSES and PRIZES.

    See you on the beach!

                                  Good luck,

                                  Stewart B. Gold

SBG:sh

Letter from President announcing contest. Reprinted with permission from Rapidata.

Advertising
A direct mail letter (fig. 14-1) explaining Rapidten benefits vs. competitive benefits.

Publicity
Press releases (fig. 14-2) for prospect industry magazines and newspapers explaining specialized features and benefits of the Rapidten system (copies of these releases were also sent to employees and stockholders).

In addition, weekly newsletters (fig. 14-3) were sent to Rapidata's field offices describing the contest status of sales and technical people, supplementing contest announcement brochures sent to salesmen's homes urging wives to encourage husbands to participate.

QUESTIONS

1. Could Rapidata's crisis have been anticipated? Discuss.
2. Could publication advertising have been used, in addition to the direct mail letter? If so, what publication(s)?
3. Comment on the writing of a letter to salesmen's wives by the company president.

15

RUSTIC ACRES

Rustic Acres, a 1,000 acre tract of land in the Pocono mountains in Pennsylvania, was turning into an expensive failure, whereupon the owners came to the Asterisk Advertising Agency with a somewhat unusual request.

Their request was based on two harsh financial realities: (1) the price of land seemed too high to both develop the land and attract prospective buyers (especially in the high-priced and competitive environment that existed in the Pocono region at that time); (2) continuing fixed costs and mortgage commitments were slowly making the developers' cash position perilous.

In light of this acute cash-flow problem the owners' request was not unusual; what was unusual, perhaps, was the request they made of an advertising agency. Specifically, they asked the Asterisk agency to prepare a plan to reverse the cash outflow and make the 1,000 acre plot profitable "as quickly as possible." Recommendations to achieve such a result would involve considerably more than preparing an advertising campaign, with attendant creative, media, direct-sales, and sales-promotion recommendations; it would involve the preparation of an entire marketing plan, including the design of product and pricing strategies, as well as the financial considerations underpinning these strategies.

FIRST STEP: DESIGN THE "PRODUCT"

The agency's first step was to inspect the raw land in the tract, as well as legislation that regulated how land could be developed, promoted and sold. From this preliminary research came two proposals designed to help the client develop and sell the land profitably.

Proposal #1: Develop a marketable "product" by constructing a golf course, a swimming pool, tennis courts, access roads, and other amenities characterizing a vacation-home development. Two assumptions underpinned this proposal: (1) the development would offer a sufficient number of unique features to differentiate it from competitive developments, and justify the higher prices that would have to be asked to cover costs and generate a reasonable profit return; (2) a sizable portion of the costs associated with the development would be consumed by a broad-based advertising and sales promotion campaign supporting the aggressive, hard-sell efforts of a corps of real-estate salesmen.

Proposal #2: Establish Rustic Acres as an "ownership campsite" situation, which would involve leaving the tract essentially untouched, except for the preparation of individual campsites, the installation of toilet facilities, and improvement of access roads leading to the campsite areas. The target market for these campsite areas would be families who vacation frequently in recreation vehicles or tents, and who would appreciate owning their own vacation campsites for a relatively inexpensive outlay without ever again having to undergo the bother of waiting for reservations or being turned away from overcrowded sites. Thus, for example, the agency investigators figured that a 1/4 acre vacation campsite lot would sell for $3,999, with other options including the installation of a mobile home on the lot, bringing the cost up to $14,000. These costs would cover improvements, promotion, and a desired rate of return on investment for the developer, and yet still be in the price range of the typically middle-class owner.

SECOND STEP: DEVELOPING THE MARKETING PLAN

The second proposal—to develop Rustic Acres as a campsite ownership property—was accepted by the developer as easier to finance and quicker to accomplish. Additionally, it was felt this approach would give the development a strong differential advantage over competitors, most of whom were developing large-scale vacation-home properties. Also, while potential profits from this campsite ownership arrangement were considerably less than they would be from a fully-developed vacation-home development, potential losses were also considerably less in the event the vacation-home market took a prolonged drop.

This decision made, the developer also immediately undertook to upgrade the property: access roads were improved, toilets installed, and arrangements made with suppliers of mobile homes and other campsite amenities to fulfill the anticipated demand created by the planned sales and sales-promotion campaigns.

While these tract development activities were underway, the Asterisk agency was developing a broad-based campaign in which a multi-faceted advertising and sales-promotion effort supported the hard-sell activities of 50 real-estate sales specialists recruited for the purpose. This campaign was carried on in four states—Pennsylvania, New York, New Jersey, and Connecticut—and featured the indirect and direct selling activities described below.

Indirect Selling Activities

Indirect selling activities in support of the hard-sell direct selling activities of the 50 real-estate salesmen consisted primarily of direct mail, brochures, and newspaper advertisements (radio and television commercials were tried but soon dropped when the number of leads produced proved to be disappointing).

Direct mail offered prospective campsite buyers a premium as an incentive to visit the Rustic Acres campsite. Premiums offered during this campaign included tents, hunting knives, and other items of camping equipment designed to preselect the prospects who visited Rustic Acres.

Brochures, sent to sporting goods stores, spelled out the benefits of campsite ownership for people shopping for campsite equipment. As with the premiums offered through the direct-mail campaign, these brochures were designed to preselect prospects seriously interested in camping to visit Rustic Acres.

Newspaper advertisements promoted the campsites as a "summer, winter, fall, and spring wonderland" and described some of the benefits of campsite ownership (retirement, recreation, long-term investment, etc.). Each advertisement also included a coupon offering "further information," as well as a toll-free number to call. The coupon, keyed to the newspapers in which it appeared, served the dual purpose of providing leads for the sales force and measuring the pulling power of each newspaper.

Direct selling activities

The hard-sell activities of the 50 salesmen recruited to sell the campsites consisted of sales calls on prospective buyers, and "homesite" and "boiler-room" sessions in which prospective buyers came to the salesmen in person, or talked to them over the telephone.

Sales calls were made on respondents to the direct-mail campaign. In such sales talks, salesmen (1) gave a presentation on the advantages of a campsite purchase and invited prospects to visit Rustic Acres, and (2) developed first-hand information on consumer attitudes toward the campsite development. This information would be used for answering objections during later stages of the direct selling portion of the campaign. In addition to calls at the prospects' homes, sales presentations were also conducted in local restaurants with groups of invited prospects. Rustic Acres management paid the meal expenses.

Homesite sessions were conducted at the Rustic Acres site. At these sessions the real-estate salesmen answered questions of prospects who had driven out to visit Rustic Acres or who had phoned in response to the "call toll-free" offer.

Boiler-room sessions. In these, real-estate salesmen telephoned prospective buyers who had returned newspaper coupons requesting "more information." Such calls were made during early evening hours when families were usually together. Salesmen stressed the benefits of campsite ownership (the price is sure to increase . . . choice campsites are being snapped up . . . your investment will appreciate in value . . . low down-payments are available . . . etc.). Families were invited to "come out and visit Rustic Acres—you'll never have another chance like this."

QUESTIONS

1. From the standpoint of the Asterisk Advertising Agency, discuss the positive and negative aspects of the agency's involvement in the financial and marketing planning as well as the Rustic Acres advertising campaign.
2. Account for the lack of success of the television and radio campaign in obtaining leads for Rustic Acres.

16

RIT HOUSEHOLD DYES

Rit household dyes, manufactured by the Best Foods company, had been a household staple for decades. Nevertheless, a number of market factors had coalesced to imperil the continued existence of the product line.

The synthetic fabric revolution was the first threat. Rit does not take well on some synthetic fibers, and, ironically, draperies, bedspreads, and curtains, traditionally the mainstay of home dyeing, were hit first by the synthetic upheaval.

Other adverse factors worked in consort. As the level of affluence rose after World War II the American woman could afford to buy time-saving convenience products, and the "make-do" aspect of Rit lost its appeal. Furthermore, in a time of inflation, paradoxically, the cost of many dyeable items, such as curtains, actually went down in price.

Because these various trends had devastated Rit sales, Best Foods considered terminating production of the product.

FROM "MAKE-DO" TO "DO IT YOURSELF"

Before implementing this plan, however, Best Foods handed the problem to its public relations agency, the Softness Group. Approaching the problem from a marketing point of view, the Softness account team decided to reposition the product application from its "make-do," refurbishing image, to a new, do-it-yourself fabric design craft. Specifically, focusing on the fad-and-trend-setting youth market, Rit was positioned as a fashion color medium. The first campaign in this repositioning strategy was developed around an emerging sports fad—surfing. Tying in with Avondale Mills, Wrangler jeans, Keds sneakers, and other manufacturers, a popular surfing champion/spokesman taught youngsters and teens how to "paint" designs on clothing with Rit dyes in store promotions, television shows, and magazine and newspaper features. A major "dye-in" at Ft. Lauderdale was organized during Easter vacation to introduce the new fad to more than 10 thousand young people. TV and press coverage was extensive, and within two months marketing research showed that 500 thousand teenagers had tried dyeing with Rit.

Then the Softness team discovered, or more correctly, rediscovered, an esoteric art known as tie-dye. This ancient craft, which had flourished in several civilizations, had been revived and practiced by a handful of "hippies" in Greenwich Village and Haight-Ashbury. Tie-dye seemed to possess all the major facets of a promotable idea: it was steeped in history; it was a legitimate art form that could be adapted for a variety of uses and aimed at divergent consumer groups; it was easy to do; and the results were self-satisfying.

TURNING TIE-DYE INTO A LIFE-STYLE

By way of exploiting tie-dye's promotable potential, the team set out to develop a multi-faceted campaign to turn the craft into a part of life. According to Donald Softness, the Softness Group's board chairman, "This was one of the few times in marketing history that a successful fad was launched as a conscious, pre-planned instrument of marketing policy."

Here is how Softness described this campaign.

Through various carefully targeted promotional activities, tie-dye became, simultaneously, a widespread "do-your-own-thing" activity among the young and an important new trend in high fashion. Tie-dyeing was made relevant to all segments of the population—from youngsters to the social set, from homemakers to senior citizens. The phenomenon culminated in a world-wide fad which gave its name to a whole era of youth—the tie-dyed generation.

Softness lists the following highlights of the campaign:

1) Developing and publicizing young creative people experimenting in the dye craft, including active participation in a memorable event of the '60s—Woodstock—where tie-dye was first universally recognized as a trend.
2) Tie-ins with top fashion designers, such as Halston, and influential life-style leaders such as Liza Minelli, Mama Cass, Janis Joplin.
3) Spotting fashion trends from London to St. Tropez, and translating the looks into tie-dyed fabric and fashion features in every major magazine and newspaper.
4) Involving high school students across the country in Dye-It Contests sponsored through magazines and home economics departments.
5) Initiating major dye promotions in department stores and malls across the country; then merchandising the activities through trade features and booklets.

6) Organizing tie-dye activities both nationally and locally, with such diverse groups as Junior Achievement, Boy Scouts, Girl Scouts, Campfire Girls, National Park Service, hospitals, city park and recreation departments.

7) Developing special dye-craft events with city and state cultural organizations such as the Metropolitan Museum of Art, the Museum of Contemporary Crafts and the Cooper-Hewitt Museum.

Through our research and experimentation with various dyeing techniques, we are constantly developing and publicizing other highly promotable dye-crafts such as easy batik, ombre, twist-dyeing and spray-dyeing.

THE MEDIA RESPONDS

Throughout this dye-craft campaign, Rit-sponsored spokespeople crisscrossed the country making television appearances on major women's and news feature programs and visiting women's and feature editors at dailies and weeklies in top markets such as New York, Chicago, Boston, Philadelphia, Los Angeles, San Francisco, Atlanta, and Miami. Within one year, for example, Rit spokespeople appeared on 86 television shows in 67 cities, reaching a combined audience of over 60 million people.

Press coverage included full-page dye features in such high circulation Sunday supplements as the *Los Angeles Herald-Examiner, Denver Post, Atlanta Journal, Sunday Oklahoman,* and the *Philadelphia Bulletin.* Among the daily newspapers featuring major dye stories were the *Miami Herald, Detroit News, St. Louis Globe Democrat, Houston Post,* and *Kansas City Times.* The combined circulation of all newspapers featuring dye stories in a single year exceeded 25 million readers.

Specially prepared magazine editorials generated by dye-craft ideas appeared in *Vogue* and *Harper's Bazaar; House & Garden* and *House Beautiful; Girl Scout Leader, Boy's Life, 4-H News, Seventeen, Mademoiselle,* and *Glamour.* Also, Rit material appeared on two *Redbook* covers in an 18-month period.

National TV coverage included segments on the "Today" and "Tonight" shows, "Mike Douglas," "Dinah Shore," and "Merv Griffin."

ADVERTISING EFFECTIVENESS IS ENHANCED

Capitalizing on the "tie-dye" public-relations campaign conceived by the Softness Group, Rit's advertising agency, SSC&B, conceived an advertising campaign which included spot TV in 40 markets as well as women's, teen, and home-economist magazines (figs. 16-1 and 16-2). A typical advertisement in this campaign explained that "Tie-dyeing is easy with Rit," and dramatized a fashion benefit of the process ("Goodbye shy legs!").

Figure 16-1.

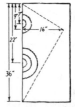

Instructional page. Reprinted courtesy of RIT Dye, with permission from Softness Group.

Figure 16-2.

Reprinted courtesy of RIT Dye, with permission from Marsteller, Inc.

QUESTIONS

1. Why was it desirable in this instance to use a public-relations and publicity approach instead of a conventional advertising approach?
2. Which—advertising or public relations—would be more likely to be successful for Rit over the long run?

17

THE EDSEL
AUTOMOBILE

Judging from the proliferation of books, articles, and case studies spawned by the short, sad story of the life and death of the Edsel automobile, it retains to this day its fascination as a study in marketing failure and frustration, although it occurred in the 1950s. In reviewing this celebrated case here we are chiefly concerned with advertising's part, if any, in the failure of the car.

Part of this fascination can probably be traced to the huge stakes involved; in all, more than $80 million was spent before a halt was called. Still, the Edsel was not the most expensive fiasco in the annals of new product failures (General Dynamic's Convair was). Perhaps, accordingly, at least part of this case's enduring fascinating lies elsewhere.

One good clue to this elusive "elsewhere" can be found in even a cursory review of the Edsel literature, which makes it quickly apparent that there are many reasons offered for the demise of the vehicle ranging from the shape of the economy to the shape of the car's "horse collar" grille.

WAS ADVERTISING TO BLAME?

One of the reasons offered by armchair and other experts puts at least a share of the blame for the Edsel's failure on the Edsel's advertising campaign, under the general assumption that, in introducing any expensive, innovative product into a highly competitive market, the advertising element in the marketing mix blazes the trail for the other elements to follow, and if the advertising campaign doesn't create a strong initial interest in the product, the other elements (price, dealer resources, product features, etc.) will never have the opportunity to assume their roles.

Authorities Disagree

While authorities generally disagree as to the extent to which advertising should be blamed in the Edsel failure, at least two such authorities maintain that the advertising for the Edsel was in no way responsible for its demise; to the contrary, both of these authorities agree that the advertising campaign for the Edsel kept a dying horse breathing much longer than anyone had any right to expect.

One of the authorities is Leo Beebe, the general advertising/sales-promotion manager for Ford at the time of the Edsel introduction and the marketing manager for the Edsel venture. (He was also, incidentally, the last man on the Edsel payroll.)

The other is Fairfax Cone, director of the Edsel account for Foote, Cone & Belding, and author of a book* giving his interpretation of the relationship between Edsel's advertising campaign and its early demise.

In order to put the viewpoints of these two spokesmen into perspective, some background facts and figures on the development and introduction of the Edsel will first be offered.

THE BIRTH OF THE EDSEL: A POSITIONING DECISION

The Edsel was the result of a decision made in 1955 to plug a gap in Ford's line of automobiles between the medium-priced Mercury and the luxury Lincoln. The logic of this decision was reinforced by years of sales figures showing that, when people reached a sufficiently high level of affluence, they would trade up from a medium-priced automobile to a Chrysler, Buick, or Oldsmobile rather than to a nonexistent Ford product. In addition to denying Ford a share of a huge, burgeoning market during the affluent '50s, this gap also adversely affected sales of Lincoln models because buyers discovering the gap were falling out of the Ford habit.

The Edsel, then, was to aim itself at this market for a full-sized automobile priced just under the "luxury car" price level.

AN AGENCY IS SELECTED

Foote, Cone & Belding, a Chicago-based advertising agency, was awarded the Edsel account after emerging as the winner in a competition with eleven other agencies. The first job undertaken by FC&B was to create a name for the automobile. The Ford Company itself was also devising names; the company had even commissioned the poetess Marianne Moore to develop a suitable name, but without success. Ford was keeping a corporate open mind in this selection process; indeed, the *only* name the company had ruled out was the name *Edsel*, because management did not want the name cf the founder's recently deceased son to be associated with a failure, should circumstances work out this way.

* Fairfax Cone, *With All Its Faults*, (Boston: Little, Brown & Co., 1969).

Foote, Cone & Belding ended with a list of 16,000 names, which was subsequently cut to 6,000, and then to 10. Finally, the agency submitted four names: Corsair, Citation, Pacer, and Ranger (names later used to identify Edsel models).

Ford's board chairman, Edward Breech, was not satisfied with any of these names and, in going over rejected names, found the name Edsel and arbitrarily decided to use this name for Ford's new car. (Interestingly, few, if any, critics of the Edsel marketing strategy attribute the demise of this automobile to its name. The name *Chevrolet*, for example, would probably have been among the first rejects in any name selection contest.)

THE PROMOTION BLITZ BEGINS

However, even before the selection of a name for Ford's new entry into the supercompetitive automobile market, the promotional drums were beginning to beat, and as the September 1957 date for the Edsel's introduction neared, the din grew deafening. The publicity effort, headed by a public relations specialist named C. Gayle Warnock, was especially effective: the press conferences he arranged were actually elaborate electronic extravaganzas featuring dramatic lighting effects, impressive gadgetry, and equally impressive refreshments served with the press kits. Thanks largely to Warnock's efforts, the Edsel introduction was covered in all of the prestigious consumer magazines of the time.

THE ADVERTISING CAMPAIGN

In appraising the role of advertising in the Edsel marketing campaign, Fairfax Cone notes that from the start the agency and the client agreed that the advertising should not compete with the publicity for the Edsel. Thus, initially at least, the advertising was to be deliberately low key.

Expanding on this point, Beebe states that the impact of this early low-key Edsel advertising was enhanced since it was "played against" the spectacular publicity the automobile was receiving. This low-key advertising, it was felt, would also convey an image of the Edsel as a "class" car. During the week of the actual introduction of the automobile, the major announcement advertisement was headed simply: "This is the Edsel."

To quote Cone: "The buildup had been so great that we felt we could do no better than to try to answer some very natural questions about the new car and let it prove itself in demonstrations."

Both in appeal and media strategy, this pre-introduction advertising was directed to the young family man of growing affluence. Both Cone and Beebe agree that the early Edsel advertising was highly successful and largely responsible for the crowded showrooms during introduction week. They credit advertising also for the often-overlooked fact that the car actually exceeded its sales goals for the first month on the market.

PRODUCT FEATURES STRESSED

After the introduction of the Edsel, the thrust of the advertising shifted to key in on some of the Edsel's innovations, including its gull-wing tail lights (considered a refreshing change from the then-fading tail-fin lights), and the electronic push button gear shifter in the hub of the steering wheel (later discovered to play hob with long female fingernails). These and other Edsel innovations represented, collectively, a significant differential for FC&B copywriter Robert Eck and artist Fred Ludekens to work with in preparing advertising for a total media blitz, including TV, radio, outdoor, magazines, and newspapers.

Figure 17-1.

FINLESS EDSELS INTO THE SWIM

In the showrooms of 1,200 automobile agencies across the country next week a widely heralded event will take place. It is the unveiling of the Ford company's Edsel, first big new car to be brought out by a major U.S. manufacturer in almost 20 years—since the Mercury's debut in 1938. Named after Henry Ford's late son, it is the Ford Motor Company's answer to a top problem. Although Ford stands with Chevrolet at the head of the low-priced field, it has lagged badly in the medium-priced range, with only the Mercury in that field.

In prosperous times too many Ford customers graduating to bigger cars have been lost to GM, which offers three medium-priced cars, and to Chrysler which has two. The Edsel will be Ford's counterpart, roughly, of the Buick, with a basic list-price range of around $2,400 to $3,600. Ford's planners, at work for almost a decade, have spent a quarter of a billion dollars to develop the Edsel. Their car will come in two sizes (118 and 124-inch wheelbases) with two different engines, each developing more than 300 hp. Altogether there will be 18 different models of the Edsel in four body series: Pacer, Ranger, Corsair and Citation. To give the car a conspicuous look, the front end has an instantly recognizable vertical grille. The body has a square appearance, and in sharp contrast with most of its rivals the Edsel will have no tail fins. The automatic shift buttons are in center of steering wheel. In its first year Ford hopes to sell 200,000 Edsels, about three percent of the total expected auto market.

MASSED EDSEL MODELS are: at top, Villager station wagon and two hardtop Citations; center, convertible Citation; bottom, Pacer convertible, hardtop Corsair. Finless Edsel has horizontal taillights.

The Edsel is launched. Reprinted with permission from Foote, Cone and Belding.

One feature of the Edsel that was *not* played up in the early advertising, and that was played down in advertising for the second Edsel model in 1958, was its front grille, which Beebe says looked like a horse

collar and which most people agreed was the worst feature of the automobile. (Later, this grille was to become a national joke, given names
like "toilet seat" and others with strong sexual connotations.)

Cone goes even further, stating that the Edsel started out as an ugly
duckling and remained an ugly duckling until the day it died, and that
advertising only emphasized this shortcoming to a disenchanted
public, which stayed away from the auto's showrooms after the early
success of the Edsel.

NOTHING WORKS

As sales lagged after the early success of the Edsel, the client insisted that the advertising approach be changed. Cone was in favor of
the original, low-key approach and states, "We might have saved the
Edsel by maintaining for it a published and broadcast personality that
would eventually have been recognized by the sophisticated segment
of the public for which the car was originally planned."

This "personality advertising," however, was not to be. The advertising took on a cliche-ridden, stereotyped, "copy cat" cast. Among
the new headlines were "The most beautiful thing that ever happened
to horsepower" and "They'll know you've arrived when you drive up in
an Edsel."

According to Cone, Ford's policy also led to mistakes in TV advertising. On October 13, 1957, Ford sponsored a grandiose "Edsel
Special" with such names as Bing Crosby, Frank Sinatra, and Rose-
mary Clooney. The show was good enough to win several Emmy
Awards, but it hardly budged Edsel sales; neither did Edsel commercials on the "Wagon Train" TV show, whose audience was made up
mostly of youngsters and old people—hardly the "young executive"
type to whom the campaign was directed.

After the first few months, with sales lagging badly, Ford, says
Cone, tried some direct action stunts to spur Edsel sales. One stunt involved giving a small model of the Edsel to anyone who came in to
test-drive the car. Another involved raffling off a pony, with chances
going to anyone who test-drove the car. According to Mr. Beebe, the
net results of these stunts were (1) a lot of people happy with their
little Edsel models, (2) the price of ponies driven sky-high because so
many were purchased by Ford, and (3) continued falling of Edsel sales.
Edsel even offered an early version of the cash rebate: a "Charter
Buyer Dividend Certificate" good for a purchase discount. This, too,
failed to raise Edsel sales to an acceptable level.

WHY DID THE EDSEL FAIL?

If Beebe and Cone are in agreement that there was nothing basically
wrong with the promotion behind the Edsel—at least, not initially—
why, then, did the product fail?

According to Cone, the main reasons were problems with the car itself (an "ugly duckling"), added to problems of a faltering economy
and the advent of the compact car. Beebe, a marketing man in general
and a Ford man in particular, concludes as follows:

There is no doubt that our research provided a car that would have done a lot better in 1955 than it did in 1957. The depressed economy in the second half of 1957 and the success of the compact car, particularly the Rambler, were, of course, important factors . . . yet, the most important reason was that people just did not like the car. The main point was probably that ugly front end and that was enough . . . It was just a bad product, and all the good advertising in the world won't save a bad product.

QUESTIONS

1. Do you agree that advertising had little to do with the failure of the Edsel? If yes, explain. If no, what would you have done differently?
2. How do you feel about the role of publicity in this case?

18

DANNON YOGURT

Here are some of the background facts and figures the Marsteller advertising agency had to work with in building a campaign for its client Dannon Milk Products, Inc., and, specifically, Dannon yogurt.

Product History

Yogurt, a fermented milk product to which certain bacteria have been added, is one of the oldest foods consumed by modern man, tracing its origins back more than four thousand years in certain parts of Russia.

However, it wasn't until 1942 that Dannon introduced yogurt into the United States in commercial quantities. Until that time, only small quantities of yogurt were sold in this country, mainly to people of European background and to a small group of health cultists.

By way of adapting yogurt to American tastes, Dannon added fruit preserves and other natural flavors to most varieties. Today, for example, dozens of flavors of yogurt can be purchased in a typical supermarket, including lemon, boysenberry, apricot, banana, dutch apple, peach, strawberry, coffee, and vanilla.

Demographic profile

In 1976, 25.9 percent of all families in the United States consumed yogurt with some degree of regularity, with 7 percent of the population qualifying as "heavy users." Comparable statistics for other dairy products:

Product	Percent of Population	Percent Heavy Users
Margarine	92	21
Ice cream	93	17
American cheese	91	20

Although yogurt's market penetration was small compared to other dairy products, its growth rate exceeded them all, including low-fat milk. Illustrative of this growth rate are per capita sales figures, which jumped 500 percent in ten years (from 0.30 in 1963 to 1.48 in 1973). Quantity consumed doubled between 1970 and 1975.

Geographically, here is how consumption for yogurt was distributed in 1976:

U.S. YOGURT CONSUMPTION, 1976 *
(By Census Regions)

New England	33.0%
Mid-Atlantic	35.0
East Central	23.0
West Central	21.9
Southeast	19.0
Southwest	16.7
Pacific	35.4

*Total consumption: 700 million cups

Today, the people most likely to consume yogurt in the United States, as compared to people who *don't* consume yogurt, have the following characteristics.

1) 94 percent more likely to be single
2) 60 percent more likely to be members of professional or managerial groups
3) 67 percent more likely to be college graduates
4) 65 percent more likely to have incomes of $15,000 to $20,000
5) 91 percent more likely to have incomes of $25,000 and over

In general, then, the typical yogurt consumer is a man or woman between the ages of 17 and 34 with a household income of over $15,000 who has at least some college education and leads an active life. However, regardless of age group, females consume more yogurt than males, and in the largest consumption group (females between the ages of 17 and 19), 31.7 percent qualify as heavy users. Among all age groups between 17 and 34, 25.8 percent of females qualify as heavy users, versus only 20.1 percent of males.

Consumer Attitudes Toward Yogurt

According to a number of research studies, most yogurt consumers think of this product as a healthful, natural food that tastes good.

Many purchase yogurt as an aid to dieting, since the number of calories is quite reasonable for the amount of nutrients supplied. Yogurt is also frequently viewed as a good dessert substitute, and it can be used in combination with many other foods.

Here are some typical responses to a survey undertaken by Dannon to determine attitudes of consumers and nonconsumers toward yogurt.

1) A young businessman: "It tastes like buttermilk, and I can't stand buttermilk."
2) A European: "I prefer it to most milk-based delicacies. Sour? Certainly not!"
3) A housewife: "I never tried it. I suppose it's like cottage cheese."
4) A high school teacher: "They give it to people on diets. I understand it has an unusual taste."
5) A student: "It's what comics on TV make jokes about."

Another survey undertaken by Dannon showed that Dannon yogurt is surprisingly well-liked by children, for these reasons: (1) its appearance is as pleasing as its taste; (2) when fruit-flavored yogurt is used, children feel they are preparing the food for themselves, because they have to stir the fruit to the top.

COMPETITIVE EXPENDITURES

In 1975, at the time Marsteller was building its campaign for Dannon yogurt, the leading yogurt producers spent the following amounts in the following media.

MEDIA EXPENDITURES FOR LEADING YOGURT PRODUCERS IN 1975

	Total	Mags.	Newsp. & Supps.	Net TV	Spot TV	Spot Radio
Dannon	$2,069,600	$ 48,100	$ 76,600	$80,000	$1,864,900	——
Delmonte	327,500	63,500	——	——	264,000	——
Hood Yogurt	300,100	——	20,500	——	279,600	——
Knudson Yogurt	356,000	——	35,000	——	321,000	——
Bryer's Yogurt	791,800	——	30,400	——	761,400	——
Light n' Lively	661,000	——	82,500	——	578,400	——
New Country	59,300	——	——	——	59,300	——
Colombo	510,700	——	91,041	——	——	$419,700
Totals	$5,076,000	$110,600	$336,000	$80,000	$4,128,700	$419,700

Sources: LNA/BAR; Media Records; RER/RAB.

A CAMPAIGN IS BORN

The campaign that emerged from Marsteller had the following creative and media rationales.

The message. The basic message Dannon wished to convey in its campaign was that yogurt is a natural, wholesome, healthful food, and to do this Marsteller sent a creative team to a region of the Soviet Union where most people consume yogurt and where a surprisingly large number of people live to be over 100.

The television commercials Dannon produced showed elderly people performing such activities as chopping wood, riding horses, working in the fields, dancing, and, of course, consuming yogurt. None of the commercials made any overt claim that eating yogurt would make people live longer, but if that was the inference viewers got from the message that was all right, too.

The most popular commercial in the series featured an old man eating a cup of yogurt with a woman next to him (fig. 18-1). As he happily eats his cup of Dannon, an announcer breaks in and says: "Eighty-nine-year-old Bagrat Topagua thought Dannon tasted so good, he ate two cups. That pleased his mother very much.

"Comrade Topagua's mother is 114."

The media. As noted on the earlier exhibit of media expenditures by leading yogurt producers, Dannon is one of the few brands to use anything like a media mix, adding magazines, Sunday supplements, and spot radio to spot television, which is their base medium. The primary reach of these media is the eastern sector of the nation from the Mississippi to the Atlantic seaboard. This geographical limitation is due to the fact that yogurt, which has a short shelf-life, must be delivered fresh every day. The fact that Dannon ships yogurt from New York in its own delivery trucks is stressed in many of its commercials.

Mr. William Camache, Marsteller's account supervisor on the Dannon account, explains Dannon's use of television as its base medium:

> We tend to use the news as the central buy and then fill it out with the late night news to get the younger viewer. We look for vehicles such as "60 Minutes" to reach the upscale audience, and "Wild Kingdom" to reach teens and young adults. Not more than 10 to 15 percent of our commercials appear in the daytime. We avoid heavy viewers.

Dannon advertisements are appearing more frequently in dual-audience magazines such as *Natural History, Scientific American,* and *Psychology Today.* Newspapers are used primarily for couponing and price promotions. During the summer months, Dannon uses sky writing along the coastline.

Figure 18-1.

Television commercial. The closing frame of this commercial gave it great memorability and appeal for television audiences. Reprinted with permission from Marsteller, Inc.

118

Dannon Yogurt.
If you don't always eat right,
it's the right thing to eat.

Every day, millions of people give up eating. For snacking.

Well, if you find yourself doing more eating on the run than at a table, make sure you're eating Dannon Yogurt.

Our label shows you that Dannon is high in protein, calcium and other things nutritionists say are good for you.

It also shows that, unlike so many snack foods, Dannon is low in fat, contains no starch, no gelatin or other thickeners. And none of those hard-to-pronounce additives. Because Dannon Yogurt is 100% natural. Not just "natural flavor," but natural everything. No artificial anything.

Dannon is reasonable in calories, too. Especially when you consider how satisfying and nutritious it is.

What's more, Dannon gives you the benefits of yogurt cultures. They make yogurt one of the easiest foods to digest, and have been credited with other healthful properties too.

Oddly enough, not all yogurts have active yogurt cultures to speak of. In some brands—mainly premixed or Swiss style—the cultures are often deactivated by the processing.

We created a whole culture of yogurt lovers.

Dannon outsells all other brands. For a number of good reasons.

For example, we go out of our way to get the best natural ingredients: to Eastern Europe for strawberries, to the West Coast for boysenberries, and we go to Canada for blueberries. (Maybe the reason that other yogurts don't come close to the taste of Dannon is that other yogurt makers don't go quite as far.)

And it's the yogurt delivered direct to your store "from Dannon to dairycase." So if it tastes fresher, that's because it *is* fresher.

Dieters aren't the only people who are big on Dannon.

Today, almost everybody's eating Dannon. Dannon Yogurt is quick and delicious at breakfast, light but filling at lunch, a high nutrition snack or dessert. Spoon it out of the cup as is, or mix with cottage cheese, fresh fruit, peanut butter, honey, or what-have-you.

A suggestion for beginners: since plain yogurt may be a bit tart, start with Dannon fruit yogurts—strawberry, blueberry, red raspberry, and others.

For more facts, including some unexpectedly delicious ways to eat Dannon, write for our booklet, "Yogurt and You."

Dannon, 22-11 38th Avenue, Long Island City, New York 11101. It's free and it will give you more reasons why Dannon is the right thing to eat— even if you always eat right.

Print advertisement. This advertisement stresses the health aspects of yogurt but makes no reference to its possible contribution to longevity. Reprinted with permission from Marsteller, Inc.

QUESTION

What would you do if you were promoting Dannon yogurt to increase male consumption of the product?

19

SHOPRITE

Of the many problems that faced the Keyes-Martin advertising agency of Springfield, New Jersey, when it first took on the Wakefern Food Corporation as a client, perhaps the most complex could be stated quite simply: What *kind* of campaign strategy is most appropriate for a supermarket advertising campaign?

To understand why this was such a complex problem requires, first, an understanding of the nature of the Wakefern Food Corporation in particular and, second, a general understanding of the nature of the fierce competitive environment in which this corporation attempts to eke out its slim profit margin.

HOW A SUPERMARKET OPERATES

Wakefern Food Corporation is the corporate name for a cooperative supermarket chain comprising 189 stores bearing the store and brand name of "ShopRite." Most of these stores are supermarkets (although liquor stores, pharmacies, gas stations, home centers and a travel agency also operate under the ShopRite label), and all of them are located on the Eastern seaboard, from Massachusetts to Delaware.

Included among the functions that Wakefern performs for its member stores are buying, warehousing, and preparing marketing and advertising plans. Wakefern has its own professional management, which works in close harmony with committees made up of independent store owners and managers.

In a recent year, the stores in the ShopRite chain generated more than $900 million in total sales, of which 30 percent resulted from the sale of ShopRite brands. About $10 million, or 1 percent of total sales volume, was invested in advertising. (Typically, about 0.1 percent of total sales is also about what the average supermarket chain earns in profits.)

THE COMPETITIVE ENVIRONMENT

A strong argument could probably be made that, among large industries in the United States, none is more competitive than the supermarket industry, as evidenced, for example, by the low profit-to-sales ratios typifying the business. Of course, a low profit percentage can translate itself into many dollars if the sales base is broad enough, but among supermarket chains the task of broadening this base is becoming increasingly difficult, for a number of reasons.

One reason is the capricious nature of supermarket customers, who will happily desert supermarket "A" for supermarket "B" at the drop of a few pennies a pound for chopped chuck. And in a business where customers must be courted assiduously in order to maintain the volume base, this mass desertion of customers can spell disaster.

However, it isn't only competitive activities and capricious customers that can adversely affect supermarket sales and profits. Almost any development in the economy or the society, including foreign grain sales, balance-of-payment deficits, price controls and decontrols, dollar devaluations, consumer movements, inflations and deflations can affect the profit-and-loss situation. Indeed, any trend or event that causes price increases, or commodity shortages, or cost increases, or changes in consumer buying patterns, often hits first, and hardest, at the supermarket industry.

Among ShopRite's competitors, when Keyes-Martin took on the account, the most aggressive were probably the Pathmark and A&P chains. At this time, Pathmark, managed by a group previously affiliated with Wakefern, had only one-third as many stores as ShopRite but was embarking on a program of building *super*-supermarkets designed for maximum per-store volume, the key to profits in the volume-oriented supermarket business.

At this time, A&P's total volume was roughly equal to ShopRite's (together making up about one-third of the total supermarket volume in ShopRite's trading area), but it was attempting to increase its volume base dramatically through its program of drastically discounted prices. A&P had about twice as many stores as ShopRite but the lowest volume per store among the three competitors. (This lack of store size was one of the main reasons for the failure of the discount program; the stores in the chain simply couldn't absorb the volume of business attracted by the discounts.)

Other, smaller supermarket chains in ShopRite's trading area included Stop and Shop, Acme, Pantry Pride, Food Fair, and Grand Union.

KEYES-MARTIN'S ROLE

As a full-service advertising agency, Keyes-Martin was retained by Wakefern on a fee basis to perform a full range of services for the supermarket chain, including the development of research, creative and media strategies; the preparation and placement of newspaper, TV, and radio advertising; the preparation of mailings and point-of-purchase promotions; and assistance in store openings and other special events. Since all advertisements were placed at local rates, without commissions, the usual agency compensation arrangement was waived in favor of fees.

In performing this full range of advertising and sales promotion services for its client, Keyes-Martin worked in close association with Wakefern and ShopRite personnel, especially the advertising and merchandising committees composed of store owners and managers who were in front-line contact with customer needs and competitive activities on an hour-to-hour basis. For example, weekly meetings were held with Keyes-Martin, Wakefern, and ShopRite people to decide on products to be advertised during the following week, and where these advertisements would be placed. Supplementing these weekly meetings were monthly, quarterly, and annual meetings to plan longer-range merchandising campaigns.

What's In An Image?

The first action taken by Keyes-Martin in its search for an effective campaign strategy was to devise a creative approach for the ShopRite chain, because the nature of the creative appeal can be as important as the nature of the market and the competition in defining campaign strategy choices. The preliminary creative strategy evolved was based on the following considerations, which applied to the supermarket field in general and Wakefern-ShopRite in particular.

1) Because the very survival of a supermarket chain, or outlet, was contingent on high-volume sales, the primary goal of the creative thrust should be to bring great numbers of customers into the store.
2) Just bringing people into stores was not, however, sufficient to assure the massive volume needed to survive and thrive. Equally important was the task of encouraging each customer to purchase heavily.
3) "Image" was also an important consideration in devising the ShopRite creative strategy, for building both customer loyalty and the kind of morale and rapport among employees that would *keep* both customers and employees loyal.

A final creative strategy emerged from the foregoing and related considerations. This strategy stressed the chain's "discounter" image while it also pointed up service and quality features including the 2,000-plus branded items (the largest number among the competitive chains).

In implementing this creative strategy, most advertisements not only featured the big, bold prices characterizing the discounter but also emphasized merchandise quality and the company's concern with housewives' problems in shopping and stretching dollars (fig. 19-1). In addition, Keyes-Martin also prepared institutional advertisements as a service to customers, such as the full-page advertisement headed "Do you make these 15 wasteful mistakes when cooking and buying meat?" (fig. 19-2). Together with the savings message, these advertisements were designed to build a ShopRite image as a modern, efficient, *concerned* merchandising operation, living up to the campaign theme "You get a lot more for a little less."

Figure 19-1.

Timely approach. Reprinted with permission from Wakefern Food Corporation.

Media Considerations

In addition to the competitive and creative considerations already mentioned, K-M developed a media strategy based on the following policy decisions.

1) Each store in the ShopRite chain would be considered a separate marketing entity, with unique demographics and competitive characteristics. These unique characteristics of individual outlets would largely define the media mix for each store—whether, for example, the stress would be on dailies, weeklies, shoppers, or circulars.

2) Supplementing this localized media mix, a chain-wide umbrella media mix would carry the ShopRite message of service and economy.

Figure 19-2.

Helpful approach. Reprinted with permission from Wakefern Food Corporation.

3) K-M was given considerable discretion in making media decisions. For example, while newspaper and circular advertising usually represented the norm for supermarket advertising campaigns, the agency was free to buy radio and even TV time if it was felt these media buys would improve the reach, impact, and cost-effectiveness of the marketing mix.

4) In making media selection decisions, K-M frequently introduced innovations. Examples: (a) Avoiding media already cluttered with competitors' commercials (such as late news fringe time on TV). (b) Seeking out unusual opportunities, such as excursions into prime time (including adjacencies to major sports events). (c) Using "sleeper" specials (such as the July 4th radio program on which the disc jockey deliberately became drunk to dramatize the hazards of drunken driving).

5) In general, cost-per-thousand was not the primary criterion in K-M's media buys. Much more important, for example, was the impact of the media on ShopRite's primary target of young (18-39) housewives.

6) Seasonal considerations would influence the nature and scope of media buys. For example, during summer months, when a mass exodus to seaside areas took place, the media mix emphasized radio commercials to extend the reach to these areas.

7) Geographic considerations also affected the media mix; for example, in densely populated metropolitan areas, greater stress was placed on dailies, while in outlying areas more use was made of circulars.

8) Still another important consideration in deciding the nature and scope of the media mix was the need for competitive flexibility characterizing the entire supermarket industry; for example, a competitive price change frequently had to be countered within hours. This consideration was instrumental in K-M's decision to make greater use of radio, which allows for changes in commercials in 24 hours, whereas putting together a full-color, 20-page, tabloid-size supplement, inserted in Sunday newspapers and mailed out to all trading areas, typically takes about six weeks from start to finish.

9) Heavy stress was placed on post-buy analyses to measure the impact of individual media buys and various media-mix combinations. This information could then be used for strategy formulation.

A TYPICAL CAMPAIGN

Starting with input from ShopRite merchandising and advertising committees as to which items various ShopRite outlets would feature during a specific period, here is how a typical campaign might look. (Note: Once strategy decisions had been arrived at by the ShopRite–K-M team, K-M would be solely responsible for implementing these decisions, including creating and producing all advertising and sales promotion materials, from 3 x 5 shelf cards to newspaper double trucks, TV commercials, 24-page full-color rotogravures, and mailer-newspaper inserts.)

Newspapers. During each week of this campaign, ShopRite advertisements will appear in 120 newspapers in its trading area, with more than half of the newspapers carrying these advertisements twice a week.

Radio. ShopRite commercials will be heard over 24 radio stations in its trading area. (In a preceding year ShopRite had used radio to introduce its line of soft drinks because it felt this was a natural medium for reaching young people. This campaign was so successful that radio was then used to promote the entire chain, as well as specials in specific stores in the chain.)

Television. ShopRite TV commercials will appear in markets in New York City, Hartford, Albany, and Philadelphia. (ShopRite's entry into TV, like its entry into radio, was also largely the result of a successful early experience: a multimedia buy for a canned vegetable promotion which, due largely to the TV component of this buy, resulted in a 100 percent increase in product movement at a cost increase of about 50 percent.)

BUDGET BREAKDOWN

As noted earlier, the cost of this campaign, added to all the other campaigns that K-M develops for ShopRite during the year, totals only 1 percent of the chain's total sales volume, and is roughly equal to its profit-to-sales ratio.

Here is how the budget breaks down for all these campaigns.

	First Year	Second Year
Newspapers	$3,000,000	$3,500,000
Spot TV	1,000,000	2,000,000
Spot radio	400,000	500,000
Direct mail	1,500,000	2,500,000
Point of purchase	500,000	500,000
Magazines		500,000
Total	$6,400,000	$9,500,000

QUESTIONS

1. What changes, if any, would you make in the amounts assigned to the different media in the campaign budget of $9,500,000?
2. Because customer loyalty to supermarkets is so fragile, what devices or stratagems might be utilized by ShopRite to keep its customers coming back?
3. If you were the president of the Keyes-Martin advertising agency, why, in view of the facts of this case, might you be reluctant to have ShopRite as a client?

20

BUSH BOAKE ALLEN

A challenge faced the New Jersey-based firm of Anderson, Dunston and Helene (ADH) in creating an advertising and sales promotion campaign for its British-headquartered client, Bush Boake Allen (BBA).

The challenge: penetrate a sophisticated, highly competitive target market with a memorable, persuasive campaign, and do it on a budget of $12,000.

PRODUCT-MARKET CONSIDERATIONS

Being promoted were a practically infinite number of natural and synthetic rose fragrances produced by BBA and used as a basic ingredient in a wide range of other products, from exotic, expensive perfumes to practical, pragmatic room air fresheners. About 200 top-level executives, such as the director of research for Avon cosmetics and the vice president in charge of product development for S. C. Johnson, are the key decision-makers in specifying fragrances, and other ingredients, for these products. Influencing these key decision-makers, however, are about 2,000 middle managers in technical and marketing positions who, in turn, are influenced by an even greater number of chemists and laboratory technicians.

MEDIA CONSIDERATIONS

Since the target audience for the campaign message would be relatively small and homogeneous, a "rifle" media strategy would be used with emphasis on direct mail and business publications serving the cosmetic and household-products field (such as *Drug and Cosmetic Industry* and *Product Management*).

At one extreme, ADH could purchase frequency and continuity advertising at the expense of reach by restricting budget expenditures to a single page in a single publication; at the other extreme, it could expand its reach at the expense of frequency and continuity by placing expensive, four-color advertisements in many business publications covering (with some duplication) its select target market. Between these extremes, ADH could recommend varying combinations of direct-mail and magazine advertising, also varying the size of individual advertisements and number of publications.

CAMPAIGN GOAL: SHORT- AND LONG-TERM IMPACT

In creating and implementing its 1976, Bicentennial-year advertising and sales promotion campaign for BBA, the ADH account team made three important, interrelated strategy decisions.

1) The campaign would feature *both* direct-mail and magazine advertising. Explaining this decision, ADH creative director William Helene said that putting all the budget dollars in one media basket would be like "sending the infantry into battle without artillery support."
2) Both the direct-mail and trade advertising components would focus on a single persuasive, dramatic appeal and, in the process, each component would reinforce the other and all the other components of BBA's marketing mix (such as the direct selling effort).
3) The magazine advertising component of the campaign would achieve strong persuasive impact over the short term, while the direct-mail component would aim to broaden the reach, continuity, and frequency of this short-term, high-impact effect.

Following are the components of the campaign that emerged from these strategy decisions.

A four-color bleed spread insert (fig. 20-1) was scheduled for two insertions in *Drug and Cosmetic Industry* and *Product Management*. Following these two insertions, a single page in each magazine would repeat the same creative appeal ("Fragrant formulations for creative concepts"). All three would feature a floral rendition of the 1776 "Bennington" flag. In addition to giving BBA a tie-in with the U.S. Bicentennial, this floral flag motif also spawned a number of sales promotion tie-ins.

An especially fragrant Johnson & Perkins rose bush was shipped to each of the 200 key buying influences for floral fragrances. The rose shipping carton contained a red, white, and blue banner insert with a "Happy Birthday, America" message from BBA. A follow-up mailing gave these rose-bush recipients a box of rose plant food, with this message over the BBA logo:

Figure 20-1.

Fragrance formulations
for creative concepts

ơ **Bush Boake Allen**

This four-color bleed spread appeared in two magazines. It provided the basis for a number of tie-ins.

Grow Bigger and Better Roses

Use this plant food as directed and, according to the manufacturer, you'll get up to 3 times more roses.

Grow More Profitable Products

Use the BBA created fragrance that complements your concept Rose. Or any other fragrance.

A reprint of the "floral flag" advertisement was sent to each of the 2,000 secondary influences and the 200 key influences. With this reprint was a challenge to "guess how many roses" made up the flag. The prize offered to each of one dozen winners: one dozen roses. This contest mailing also included this promotional message from BBA:

How Many Roses: No Contest

For a rose fragrance that identifies your product, one that will help it sell, call us. You get *your* identity, the right rose from the thousands in the BBA garden of formulations. Roses. No contest . . . And call us for hyacinth, honeysuckle, muguet, narcissus, etc.

As with the mailing to the 200 key buying influences, a follow-up mailing also went out to announce the winners of this contest (fig. 20-2). Included with this follow-up mailing was a vintage table (fig. 20-3) carrying the evaluations of the International Wine and Food Society to simplify wine selection, and this message:

Figure 20-2.

How Many Roses Contest Winners

The right answer—to how many fresh fragrant roses it took
to make up the Bennington flag—wasn't submitted.
But these entrants were closest
to that number, 3,800. To the hundreds who entered,
thanks for participating.
And to the dozen winners, one dozen roses.
From BBA.

> S. M. Boccanfuso—Piscataway, New Jersey
> Robert F. Zwinak—Cincinnati, Ohio
> Robert N. Pollack—Boston, Massachusetts
> Richard Kaplan—Suffern, New York
> Ms. R. Fox—Brooklyn, New York
> Morris Herstein—Princeton, New Jersey
> Wilson Lee—Nutley, New Jersey
> George Andrassy—Los Angeles, California
> T. Stepanski—Port Jervis, New York
> Stephen Shymon—Piscataway, New Jersey
> Robert Price—New York, New York
> Jerry Fields—Cincinnati, Ohio

Bush Boake Allen

Follow-up mailing announcing winners of contest.

Figure 20-3.

For Days of Wine; Not Roses.

Guessing about roses may be fun. Not so with wine.
So, to simplify wine selection,
here's a vintage table carrying the evaluations
of the International Wine and Food Society.
Want additional cards?
Call or send us the enclosed request card.
And when you seek confidence
in creative fragrance formulations
plus dependable supply,
call Bush Boake Allen. We're creative.
And basic. 201/767-3010

	Claret	Red Burgundy	White Burgundy	Sauternes	Loire	Rhone	Rhine	Moselle	Champagne	Port
1945	7	6		7		5	4		5	7
1947	6	5		6	4	5	4		4	7
1948	4	4		5		4				7
1949	6	5	2	6		6	5	5	4	
1950	4	1		6		5	2			4
1952	5	5	3	6		6	2	2	4	
1953	5	5	3	6		6	6	5	3	
1954	2	2	1	1		3				5
1955	5	4	3	7		6	3	4	4	7
1957	3	4	4	5		6	2	3		
1958	3	1	1	3		4	2	2		5
1959	6	6	4	6		6	6	7	5	
1960	2	0	0	2		6	1	1		6
1961	7	5	5	6		7	5	4	6	
1962	6	6	6	7		6	3	3	5	
1963	1	1	1	0		2	2	2		7
1964	5	6	6	3	4	6	6	6	7	
1965	1	0	0	1		2				
1966	6	4	6	3	3	6	4	4	7	7*
1967	5	5	6	6	5	6	3	3		7*
1968	0	1	1	0	0	2	3	2		
1969	3	6	6	4	7	6	5	6	7	
1970	7*	5	6	6*	6	6	5	4		7*
1971	6*	7*	7	6*	6	5	7	7		
1972	3*	4*	5	4*	4	5*	2	2		6*
1973	4*	3*	4	4*	5	4*	4	5		
1974	3*	5*	6	1	6	3*	3	3		

7 the best 0 no good
* recommended for laying down

Inclusion with follow-up mailing shown in Figure 20-2.

Want additional cards?

Call or send us the enclosed request card. And when you seek confidence in creative fragrance formulations, plus dependable supply, call Bush Boake Allen. We're creative. And basic.

Publicity generated by the campaign included a writeup in *Industrial Marketing* describing the specifics of the BBA promotion ("U.K.'s Bush Boake Allen ads hail U.S. Bicentennial") and articles in New York and New Jersey newspapers (fig. 20-4) describing the challenge of designing the floral flag (which so diminished the area rose supply that roses were flown into the New York metropolitan area from California), and the disposition of the 3,800 roses (they were given to a children's hospital in New Jersey).

Commenting on the campaign, creative director Helen said:

Our idea was to compensate for the shortness of the magazine campaign with a direct mail campaign, in such a way that each campaign would support the other. However, for this idea to work, it was important that our centerpiece ad, the floral Bennington flag, be intrusive without being obnoxious—a real "uptown" piece; a visual carrot instead of a visual sledgehammer.

Figure 20-4.

From: Anderson, Dunston & Helene
              701 East Linden Avenue
              Linden, New Jersey 07036

Contact: Lorraine Sheehy

Phone: (201) 862-7400

<u>Floral tribute to '76</u> was presented to Children's Specialized Hospital,

Mountainside, NJ, by Bush Boake Allen, London-based producer of fragrances.

The floral rendition of the 1776 Bennington Flag was made up from 3,800

roses, each of which was implanted in a separate vial of water. The

presentation was made by Roger Rich, BBA vice president, and received on

behalf of the children by Richard Ahlfeld, hospital administrator. The

floral flag was prepared under the direction of Bush Boake Allen's advertising

agency, Anderson, Dunston & Helene of Linden, NJ, and was featured in a

company ad.

Article appearing in New York and New Jersey newspapers about the promotion.

QUESTION

Each promotional "package" sent to the 200 key buying influences cost about $20. This package included the rose bush, its container, the fertilizer, the contest mailings, and the prizes offered. Would it have been better to have salesmen call upon the prospects to tell the Bush Boake Allen story instead of using the promotional package approach?

21

UTILCO CORPORATION

As the manufacturing and distribution division of a large public utility, Utilco Corporation controlled eight widely separated plants. In addition, the division had 20 distribution locations around the country.

Supplied to the parent utility by Utilco Corporation was a variety of communications equipment manufactured in the various plants. This equipment included such items as cables, telephones, mechanical and electronic switching systems, wire, and PBX stations. There were many other items of a similar nature.

Little or no public awareness of the division's relationship to these products was evident. The parent organization was well known, however, through its extensive corporate advertising campaigns and its public-relations efforts. The latter were systematic, and consistent. Both the advertising and public relations stressed the utility's service.

In the words of one of the top management men of the parent company: "The result of our concentrating on the service angle is that we now have a very low profile for the manufacturing and distribution arm of our company." Concern over this "low profile," or unawareness, grew in the company as they surmised that in the plant cities problems might arise in the areas of community attitudes, employee morale, and efforts to recruit personnel locally.

As a first step in attacking the problem, or problems, the division consulted with its advertising agency. Some of the questions posed to the agency were:

1) Would an advertising campaign help to overcome the problems?
2) Would a public-relations campaign be more effective than an advertising campaign?

3) Should whatever action was undertaken be considered an overall project, or should it be broken down city by city to embrace the various plant locations?

Considering the first two questions, agency and company executives decided that both advertising and public-relations efforts would be needed to resolve the problems. It was not thought that one would be superior to the other, or "more efficient." Instead, maximum benefit could be achieved, it was thought, by a careful blending of advertising and public relations.

On the third question, it was felt that there would inevitably be differences in the plant cities and distribution locations that would make it impossible to evolve an overall advertising and public-relations campaign that would answer all the individual problems. Thus, it was decided to individualize as much as possible.

Once this agreement was reached, it was reflected in the extensive research project that was begun. For example, detailed questionnaires were framed that applied to the eight manufacturing plant cities. Also, by agreement, six of the warehouse and distribution-point cities were included. It was not felt that all 20 such locations need be covered with the questionnaires.

A survey, using the questionnaires, was to be conducted over a two-month period by a major opinion research organization. This was to be a two-pronged effort.

1) Respondents were to be selected carefully among the business-men of each city. These would include owners of other industrial firms, as well as middle to upper management of those firms. Editors and broadcasters were to be included also. Other respondents would be key elected officials and local educators.
2) Respondents for part two of the project would be the rank and file of the labor pool in each city but would not include current employees of the company.

Although all questions were considered important, the key questions of the research concerned the division's reputation as a manufacturer and employer. The chief probes developing from these questions sought to discover—

1) the levels of awareness of the division;
2) the division's role within the parent utility;
3) its reputation for quality products;
4) its role as an important operation in the community in which it was located;
5) its standing as an active force in helping to improve the community in which it was located (i.e., was it a "good citizen"?); and
6) its reputation as a place to work.

A total of 40 questions was asked at each interview. To facilitate easy tabulation, each attitudinal question had a range of answers from which to pick:

Excellent _____
Above Average _____
Good _____
Below Average _____
Fair _____
Poor _____

A number of questions could be answered with "Yes," "No," "Don't know." These questions related to general awareness, specific association with the parent utility, location, etc.

When the tabulated results were available from the research, they were studied intensively for three weeks by the division and its advertising agency. As had been expected, upper demographic respondents had a relatively high awareness of the division (73 percent) and an understanding of its relationship to the utility (54 percent). They scored lower, however, in their judgment of its economic importance to the community. Forty-six percent responded with a nearly accurate estimate of annual gross figures. Only 37 percent were reasonably aware of the extent and variety of communications equipment manufactured by the division.

Not unexpectedly, the answers of the rank and file varied widely. Answers were fairly complete from the many respondents whose relatives, friends, and neighbors worked—or had worked—for the division. These respondents answered with confidence and satisfactory accuracy.

Almost half the respondents, however, (42 percent) knew little or nothing about the division except that they "had heard of it" or had "seen the plant when driving by."

In answer to the question about the division's reputation as a place to work, opinion was fairly well split, since 48 percent said it was a good place to work, 3 percent said excellent, 38 percent said fair, and 11 percent had no opinion.

To the surprise and dismay of division management people, replies about the division's community involvement or social consciousness were far short of an expected "Above Average" rating. Because of the division's excellent showings in recent United Fund drives the public relations department was especially disappointed.

As a result of the answers obtained through the survey it was decided that some kind of campaign was indeed needed to improve the division's image. Furthermore, it was agreed that after the campaign had been conducted for a suitable time, a follow-up research study should be made in order to see if any changes had occurred since the original benchmark research. It was hoped that gains would be made in such important areas as awareness, attitude/appreciation and understanding, and community involvement.

QUESTIONS

Outline what kind of campaign you would recommend for the division in the light of the research findings. Assume that the campaign would be an advertising campaign with public-relations overtones. Present your ideas on the following:

1. What local media should be used in the various plant cities?
2. What local media should be used in the various distribution cities?
3. If television is decided upon, how should it be used? Straight spots? Programs? If programs, what kind of programs?
4. If television is used, what kind of creative approach should be used for the commercials?
5. What creative approach should be used if media other than television are used?

22

METER-RITE COMPANY

When the Meter-Rite Company was founded, the industrial meter field, an expanding industry, had reached total sales estimated at $160 million annually.

Industrial meter companies provide other industries with panel controls for measurements of countless test requirements during production. These meters must often be tailored to fit the needs of a particular manufacturing situation. Under all situations, however, meters must be precise enough to furnish close tolerances. Industries using such meters range from automotive plants to chemical, aerospace, and missile fields. The latter two have demonstrated especially strong growth potential in recent years.

Despite the vigor of the meter manufacturing industry, the four men founding a new company to manufacture industrial meters in Hoboken, New Jersey, were under no illusions about the difficulties of establishing a foothold in an industry that seemed closed to new firms.

Heading the small newcomer to the field was Jefferson Hurwitz. His brother, Henry, was sales manager, and Sidney Pacci was chief engineer. In charge of business operations was William Soklow. Typical of the kind of background acquired by the four men was that of Hurwitz, who had been in radio repair work for 20 years. After some experimental work with industrial meters, he worked in a production capacity with a meter manufacturer for 10 years, thus acquiring a thorough knowledge of the field.

All four men heading the new company realized that they were starting with little more than the confidence that they were capable of producing quality meters. The company was financed satisfactorily;

but compared to their competitors, a number of whom had been in the field for more than 50 years, they were in a decidedly minor bracket, and the smallest firm by any standard in the field.

Adding to the uncertainty of success for the new company was the fact that a dozen firms already established in the field seemed quite capable of supplying all the industrial meters needed. Few of these companies did any advertising. Those that did advertise were modest, occasional advertisers. Most companies in the field, furthermore, did not even have sales forces. Another interesting and somewhat discouraging fact was that many companies requiring meters in their manufacturing process made their own instead of buying them.

Specific companies supplied by meter manufacturers of which Meter-Rite was one included such enterprises as auto makers (engine tachometers), aircraft makers (glide slope indicators), makers of X-ray machines, and innumerable others.

Hurwitz, commenting on marketing conditions existing when Meter-Rite entered the field, said:

"When we began, our competitors were sitting pretty. They felt, and with some justification, that they didn't have to advertise, or even look for business. Companies needing meters sought out meter manufacturers.

"Naturally, we couldn't enter a field where this kind of situation existed and just sit still."

QUESTIONS

1. Considering the marketing conditions existing in the meter industry at the time Meter-Rite entered the field, what would you say was the first step to be taken by the company?
2. At what point (if any) in the company's developing period should advertising enter the marketing-mix at Meter-Rite?
3. What generalization could be offered about the amount of emphasis that should be placed on personal selling and/or advertising? Consider the size of the company, and other circumstances, in arriving at your conclusions.

23

MARINE SUPPLY COMPANY

With the power boat industry getting more popular every year, Marine Supply Company had hoped to be able to show a corresponding growth in market share. The company had always maintained a position as one of the top ten manufacturers in selling marine "hardware" components such as propellers ever since it was started at the turn of the century, in 1900.

Although the company made many of its sales directly to boat manufacturers, a large proportion of total sales resulted from consumer sales through boating dealers, who sold boats, parts, and accessories for both inboard and outboard models. With both manufacturers and dealers, Marine Supply had developed an excellent reputation for reliable, high-quality components, especially propellers. (Sales to manufacturers were relatively stable, leaving the dealer outlets as the primary area for growth.)

While the dealers knew the name Marine Supply, their customers did not; and brand loyalty to Marine Supply or any other name in the field was virtually nonexistent. And as the vice president of the company advertising agency pointed out, "The customer buys what's available at the point of sale, and this was the problem we had to overcome. We had to get the marine dealers to recommend Marine Supply Company."

In addition to wanting to keep pace with competition and improve sales generally, Marine Supply was also planning a revolutionary propeller innovation that company executives wanted to introduce only after a better sales position was achieved. The new propeller included a depth-sounding feature that would be a unique and valuable addition to any boat. This new sonar device detected nearby fish and warned boaters against running aground. As part of a propeller, it was an improvement over existing detectors.

Boaters were dissatisfied with present depth sounders because they were installed in a hole made in the bottom of the boat. This meant boating was impossible whenever the device needed repair.

The proposed "Bottom-Vu," as the new depth sounder would be called, was sure to be a success, the company felt.

QUESTIONS

1. Should Marine Supply aim at the consumer himself or at the dealer to increase consumer awareness and sales of Marine Supply propellers?
2. What media and what advertising themes should be stressed? Company image or company product? Would in-store promotion help?
3. Do you feel the company should strengthen its market share first and then introduce "Bottom-Vu," or should the company try to beat the competition by advertising "Bottom-Vu" immediately to improve market share?

PART IV
CREATING
THE APPEAL

The cases in this section illustrate what is frequently the single most important and difficult task in the entire campaign-planning process—creating the "appeal" that will motivate people to do something consistent with your marketing and promotional goals, such as buying a used car, or feeling friendlier toward a utility, or developing a better understanding of the free-enterprise system.

The reason the appeal is so important is that it must *do* so much—in effect, boil down everything of significance you want to say about the product, or product mix, into a single short statement, which spearheads the entire campaign for this product.

The reason the process of creating this appeal is so difficult is that this appeal must *be* so much. Thus, it isn't enough that it manages to capture the significant essence of the product; it must capture this essence in a way that is *meaningful* to broad and diverse groups of people who are using the product, or could use the product, or might sell the product, or even who help make the product. Somehow, this appeal must be persuasively versatile enough to push a lot of motivational "hot buttons."

But meaningfulness isn't enough either. The appeal must also be *believable*, or its motivational job will never get started.

Even meaningfulness and believability aren't quite enough. Unless the appeal is *distinctive* in some way, these admirable attributes will get flipped over or turned off.

GUIDELINES FOR APPRAISING APPEALS

As you read the cases in this section and develop a better understanding of the occasionally agonizing process of generating appeals to spearhead campaigns, you might find it helpful to apply these meaningful-believable-distinctive criteria to the end-products of this process.

In applying these criteria, you might also find it helpful to consider the effect that the marketing environment has on the crafting of an appeal. This environment includes things like the life-cycle stage of the product, the nature and scope of the competition, and the degree of interest and sophistication among members of target markets.

For example, six appeals illustrated in this section were directed toward target markets in which the product was either misunderstood (Dr Pepper, Blue Nun, Amerchol), or not understood at all (Berger Chemical, AMF, Red Rose).

Contrast this environment with the environment in which the product occupies a solid leadership position in which loyal customers only have to be reminded to use it now and then (Prestone, Eastman Kodak, Trancol), and an entirely different *type* of appeal emerges.

Still another type of appeal emerges in situations where the product is in the thick of a competitive dogfight (Irving Trust, Sherman Toyota), with differentials as difficult to come by as necklocks.

A useful starting point for getting into this section is via the Five Campaigns case, which compares and contrasts a number of appeals emerging from a diversity of marketing environments.

FIVE CAMPAIGNS

During a typical period during the middle and late 1970s, the major competitors in the supercompetitive soft-drink field lined up in this order: #1, Coca-Cola; #2, Pepsi-Cola; #3, 7-Up; #4 and #5, Dr Pepper and Royal Crown Cola, the order depending, mainly, on who happened to have won the latest promotional battle in the ongoing war of the brands.

Also, during this typical time period, the advertising campaigns of the five competitors seemed to have at least two things in common: (1) each reflected the relative standing of the advertising company on the competitive ladder, and (2) in terms of basic appeal, each was markedly different from the others, although both the target market and media strategy of each competitor were quite similar.

Generally, this "heavy user" target market comprised an age group of between 15 and 30 years, with few characteristics among subgroups in this overall group that would differentiate drinkers of one soft drink from drinkers of the other soft drinks. The media strategy employed to reach members of this target market assigned the largest share-of-budget to network television, with print media—notably, news-papers—playing a secondary, supportive role on the local level.

Following are thumbnail profiles of these five campaigns.

Coca-Cola has established, over the years, a strong position of brand leadership and brand insistence, and has adopted a marketing strategy in which reminder advertising, with little stress on product differentials, is believed to be sufficient to maintain its consumer franchise ("Drink Coca-Cola" is the essential message projected by this advertising). Because of Coke's strong leadership position in a mass, worldwide consumer market, it is the reference product against which competitive products compare themselves in such areas as price, flavor, and availability. In its vast, worldwide market, Coke uses a broad-based approach, avoiding segmentation strategies to define and exploit specific market segments. Primarily in response to Pepsi-Cola's advertising, Coca-Cola changed its creative appeal in certain campaigns, including a youth-oriented campaign ("Coke Adds Life"), and a campaign satirizing Pepsi's "taste test" campaign (in one advertisement, tennis balls are used in the taste test and ranked in terms of "fuzziness").

Pepsi-Cola, whose number two share-of-market rank behind Coca-Cola has changed only a few percentage points either way over a period of 30-plus years, is in the difficult position of having to gain ground on Coke while, at the same time, carry on rear-guard actions to protect its market share against companies behind it on the competitive ladder. Unlike Coke, Pepsi uses a highly competitive advertising strategy which features product differentials (the Pepsi comparative taste test) and market segmentation strategies (the Pepsi generation). On top of these was the "Have A Pepsi Day" campaign, part of a continuing theme associating Pepsi and fun.

7-Up, the third-ranked competitor in the soft drink industry, had adopted a marketing strategy designed to position it, in effect, in the "introduction" or "growth" stage of the product life cycle. Specifically, instead of competing head-on with Coke and Pepsi as a soft drink in the maturity stage of the life cycle, 7-Up had attempted to establish itself as a product completely *different* from these cola products by referring to itself in all its promotions as the "uncola." In so doing, it had also attempted to reposition itself as a new product in the collective consumer mind, although, in fact, the product itself is essentially the same soft drink that positioned itself against these leader soft drinks for decades ("Wet and Wild") without appreciably changing the share-of-market standings. In general, the 7-Up strategy differed from the Pepsi-Cola strategy in that 7-Up was not seeking out specific target market segments in which to establish strong competitive positions but, rather, was attempting to establish such positions in the minds of members of the entire soft drink market.

In 1979, alarmed by a declining share of the market, 7-Up initiated a new advertising campaign that stressed an outdoor identity and a "macho" image. The new direction resulted from research that revealed that the product had a feminine image and that it was considered an alternative beverage. To turn the sales trend around, the new campaign shows 7-Up imbibers engaged in jogging, tennis, softball, and other sports. Most of the persons appearing in commercials and print are male. This fits in with the selection of shows used by the company, such as "Pro Bowl," and publications such as *Runner's World*. Using a theme line of "America's Turning 7-Up," the company stressed the universal appeal of the product but never lost sight of the vigorous market that seemed to hold such promise for sales.

Dr Pepper, competing with Royal Crown cola for the fourth rung on the competitive ladder, was actually in two (or more) stages of the life cycle at the same time. In the South, where it had been a well-known

Figure 24-1.

7UP goes after macho image

By Jerry C. Davis

This week, 7UP launches a major new advertising campaign by trying to build an identity with outdoors activity and "macho" appeal.

The company's heavy Wednesday night prime time television advertising was only the start of a

Marketing

campaign that will remove it "from the pedestal among soft drinks to the new lifestyle that is emerging," according to John Kidwell, president of 7UP of the United States.

"We found ourselves in trouble with our regular 7UP product, with a declining share of the market that has never been entirely corrected," Kidwell said. "We knew we needed a new direction, so we undertook an extensive consumer research campaign that lasted for two years."

The company discovered that 7UP had a feminine image, "pristine, though of very high quality," Kidwell said. "You could hardly go into a home in America that didn't have some 7UP, but people don't drink it as frequently as other beverages. Our product is highly regarded for quality, but it's considered to be an alternative, rather than the first order."

JUST AS the company decided what it needed to do, and changed ad agencies to N.W. Ayer ABH International in New York to accomplish it, Philip Morris acquired 7UP. Philip Morris has depended heavily on imaginative advertising campaigns to turn around its acquisitions, most notably Miller Brewing Co.

"Philip Morris wanted to review our decision to appoint N.W. Ayer," Kidwell said. "But when they saw what we planned to do, they said it was a good decision, and have been nothing but supportive They comprehend how absolutely essential it is to invest money to get a product turned around in the marketplace."

The new ad spots, replacing the old "uncola campaign," depict 7UP drinkers engaged in jogging, tennis, softball and other sports. Most of the principal figures shown are male, which 7UP plans to carry through into its advertising buy

"Peer pressure is important to the brand selection, and our research showed we were more identified with Elton John than Telly Savalas or John Travolta," Kidwell said. "So the ads will have a heavy male skew, and we'll advertise it on sports shows, such as the Pro Bowl, and in Runner's World. That's the audience we especially want to play to."

KIDWELL HIMSELF is a long-distance runner He finished the New York and St. Louis marathon races last year.

"We think it's a beautiful fit for vital, alert, active people to have this bright, sparkling, less-filling beverage," he said.

In its whole marketing program, including new packaging and promotions at the point of sale, 7UP plans to spend about 40 per cent more this year than in 1977. The company even achieved its own version of the coups pulled off by Pepsi with its exclusive fran-

NEW LOOK for 7UP claims an affinity with the more active kind of life.

chise in Russia, and Coca Cola with its new China market.

"We moved into Egypt three months ago, and sales have been going like a house afire," Kidwell said.

Spots

Lorillard Co., a unit of Loew's Corp., introduced a new brand of low-tar cigaret, Kent III, which sold better than Kent Golden Lights in test markets. The new brand has 3 milligrams of tar.

Doyle Dane Bernbach was appointed advertising agency for H.J. Heinz Co.'s Weight Watchers International and Foodways National Inc. subsidiaries. Both companies were acquired by Heinz last year.

News about new campaign.

soft drink for generations, it was in the maturity stage of the cycle. In the North, however, where it was a newcomer of relatively unknown credentials, it was in the introductory stage of the life cycle. Since the greatest share of its advertising budget was being spent to penetrate the Northern market, its advertising tended to be of the "pioneering" variety, although elements of all the other campaigns were present. Thus, as with 7-Up, the campaign attempted to position the product away from all other soft drinks with the appeal that it was "the most original soft drink in the whole wide world." Also, it seemed apparent from the youth-oriented content of its advertising that this was the market segment of most pertinent interest, as with Pepsi and Coke.

However, as a product in the introductory stage of the life cycle, Dr Pepper also faced an identity crisis that the others didn't, i.e., people weren't sure just what kind of a soft drink it was (or even, for that matter, if it *was* a soft drink, with research showing that many considered it a medicine). Thus, in addition to telling people what Dr Pepper *was*, a large part of its promotional strategy was devoted to telling people what Dr Pepper *wasn't* ("It's not a root beer, there are root beers by the score").

Royal Crown: Unlike the other competitors, which had managed, in general, to create well-focused images of themselves in the minds of consumers (the leader, the uncola, the Pepsi generation drink, the "most original" drink), Royal Crown's problem seemed to be a lack of any such clearly focused image which would generate feelings of loyalty, or attitudes of brand insistence, toward the product. This image ambiguity tended to categorize Royal Crown as a "follower" product on the trail of Coke and Pepsi, with no significant differential to make it unique.

This lack of a clearly focused "image" was the main reason for the "Me and My R-C" appeal underpinning Royal Crown's competitive campaign. This appeal was used primarily in television commercials relating to life-style values of the youth market, such as having fun together in adventurous ways, or returning to basic values. In all these undertakings, R-C cola was the constant companion, and the tag line on the folksy song accompanying the action.

The rationalization for this appeal was that it exhibited strong associations with comradeship and "possessiveness"—characteristics generally favored in society and usually associated with youth lifestyles. Presumably, these favorable associations would transfer to the product, giving it a distinct "personality."

QUESTIONS

Five of the advertising strategies used by today's marketers are illustrated by the approaches employed by the five companies described in the case material. Tell what strategy is used by each and discuss its possible, or actual, effectiveness.

25

DR PEPPER –
No Longer Misunderstood

In recent years, most Americans have become familiar with the growing popularity of Dr Pepper—the soft drink from Texas. Contributing to this interest is its strange name, its unusual taste, and its individual advertising. Few, however, realize that Dr Pepper is older than Coca-Cola (by one year). It was originally introduced in a corner drugstore in Waco, Texas, in 1885. The founders, the Lazenby family, were happy with its success in the Southwest and did not have the expansionist ambitions of Asa Candler, who started Coca-Cola on its way to national fame.

GOING NATIONAL

Although Dr Pepper did expand into other areas in the South on a modest basis over the years, it was not until the 1960s, when several fortuitous events occurred almost simultaneously, that the stage was set for Dr Pepper's emergence as a strong, national contender.

In the late 1950s and early 1960s, soft drink bottlers began to discover that they could increase their sales volume and profits more rapidly with two, three, or four noncompeting brands of soft drinks than with all of their efforts concentrated behind one brand. It was reasoned that each truck stop costs so much money. Thus, if the driver is able to deliver three or four brands to a store, he can sell more cases, earn more in commissions, and make better use of the bottler's distribution system. (Until 1955, Coca-Cola bottlers sold only Coca-Cola and in only one size, the familiar, returnable 6-½ oz. bottle.) Today, the typical bottler markets three or four brands in six to ten different package sizes and types.

COURT DECISION

In 1958, the Supreme Court ruled that Dr Pepper was not a cola-type drink and that, therefore, it could be bottled by cola bottlers without fear of restraint-of-trade claims. This decision provided access to the major Coca-Cola, Pepsi Cola, and Royal Crown Cola bottlers for Dr Pepper—if Dr Pepper Co. could convince these bottlers of the added potential that their brand represented.

At about this time, W.W. (Foots) Clements, who had started with Dr Pepper as a route salesman in Tuscaloosa, Alabama, in 1938, was elected vice president-marketing. (Mr. Clements was elected president of Dr Pepper Co. in March 1970 and subsequently gained the added responsibilities of chief executive officer and chairman of the board.) Foots, as he liked to be called, had proved to be one of America's most dynamic marketing and sales executives. During the '60s, he developed a strong marketing organization and together they franchised more than 200 Coca-Cola bottlers, more than 170 Pepsi Cola bottlers, and nearly 200 7-Up bottlers for Dr Pepper. From a small Southwestern origin, a strong, national bottler organization had been built for Dr Pepper. (The last open territory, Presque Isle, Maine, was franchised to a Coca-Cola bottler in the spring of 1974.)

During the 1960s Dr Pepper's rate of growth had been better than double that of the industry and of its major competitors. In 1969, it was in fifth place nationally in case sales behind Coke, Pepsi, 7-Up, and Royal Crown. Its growth had stemmed obviously from increased availability nationally, but of equal importance was its continued share growth in the Southwest.

ENTER Y&R

The company had grown to a point by 1969 where the need was felt for a large, full-service advertising agency with a strong reputation for creativity. In the early summer of 1969, the Dr Pepper account was awarded to Young & Rubicam.

Consumer research undertaken at this time indicated that there was a high degree of awareness (on an aided basis) that Dr Pepper was a soft drink. However, there were the following misconceptions about the brand: It is made from prune juice; it contains peppers or pepper sauce; it is medicinal; it aids regularity; etc. Even in the Southwest, where the brand was second only to Coke in sales, these myths persisted. These misconceptions made many people reluctant to try Dr Pepper. Also, first-time triers were often disappointed because they had not been properly prepared for its taste difference (because of its brown color, many expected it to taste like a cola).

Lastly, Dr Pepper was heavily outspent in media by Coke, Pepsi, and 7-Up. As a result brand power and recognition were low.

Based upon analysis of this research, along with other market data, the advertising objectives that followed seemed obvious: convince prospects, 12 to 34 years of age, that Dr Pepper is a deliciously different-tasting soft drink. However, the "how" was more difficult.

CREATIVE GUIDELINES

The creative guidelines that were developed detail the extent of the challenge to the creative group.

1) The advertising must be *meaningfully different* from competitive advertising. In order to stand apart from competition, the advertising cannot fall into the traditional syndrome of the "icy" bottle and teenagers frolicking on the beach.
2) The product must be the hero of each commercial. Any entertainment included must be relevant to the product and the copy message.
3) Copy must avoid soft-drink cliches.
4) Commercials should be designed to be involving and not just present the selling message in voice-over copy against a background of happy people at recreation.

The campaign that emerged has since become very familiar:

DR PEPPER
AMERICA'S MOST MISUNDERSTOOD SOFT DRINK

The copy initially met the misconceptions head-on and used them as a handle in explaining that Dr Pepper is a good-tasting, unique soft drink. Originally, "misunderstood" commercials positioned Dr Pepper as an underdog fighting to gain awareness and used company spokesmen setting out to dispel the misconception and gain new "triers"—in warm, larger-than-life situations. Over the years, the campaign evolved and the company spokesmen were replaced with recent converts attempting to convince "hold-outs" to try Dr Pepper.

Did the "misunderstood" campaign work? By all available measurements it did. It was successful not only in building a bright new characterization for Dr Pepper but also in terms of adding to sales increases. Dr Pepper, from 1969 to 1974, grew at a rate better than double that of the industry, and in 1972 it passed Royal Crown in sales, to move into fourth position nationally. On a five-year basis, Gallup & Robinson tests reported that Proved Commercial Recall scores for Dr Pepper commercials were almost 90 percent above G&R's soft-drink norms.

By 1974, top-of-mind awareness had increased dramatically. The brand was in fourth position in sales and moving up on third place. In 1979 Dr Pepper aimed at displacing 7-Up either in that year or in 1980, and by 1985, its 100th year, it expected to be double its size in 1979.

NO LONGER MISUNDERSTOOD

In truth, Dr Pepper was no longer misunderstood. It had come into its own. As successful as the "misunderstood" campaign had been, it was time for a change. With the change in market position, the underdog stance in copy was no longer appropriate; it was time for Dr Pepper to behave and talk like the contender that it had become. It seemed only logical that the new advertising should be more positive and even more aggressive.

However, many of the factors that originally made Dr Pepper misunderstood were what had made Dr Pepper unique. No matter how understood it had become, Dr Pepper still had the most distinctive taste of any soft drink, the most distinctive name of any soft drink, and the most individual personality of any soft drink. In the soft-drink spectrum, it stands alone as a true original. In the words of Y&R creative supervisor Curvin O'Reilly—THE MOST ORIGINAL SOFT DRINK EVER. And that, of course, is the way that the new advertising positioned this unique drink, as The Most Original Soft Drink Ever.

MOST ORIGINAL ADVERTISING

Naturally enough it was hoped that The Most Original Soft Drink Ever should have the most original advertising ever. O'Reilly, in team with Jim Swan and Dennis Powers, creative supervisors, and associate creative director Lou DiJoseph, created a television campaign against some very tough guidelines. They needed to continue to be different from other soft-drink commercials. They had to tell the "unique taste" story. They had to be entertaining (viewers have come to expect entertainment from Dr Pepper commercials), and they wanted to use music in an important way, particularly after the musical success of the "misunderstood" campaign.

An effective medium for telling stories with music is the Broadway musical. Accordingly, the agency creative team created five mini-Broadway productions for the television campaign. And productions is what they were. Even though they were all subsequently filmed on a theatre stage, they were all different. Each in its own right was a story about Dr Pepper.

One took place in an executive board room as the board members were about to work through lunch. A young maverick, resisting the usual soft drink when ordering, converts the boss and the rest of the board to Dr Pepper. Another was situated at a classic 1950s high school prom as Herbie the Square uses his preference for Dr Pepper to get the attention of Mary Lou, belle of the ball. Others took place outside a factory during lunch (Meals on Wheels); in a college library where a stuffy librarian discovers Dr Pepper; and, finally, in a Texas town of the 1930s, where a Yankee salesman learns that Texas is not only big—it's original.

In order to achieve an original sound for the theme music, the agency asked a young composer named Randy Newman to write the music based on the most original concept. Randy, one of the rising

Figure 25-1.

Example of "misunderstood" campaign commercial. Reprinted with permission of Young & Rubicam New York.

152

stars of the popular music field, not only came from a musical family but also had three highly successful albums. In his assignment from Dr Pepper, he created memorable sound and timely lyrics that positioned Dr Pepper in a competitive way.

It's not a Cola
It's something much, much more
It's not a Root Beer
There are Root Beers by the score
Drink Doctor Pepper
The joy of every boy and girl
It's the most original soft drink ever in the whole wide world!
Doctor Pepper! Doctor Pepper!

In radio, to add further originality to the campaign, the agency sought out some of the true "originals" of the music field—Doc Watson, Eubie Blake, Muddy Waters, Anita O'Day, and Grandpa Jones. Many of the scores considered as contemporary in music today originated with performers such as these. While Newman composed the music, all of the arrangements were created and produced by Dick Behrke, Jake Holmes, and Susan Hamilton.

Both the television and radio commercials expressed the Dr Pepper selling theme profoundly. They celebrated the product. They were joyful. The agency felt that the new commercials were among the most original soft drink commercials ever produced.

QUESTIONS

1. Assess the chances of success for the "most original" campaign for Dr Pepper. Explain your reasoning. What are your criteria for success or failure?
2. Weigh the relative merits of the 7-Up theme—America's Turning 7-Up—developed at the time of this case, and the Dr Pepper "most original" theme.

26

BLUE NUN WINE

Blue Nun is a white wine made by the H. Sichel & Sons winery of Mainz, Germany, and imported in the United States by Schieffelin & Co. of New York. Before 1970, when the Della Femina, Travisano & Partners agency took over the account, Blue Nun had been promoted as a gourmet wine, with most of its $80,000 annual advertising budget concentrated in gourmet and connoisseur magazines with nationwide distribution. Until 1970, annual sales of Blue Nun totaled about 70 thousand cases a year, a figure which had grown slowly but steadily over the decades. The wine retailed for about $4.00 a bottle.

KEY FINDING: WINE SCARES PEOPLE

From the initial research undertaken by DFT&P, three findings emerged which were to play a significant role in the agency's future campaign planning for Blue Nun.

1) Slightly sweeter than many white wines, Blue Nun was perfectly suited to drink with any kind of meal, from white fish to red meat.
2) Most people are not wine connoisseurs, and do not know which wine to order with any type of meal. These people typically harbor a strong subconscious fear that their ignorance will be exposed.
3) Unlike most of the names on a typical wine menu, which only serve to further befuddle the already unsettled diner, *Blue Nun* is eye-catching, simple to understand, and extremely easy to remember.

With these findings in mind, DFT&P, using the same $80,000 annual budget of past Blue Nun campaigns, proceeded to revamp the entire campaign.

Here are some of the features, and results, of this revamping.

Figure 26-1.

Typical off-beat print advertisement. Reprinted with permission from Schieffelin & Co.

The **market**—Because people between the ages of 18 and 40 buy more wine and go out to dinner more often than any other age group, the account team identified this as Blue Nun's demographic target market. Geographically, the team decided to concentrate the entire campaign in the New York market, rather than attempt to stretch the budget over all 50 states, as was done previously.

The **media**—Radio was chosen as the primary medium since television was much too expensive and print would not be sufficiently selective to focus on their target market. Supplementing radio, smaller advertising schedules were placed in consumer and trade magazines.

The **message**—Perhaps the most significant decision of the entire campaign was the hiring of the comedy team of Stiller and Meara to convey the Blue Nun message to the New York target market. The aim of the message was to implant the "Blue Nun" name in listeners' minds in a hilarious, often outrageous, manner that sometimes gently spoofed the Sisters of the Church. (In one typical example, a couple in a fine restaurant cannot decide on a wine to go with both Boeuf

Figure 26-2.

How to tell Blue Nun from the rest of the flock.

How often have you sat in a restaurant and wondered what they're drinking at the next table?

If you see a distinctive white cap with blue stripes and the name Sichel you don't have to wonder.

You'll know it's Blue Nun, the distinctive white wine that's as good with meat as it is with fish.

Only Blue Nun has this cap. So if you want to be sure you're getting the most popular imported premium white wine on the market, start at the top.

By looking at the top.

Blue Nun. The delicious white wine that's correct with any dish.

IMPORTED BY SCHIEFFELIN & CO. N.Y.

Stress on point of difference. Reprinted with permission of Schieffelin & Co.

Wellington and Dover Sole. The man suggests that a Blue Nun might solve the problem. The woman replies, "I don't want a miracle, I just want some wine!") A second aim of these commercials was to take the fear out of buying or ordering wine.

Figure 26-3.

```
Announcer:  Stiller and Meara.

Stiller:    May I help you?

Meara:      What? Oh -- you scared me.

Stiller:    I work here.

Meara:      Oh, well, I'm just looking, uh -- I need some wine for dinner.

Stiller:    I see.

Meara:      I need a wine to go with shrimp cocktail.  A white wine.

Stiller:    I see, well --

Meara:      You know, seafood, white wine and a --

Stiller:    I have a number of wines --

Meara:      Well, I need a red wine to go with the beef stroganoff.

Stiller:    Well --

Meara:      Do I need two red wines?  I mean, one for the beef and

            one for the stroganoff?

Stiller:    Well, actually, there is a wine that --

Meara:      And then there's the brussels sprouts.  I mean, they're so

            ugly.  Do you have anything to suggest for brussels sprouts?

Stiller:    My dear lady, I have been trying desperately to suggest Blue

            Nun.

Meara:      Didn't she sing on the Ed Sullivan Show?

Stiller:    No, No, it's a wine.  A delicious white wine that's correct

            with any dish.

Meara:      Shrimp cocktail?

Stiller:    Shrimp cocktail.  You see, you can never make a mistake

            when you're asking for Blue Nun.

Meara:      Beef stroganoff?  Brussels sprouts?

Stiller:    Everything.
(under his
breath)

Meara:      Everything.

Stiller:    Everything.

Meara:      Do you deliver?

Announcer:  Blue Nun, the delicious white wine that's correct with any

            dish.  Imported by Schieffelin and Company, New York.
```

Example of popular radio commercial. Reprinted with permission of Schieffelin & Co.

QUESTIONS

1. Comment on the suitability (pro and con) of the humorous approach in the selling of wine, via the Stiller and Meara radio commercials.
2. Was it wise to concentrate the campaign for Blue Nun wine in the New York market?

27

AMERCHOL

Anderson, Dunston & Helene does not call itself, or even think of itself as, an "advertising agency," although creating business-to-business advertising campaigns is what it does. Instead, ADH refers to its offerings as "Market Development Services."

"We're just applying to ourselves a basic philosophy we apply to all our advertising," says William Helene, ADH's vice president and creative director: "Sell end benefits!"

Illustrative of this philosophy in action was ADH's creation of a "new look" advertising campaign for Amerchol Corporation, a unit of CPC International Inc., a manufacturer of lanolin derivatives used in many products of the cosmetics industry.

THE MARKET: INTUITION AND ALCHEMY

Describing the unusual nature and needs of the market for lanolin derivatives, Helene notes first that it is "much more responsive to effective communications than other segments of the industrial market," because so much of the product development work is intuitive in nature: "Much closer to alchemy than chemistry."

"At any given time, there are thousands of lab technicians, product managers, and promotion specialists working on new product formulations in a white-hot competitive environment," says Helene, "and intuitive judgment plays at least as important a role in the selection process as technical knowledge."

In general, though, he notes, there is one practically universal attribute of the ingredient selection process—"an emphasis on quality."

APPEAL #1: MAKE THE AMERCHOL CALL

At the time ADH took over the Amerchol account, its advertising campaign, using business magazines as the primary medium, was built around the theme "Make the Amerchol Call." Typical advertisements in this campaign (fig. 27-1) featured a curiosity-arousing head-

Figure 27-1.

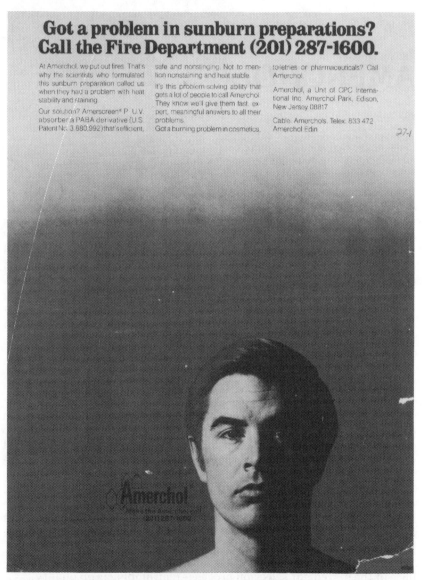

Typical advertisement in the advertising campaign devised by the advertising agency preceding Anderson, Dunston & Helene.

Figure 27-2.

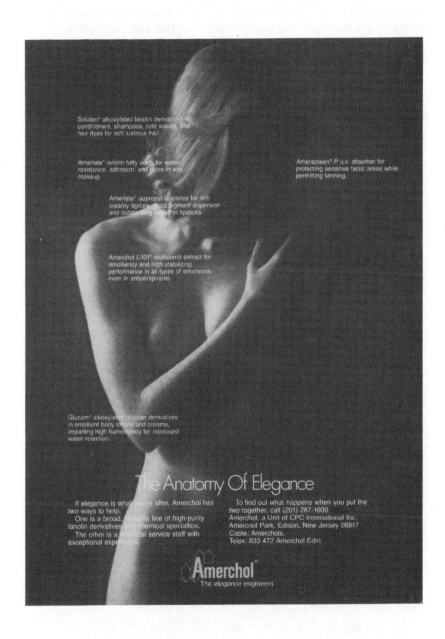

New campaign featuring the female body.

line and a suggestion that the reader "call Amerchol for creative solutions to cosmetic, pharmaceutical, and toiletry problems." Also featured, and visualized, in each advertisement was one of these "creative solutions," such as an emulsifier which holds four times its weight in water, or a non-staining ingredient in sunburn preparations.

APPEAL #2: THE ELEGANCE ENGINEERS

The new-look campaign developed for Amerchol by ADH featured a dramatically different visual treatment built around an equally different creative appeal: "Amerchol—the Elegance Engineers." Says Helene:

We wanted this campaign to convey a *feeling* of what Amerchol could contribute to a product sold in the cosmetic market, and whether this product is a body lotion or a lipstick or a hand cream or a deodorant or a shampoo, it's essentially a product for the female body—a *feminine* product.

So that's the 'look' we tried to impart to all the advertisements in the campaign—a look of feminine style and sophistication. We wanted to get away from the "trade magazine" look with advertisements that could just as easily have appeared in *Cosmopolitan* or *Mademoiselle* or the *New York Times* Sunday magazine.

Figure 27-3.

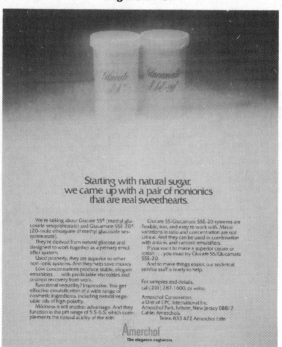

New campaign featuring the "elegance engineers" theme.

The same reasoning led the ADH team to create the new campaign theme, "The Elegance Engineers."

We felt the single word *elegance* effectively connoted quality and femininity, and, when associated with the world 'engineers' really described Amerchol's distinctive role in a fresh, meaningful way. We also felt it put across the technological capabilities of Amerchol, and the idea that there just were no equivalents for this product.

In sum, says Helene, "We wanted to get the same high-key look and feeling into our advertising for Amerchol that Amerchol accounts, such as Revlon and Jean Naté, get into their advertising."

The "High Key" Look

In the implementation of this stylized, sophisticated look, all the advertisements in the Amerchol campaign were in four colors (the previous campaign used two-color advertisements), high fashion photography was used, and the nude female body was prominently displayed in many of the advertisements (fig. 27-2).

Helene admits to some trepidation in arriving at the decision to use nude models in the campaign. "There are many women executives in the cosmetics field," he says, "and there was some initial concern that some might consider our approach chauvinistic, which was the last thing we had in mind. . . ."

QUESTIONS

1. Readex, Inc., a firm that researches business magazine advertisements by determining the degree of interest of readers in the individual advertisements appearing in a magazine, tested the Amerchol advertisement shown in figure 27.3. This was a one-page, four-color advertisement. Out of 10,818 advertisements tested for reader interest, 1,633 were one-page, four-color advertisements. The median reader interest score for such advertisements was 17 percent. The range of reader interest in such advertisements was 1 percent to 69 percent. With the foregoing data in mind, estimate the reader-interest score for the advertisement shown in figure 27.3. Account for your estimated score. If higher than the median, why? If lower, why?
2. Comment on the "nude" campaign.

28

BERGER CHEMICAL COMPANY (A)
I. The Appeal

Facing a seemingly unlimited supply of competitors in the tight summer-job market, Kurt Berger, newly graduated from high school, decided to manufacture his own job and had a good idea of how to go about it. During previous summers, he had earned money by servicing swimming pools in his relatively affluent suburban neighborhood. Typically, this job involved chlorinating, skimming pool surfaces, and performing minor maintenance on pump and filtration systems.

Now, however, it occurred to him that he might expand his servicing of swimming pools into a profitable full-time summer job, or perhaps even a lifetime career. Motivated by this goal, Berger set out to develop a customer list, and to increase the number of services offered to each customer.

INCREASING CUSTOMER SERVICE OPTIONS

Increasing the number of service options available to customers was not especially difficult. During past summers, Berger had purchased supplies of pool chlorine from a large local wholesaler, and now this wholesaler assured Berger of continuing assistance. As long as Berger would purchase at wholesale prices from the wholesaler's complete line of swimming pools, supplies, and accessories, the wholesaler would arrange direct delivery to customers. Being relieved of this stocking burden would make it possible for Berger to offer customers a complete pool service at discount prices of approximately 20 percent under competitive prices because his overhead would be almost nothing.

BUILDING A CUSTOMER LIST

With his supply problem solved, Berger now focused on the problem of building a customer list which would permit him to buy from the wholesaler in large enough quantities to justify the wholesaler's discounts and services. In order to build a customer list it was necessary first to develop a persuasive appeal to attract customers and second to direct this appeal to "hot" prospects, i.e., owners of in-ground swimming pools.

To convey the appeal Berger decided to use the following business card.

E. KURT BERGER

POOL SERVICE AND SUPPLIES

245-8200

After he ordered and paid for the cards, Berger was dissatisfied because they said nothing about the *kinds* of "pool service and supplies" offered by E. Kurt Berger and seemed suited only for a part-time, one-man operation. He wanted to make clear what he could offer that would meet the needs of customers and prospective customers. Likewise, he wanted to erase the impression that he offered only part-time service.

What was needed was a trade name that would have a professional sound, yet would be familiar to his present customers. After experimenting with a number of possibilities—from acronyms to complicated explanatory titles—he finally chose between "Berger Chemical" and "Berger Pools." The former was selected for two reasons: (1) because many competitors had the word *pools* in their trade names, the word *chemical* stressed a helpful differential; (2) because the use of chemicals would represent the biggest portion of his business, it seemed sensible to promote this fact in the trade name.

Having selected the new name, Berger ordered a second batch of calling cards that featured the name and described the products and services he had to offer—and to whom.

Although Berger felt that the new card was an improvement, he still was not completely satisfied. The complete range of services he could give customers was not shown on the card; nor had he given compelling reasons for choosing his firm over rival companies. Until he

RESIDENTIAL   COMMERCIAL

Berger Chemical

POOL CHLORINE AND SUPPLY
WATER PURIFICATION SYSTEMS
SALES · SERVICE

KENILWORTH, N. J.   (201) 245-8200

could produce a persuasive appeal dramatizing his services and then direct this appeal efficiently to prospective customers, his problem of expanding his customer base was not going to be solved.

Calling cards, while a step in the right direction, were a weak substitute for a well-conceived and -directed promotional program. Yet Berger knew that the $17.50 he had as cash on hand was hardly suitable for undertaking an ambitious promotional effort.

Flyers vs. Calling Cards

At this point he considered flyers, because a thousand could be printed for only $14.00. Furthermore, he could distribute them by handing them to customers, placing them on supermarket counters, and slipping them under automobile windshield wipers.

To be effective the flyers, Berger decided, must be crammed with persuasive copy. One such flyer designed by Berger was produced by a local print shop. Especially pleasing to him was the appeal "Save gas,

Figure 28-1.

beat the traffic—enjoy your summer fun right at home." These appeals, Berger judged, capitalized on a trend to home vacations resulting from inflated prices in general, and high gas prices in particular.

Also pleasing was the "Double your swimming season" appeal, next to the mention of "heaters," because it seemed that the development of this year-round segment would help assure him a year-round income. In addition, the "Water purification specialists" and "Free testing and delivery" lines looked promising because they gave him a point-of-difference from some of his competitors.

One disturbing note was the "Discount pool supply" line, which had a cheap and unprofessional tone that clashed with his overall quality approach. Still, he felt compelled to convey a low-price appeal to potential customers because the mention of "pool supplies" pushed him into a competitive, price-conscious field. As a compromise, however, he buried the "discount" line to prevent its playing a dominant role.

QUESTIONS

1. Do you agree, or disagree, with the use of "chemical" in the company name?
2. Look over Berger's flyer. As a reader, what would you say is the main appeal that would be derived? If you don't agree with this emphasis, what appeal would you stress?
3. What might be done to improve the flyer, graphically speaking?

29

AMF INCORPORATED

AMF Incorporated and the many sporting goods companies it manages market a large variety of high-quality leisure equipment items, ranging in price from $7.00 to $700,000.

Although AMF is the leader in the leisure products field, a distinguishing feature of this field is the hundreds of small companies competing with one another in a number of sports-leisure categories. Some of the manufacturers and brands that compete with AMF products in these categories are the following:

Category	AMF Products	Competitive Products
Motorcycles and Travel Vehicles	Harley-Davidson motorcycles	Honda, Suzuki, Yamaha, Kawasaki motorcycles
	Skamper trailers	Winnebago, Streamline travel vehicles
Marine and Sports Products	Alcort Sunfish sailboats	Chris-Craft, Trojan, Whittaker, Laser, Pearson, Sea Ray, Glastron, Mako
	Slickcraft powerboats	
	Crestliner runabouts	
	Hatteras yachts	
	Ben Hogan golf clubs and balls	MacGregor, Wilson, Bancroft, White Stag ski apparel, Acushnet, Spalding, Dunlop, Slazenger
	Head Ski, tennis equipment	
	Tyrolia ski bindings	
	Voit balls, skin diving and racquetball equipment	
	Wing archery equipment	

Lawn and Garden Products	AMF Snow throwers and mowers	Sears, Toro, Jacobson
Bowling Products	Dick Weber bowling ball	Brunswick Corp., Fair Lanes,
	AMF Bowling Center operations	Columbia
	AMF MagicScore bowling scorer	

This scrambled situation, with products in many sports-leisure categories competing against AMF products, posed a difficult dilemma for AMF and its advertising agency, Benton & Bowles, in devising an advertising campaign strategy. On the one hand, the company simply couldn't afford to match, dollar for dollar, the advertising budgets of its major competitors. On the other hand, how could AMF expect to maintain its leadership position in the field without demonstrating some kind of a strong differential over its competitors?

Pondering this dilemma, the AMF team decided to go with one of three possible strategic campaign options:

1) *A Product Campaign*—Select six or more profitable products that are well established, promote them, and expect the advertising to create demand for the remaining unadvertised items.
2) *An Image Campaign*—Concentrate on improving the AMF reputation as a maker of top-of-line, quality leisure products. A few better-established items would be mentioned to add support and specifics to the messages. Eventually, it was hoped, this corporate approach would create consumer preference for the complete product line.
3) *A Combination Campaign*—Combine a corporate campaign with advertising for individual products. Each item would have a unit cost/profit high enough to justify a separate budget, and be in a field where competition is strong and visible.

CREATIVE STRATEGY

As the main goal, AMF decided to tell prospects that they should get up off their chairs, out of their ruts, and participate in some form of sport. The messages would assure consumers that AMF makes a variety of quality products for major sports and recreation that enable people to enjoy recreation with greater satisfaction. Consumer preference would also be encouraged to spur prospects to select AMF brands when they buy.

Campaign slogan: "AMF—We make weekends."

Creative tactics: As part of the campaign, well-known personalities would be featured as they stress the value of recreation for themselves

Figure 29-1.

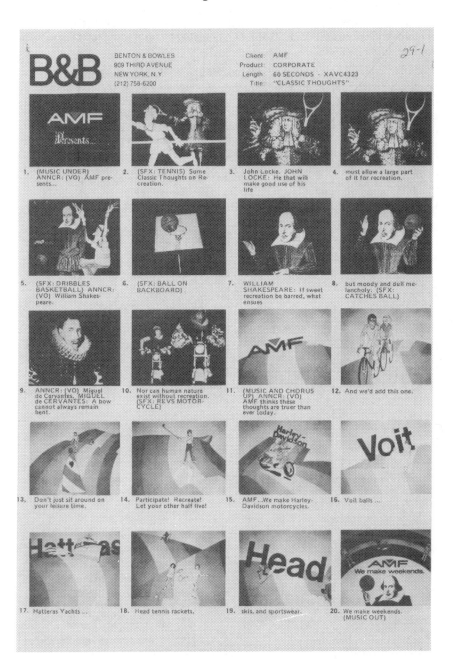

Combination approach in television. Reprinted with permission from American Association of Advertising Agencies.

and, by so doing, recommend it for others. Copy would be in the form of a question-answer interview.

Another aspect of the campaign would be the showing of imaginative and symbolic situations that capture the feeling of recreation and activity.

Figure 29-2.

Q. Strong words. What do you mean?

A. I've reviewed every fact I could find on the subject. The statistics are clear: A man who becomes sedentary after a normally vigorous youth is shortening his life by about 18 months.

Q. But as a kid, almost everyone plays baseball, football, or basketball.

A. And they're fine for kids. But our high schools and colleges are shortchanging us in not teaching us other sports we can play as adults.

Q. And as a result, we play nothing?

A. Too often. We sit around watching younger people play our games. We drop out of body conditioning in the critical years. Career pressures, stress, tension dominate our lives and absorb our interests.

Q. Is it the same with women?

A. It doesn't seem to be. Not up until menopause, anyway. But afterward, they tend toward the male pattern.

Q. What do you recommend?

A. With your doctor's advice, easing back into recreation. It's difficult, but it's vital. For example, authorities I respect agree that even jogging can be a big help.

Q. Do you jog?

A. No, it bores me. I play tennis. Winter and summer. Even at 20°, with the snow bulldozed off the court. I need the competition, the spiritual contest, the game structure.

Q. What's the prognosis for a regenerated dropout?

A. Excellent. The body can come back awfully quickly with relatively little consequence. But the longer you wait, the more you lose.

This is one in a series of messages brought to you by AMF. We make Voit Balls, Head Skis, Tennis Rackets and Sports Wear, Skamper Trailers, Roadmaster Bicycles, AMF Bowling Products, Slickcraft Boats, Sunfish Sailboats, Hatteras Yachts, Crestliner Boats, Ben Hogan Golf Equipment, Harley-Davidson Motorcycles.

AMF
We make weekends

Magazine advertisement. Accompanying the question-answer material was a full-page picture of a prominent writer. The headline over the picture was: "A man who drops out of recreation after an active youth is committing slow suicide." Reprinted with permission from American Association of Advertising Agencies.

Figure 29-3.

"You've got to keep your body in shape. First your career depends on it, then your life does."

Mickey Mantle

(Mickey Mantle has been justly called the premier athlete of his decade. Four times American League home run king, three times most valuable player, he retired in 1968 and was elected to the Hall of Fame in 1974. He and Whitey Ford are the subjects of a popular new book, "Whitey and Mickey," published by Viking Press.)

Q. That must be rough to do. After running for 20 years, the body probably wants to take it easy.

A. That's right, but you can't let up. There's too many banquets, too many guys buying you drinks.

It's easy to balloon up and become a walking heart attack.

Q. Do most former athletes stay in good shape?

A. They want to, because they have pride in their bodies. But it's hard, especially if you retired because of an injury.

Q. You mean the injury keeps you from playing other sports?

A. Sure. With my knee, I can never play tennis or handball. If I could play tennis, I could still be playing baseball.

Q. How do you keep in shape?

A. I ride a bike, I play golf and swim. I can walk about nine holes of golf, then my knee starts getting worse. That's what's good about a bike. It's like an exercise machine, only a lot more fun. I need it.

Q. So once your body is used to athletics, you can't ever really quit.

A. That's true. Of course, I've always enjoyed athletics and I still do. I just miss getting paid for it.

This is one in a series of messages brought to you by AMF. We make Voit Balls, Head Skis, Tennis Rackets and Sports Wear, Skamper Trailers, Roadmaster Bicycles, AMF Bowling Products, Slickcraft Boats, Sunfish Sailboats, Hatteras Yachts, Crestliner Boats, Ben Hogan Golf Equipment, Harley-Davidson Motorcycles.

AMF
We make weekends

29-3

54%

Celebrity approach. Reprinted with permission from American Association of Advertising Agencies.

QUESTIONS

1. Which of the three possible strategic campaign options should be selected? Provide a rationale for your choice.
2. Create a profile of what you consider to be the target market for the campaign.
3. Work up a media approach for the campaign based upon your assessment of the target market and the creative approach being used. Be specific in media selections if print is being used.

30

RED ROSE TEA

Illustrative of the way research can support every step of an advertising campaign, from first concept to final closing date, is the Warwick, Welsh and Miller campaign on behalf of Red Rose tea.

Red Rose tea is a product of Brooke Bond Foods, Inc., a subsidiary of Brooke Bond Liebig, headquartered in London. Brooke Bond purchased the Red Rose tea brand in Canada in the early 1930s and began selling Red Rose in the United States in the 1950s. In the 1960s, Brooke Bond purchased Ehler's Coffee, Spice & Tea Company to strengthen its expansion into the United States. Prior to its affiliation with WW&M, Red Rose experienced only a limited growth in the highly competitive U.S. market, where seven major tea companies fight for market shares.

Here is how WW&M, a strong practitioner of research-based advertising, employed research to help answer some of the important questions pertaining to the Red Rose campaign:

How can we differentiate the product? To answer this basic question WW&M consulted such reference sources as *Target Group Index* and *Simmons Market Digest* to identify the "heavy user" tea market, and define the needs, attitudes, preferences, and characteristics of this group. These secondary sources, combined with primary source interviews among members of the "heavy user" group, produced these significant facts and figures:

1) About 25 percent of tea drinkers drink 80 percent of all tea consumed on the North American continent, with consumption about equally divided between men and women.
2) Women are the primary purchasers and decision makers for tea products.

3) Canadians drink tea as often as they drink coffee.
4) In general, heavy users of tea products in both the Canadian and United States markets exhibit a preference for "a strong tea flavor."
5) Red Rose consumption skewed to older tea drinkers (45+), while the greatest growth in tea consumption was among younger people (25 to 34).

Thus, the creative strategy the WW&M account team decided to employ was to convince tea drinkers—primarily women in the 25-to-49-year age bracket—that Red Rose had a good, strong flavor. Following up this decision, the team devised five basic advertising themes (fig. 30-1), which were presented to consumer viewing panels chosen through survey questionnaires (figs. 30-2 and 30-3). The themes were presented in the form of animatics (filmed story boards) to hold down the cost of testing. The five commercials were labeled as follows:

1) Canada's Cup of Tea
2) The Things People Do (adding sugar, lemon, milk, etc.)
3) Gets You Going in the Morning
4) A Potent Cup of Tea
5) Everybody's Favorite Tea

Figure 30-1.

(1)	Canada's Cup of Tea.	(Shows a mountain lake. Seaplane is moored by shore. Nearby is simple cabin and smoke arises from outdoor fire. In background are rugged mountains).
(2)	The Things People Do.	(A man is shown in close-up pouring cream and sugar into a large container of tea.)
(3)	Gets You Going In The Morning.	(Three men are shown with breakfast trays in front of them. The trays are loaded with food. They are talking animatedly. Two of them are holding sizable tankards of tea.)
(4)	A Potent Cup of Tea.	(A woman is shown holding a cup of tea close to her mouth. Shown in close-up at the bottom of the screen is a package of Red Rose tea with the name clearly visible.)
(5)	Everybody's Favorite Tea.	(Two waitresses are talking to each other in a kitchen. One of them is preparing a pot of tea. In front of them in foreground are lined up six cups of tea sitting in saucers.)

Five commercial approaches that were tested in animatic form.

Figure 30-2.

```
                    TEA SURVEY
               QUALIFYING QUESTIONNAIRE
                 July - RPO #2044


Hello,

I'm from Metropolitan Research Associates.  We are conducting a
study on advertising and would like to get your opinion.

Before I do, however, could you please tell me if you, yourself, use
any of the following products?

     Coffee  ( )        Cocoa      ( )      Baking Powder   ( )
     Tea     ( )        Olive Oil  ( )      Salad Dressings ( )

IF NOT TEA, DISCONTINUE.  DO NOT COUNT AS INTERVIEW.

I notice that you use tea.  Would you please tell me which of the following
types of tea you use?

     Bags  ( )         Instant  ( )      Iced Tea Mix ( )     Loose Tea ( )

IF NOT BAGS, DISCONTINUE.  DO NOT COUNT AS INTERVIEW.

Which brand of tea do you usually buy?

     Red Rose ( )    Lipton ( )    Salada ( )    Tetley ( )   Other:_____

IF RED ROSE MENTIONED, DISCONTINUE.*  DO NOT COUNT AS INTERVIEW.

About how many cups of tea do you usually drink a week?

     1-4 ( )    5-9 ( )    10-15 ( )    16-20 ( )    20 or over ( )

IF LESS THAN FIVE, DISCONTINUE.  DO NOT COUNT AS INTERVIEW.

     *Note that "anamatic" test group was comprised of people that drank
      competitive tea brands, in order to effectively gauge the persuasive
      effect of each advertisement.

W RESPONDENT CARD "A"

On this card are a number of statements which describe how a person might feel
about buying a particular brand of tea.  Would you please tell me which letter on
this card comes closest to how you feel about buying, if your present brand were
not available.
```

	Certain I Would Buy	Almost Certain I Would Buy	Probably Buy	Not Sure	Probably Not Buy	Almost Certain Would Not Buy	Certain Would Not Buy
A. Lipton Tea	( )	( )	( )	( )	( )	( )	( )
B. Red Rose Tea	( )	( )	( )	( )	( )	( )	( )
C. Tetley Tea	( )	( )	( )	( )	( )	( )	( )
D. Salada Tea	( )	( )	( )	( )	( )	( )	( )

```
Why did you say that about Lipton Tea?

_____

_____

_____

Why did you say that about Red Rose Tea?

_____

_____

_____

Now would you watch this commercial.
```

This questionnaire was devised to help choose the test panelists.

Figure 30-3.

TEA SURVEY
QUESTIONNAIRE #2
July - RPO #2044

NEW RESPONDENT CARD "A"

Which letter on this card comes closest to how you would feel about buying Red Rose tea, if your present brand were not available.

A. Certain I would buy ( )   E. Probably would not buy ( )
B. Almost certain I would buy ( )   F. Almost certain would not buy ( )
C. Probably would buy ( )   G. Certain I would not buy ( )
D. Not sure ( )

Would you please tell me why you said that?

_____

_____

Thinking about the Red Rose tea commercial - apart from trying to get you to buy the product, what do you think they were trying to tell you about Red Rose tea?

_____

_____

What was the one most important thing they told you about Red Rose tea?

_____

_____

Just from what you saw and heard in this commercial, what disadvantages, if any, do you think Red Rose tea might have?

_____

_____

Now, just from what you saw and heard in this commercial, what advantages, if any, do you think Red Rose tea might have?

_____

_____

Is there anything about the commercial you just saw that you found hard to understand or believe?

_____

_____

Please mark all the words you feel come closest to describing the commercial you've just seen.

Amateurish	( )	Interesting	( )
Appealing	( )	Original	( )
Clever	( )	Realistic	( )
Convincing	( )	Repetitious	( )
Dull	( )	Silly	( )
Effective	( )	Slow	( )
Entertaining	( )	Unbelievable	( )
Fast-moving	( )	Unclear	( )
Genuine	( )	Unimportant	( )
Imaginative	( )	Uninteresting	( )
Informative	( )	Unusual	( )

NEW RESPONDENT CARD "B"

Based on this commercial, which letter on this card comes closest to how you would rate the overall quality of Red Rose tea? (RECORD BELOW)
How about the strength of the tea? (RECORD BELOW)
The flavor of the tea? (RECORD BELOW)
The color of the tea? (RECORD BELOW)

	9a. Overall Quality	9b. Strength	9c. Flavor	9d. Color
Excellent	( )	( )	( )	( )
Good	( )	( )	( )	( )
Fair	( )	( )	( )	( )
Poor	( )	( )	( )	( )

This questionnaire was devised to help decide the best test commercial.

All these commercials positioned Red Rose as a stronger, heartier, more flavorful tea, and unstructured interviews with viewers following the showing of the animatics indicated that, while the "Canadian Heritage" appeal of the "Canada's Cup of Tea" commercial was perceived as largely irrelevant, and the "coffee confrontation" appeals of the "Gets You Going" and "Everybody's Favorite" commercials were perceived as "not believable," both the "Things People Do" and the "Potent Cup" appeals were perceived as believable and persuasive.

Here is how a WW&M spokesman summarized the results of these research findings.

An especially critical measure of each potential campaign's effectiveness is its ability to move respondents to a more positive purchase intent. "The Things People Do" scored highest in this important category as well as in most other areas under measurement. It was closely followed by "A Potent Cup of Tea."

Now, one of the fascinating aspects of research is that its interpretation is just as vital as the statistics it provides. In this case the statistics indicated that both campaigns would provide effective advertising for the brand. But a meticulous analysis indicated that "A Potent Cup of Tea" had slightly more intrusive value. Thus . . . it would be able to achieve one of Red Rose's key marketing objectives . . . the building of brand awareness. In addition, it was believed that the *form* of the test (animatic commercials) might have adversely affected the score of this particular commercial.

The "intrusive value" of the "potent tea" theme resulted, according to test interpretations, from the connotation of the word "potent," and the positive ending of the commercial.

What is the most effective media strategy? Having created an appeal that they believed would effectively and dramatically position Red Rose tea in the consumer's mind, the WW&M account team next set about positioning this appeal in media that would best achieve reach-frequency-continuity goals.

Once again, research provided the key information on which to base a key decision. First, secondary sources, in the form of various media trade publications, were examined to determine media appealing to heavy tea drinkers. Television was found to cover a greater proportion of the target group than did radio or magazines, by virtue of its diverse programming, convenient time scheduling, and access to consumers. Also, TV's cost for reaching each thousand members of Red Rose's target market was found to be the lowest of the three media—an especially important consideration since this campaign would emphasize media frequency as a means of encouraging product trial and repeat sales.

How can we control campaign effectiveness? Once the "potent tea" TV campaign was launched, research continued to assume an important role by ascertaining whether advertising goals were being met, and whether the most persuasive commercials were being shown. For example, when the first commercial in the series was being shown, the WW&M research department engaged in a telephone survey among a random sample of metropolitan viewers to measure its actual impact. This same procedure was used again for the next commercial in the series, and for subsequent commercials in the "potent tea" campaign, with revisions made on the basis of these impact studies. For example, the No. 4 commercial was shown to be more persuasive than the No. 3 commercial, in terms of recognition and later sales, and was therefore scheduled more frequently (the apparent reason for the greater impact of the second commercial was its stronger appeal to women, the major purchasers of tea).

Revisions of early commercials in the Red Rose campaign were also made frequently to keep viewers involved. As a result, numerous commercials featuring different characters were devised to maintain the entertainment value of the campaign which early studies had found to be so important. Costly follow-up surveys indicated the expense was justified in terms of heightened product recognition and sales.

RESEARCH'S ROLE: THROUGHOUT THE CAMPAIGN

Throughout the Red Rose campaign, WW&M used statistical research to monitor and measure campaign effectiveness, instead of merely relying on sales results over the period of the campaign, although, according to a WW&M spokesman, "the decision to produce 'A Potent Cup of Tea' was justified when Red Rose tea's share of mind and share of market reached unprecedented heights despite an advertising budget markedly smaller than that of its major competitor." By focusing on such intermediate goals as brand recognition and intent to purchase, rather than on actual sales results, WW&M believes much more useful and conclusive results are derived, especially since so many factors other than advertising affect sales.

The survey method that WW&M found most useful in appraising the immediate impact of Red Rose commercials was the "Burke Test," a random telephone survey taken within 24 hours after a commercial presentation. Viewers are asked what advertisements they recall, in given product groups, with an increase of 25 percent or more in customer recognition of the product considered acceptable.

Shopper surveys are rarely used by WW&M in any campaigns, because of the belief that insufficient information is gained for the cost involved. Likewise, motivational studies are seldom used at Warwick, because it is felt they have a low reliability. When market model studies are used by Warwick, they are usually of the "behavioral" type, and are generally relied on only in "disaster" situations when nothing about the advertising seems to be working.

QUESTIONS

1. Various research organizations and terms appear in the discussion of this case. Define and/or explain fully the following:
   a. Target Group Index
   b. Simmons Market Digest
   c. Random sample
   d. Burke Test
   e. Motivational research
   f. Behavioral research
   g. Focus group interviewing (not mentioned in the discussion but used by the advertising agency)

31

UNION CARBIDE (PRESTONE ANTIFREEZE)

In planning various campaigns over the years for its client Prestone Antifreeze, the Ogilvy & Mather advertising agency found there were pluses and minuses. (Note: Leo Burnett, Chicago, became Prestone's agency of record as of the 1978 season.)

Perhaps the biggest plus was the fact that Prestone held a 70 percent share of the domestic market for antifreeze, and the leverage provided by a dominant leadership position in practically any field can hardly be underestimated. (For example, studies have shown that "leader" brands such as Goodyear and Anacin often benefit as much from competitors' advertising as the competitors do.) Another strong plus was the fact that Prestone could be advertised profitably because of a highly respected and identifiable trademark, broad and varied distribution (including supermarkets, mass merchandise outlets, and drug stores), and a reputation for consistency, quality, and reliability.

Indeed, the only significant minus for the product was the lack of a strong product differential, a "minus" that can often offset a lot of pluses. Although Prestone does have an exclusive patented formula, consumers believe that an antifreeze is an antifreeze is an antifreeze, with no significant difference in formula from one brand to the next.

Another minus with which the agency had to cope in preparing advertising campaigns for Prestone was the nature and scope of the target market for antifreeze, i.e., men concerned with driving automobiles or, for all practical purposes, *all* men of driving age in the country. The extraordinary diversity of this market, from teen-age hot rodders to board chairmen, made it particularly difficult to tailor an appeal that would relate to all segments and sub-segments.

Still another minus was the seasonal nature of antifreeze sales, with 70 percent of all purchases made in the September-November period. This reflected a widespread misconception among customers that antifreeze, as its name (perhaps unfortunately) suggested, was useful only in preventing auto radiator freeze-ups and cracked blocks during winter months. Actually, it was equally or *more* useful in preventing overheated radiators during summer months, particularly with the widespread installation of air-conditioning units in automobiles.

Other minuses listed by W.J. McDermott, Director of Advertising for the Home and Automotive Products Division of the Union Carbide Corporation (Prestone's parent), included the following:

1) Shifting distribution patterns, with the trade looking for more promotional deals and stocking more than one national brand along with private-label brands.
2) The tendency for engine sizes, and cooling systems, to get smaller and smaller in response to political and ecological pressures.
3) "Disbelieving consumers" who can't see what's going on in their automobile cooling systems the way they can see the filter on an advertised cigarette, or the bucket seats in an advertised sports car.

STRATEGY GUIDELINES EMERGE

Joining these pluses and minuses to build campaign strategies that would accentuate the former and sidestep the latter, the Ogilvy & Mather account team agreed to the following guidelines:

1) In general, advertising campaigns for Prestone should aim to expand the entire antifreeze market, rather than simply focus on Prestone's competitive differentials (the fact that few such differentials existed made this guideline relatively easy to follow). The rationale behind this guideline was that Prestone, as the product leader, would profit more by maintaining its present percentage share of a larger share of market than it would by simply increasing *its* slice of the market. That it *would* maintain this market percentage seemed amply evidenced by the share-of-market experience of other such leader products, including Goodyear, Chevrolet, and Coca-Cola.
2) However, the thrust of this advertising would not be entirely generic. Thus, while not specifically spelling out competitive differentials, the campaigns would certainly emphasize the Prestone name, and what this name stands for (i.e., trust, reliability, and number-one brand status).
3) Campaign tactics would be modified, periodically, to emphasize other attributes of antifreeze, such as its anti-boilover and corrosion-resistant properties.
4) The narrative context in which the Prestone message would be conveyed would be a problem-solution format, which research had indicated generates higher recall and customer involvement.

PRESTONE CAMPAIGN CONCEPTS PRESENTED TO THE CLIENT BY OGILVY & MATHER

1) The scene is in front of a movie theater on a wintry, snowy late afternoon. The picture has ended and, one by one, parents arrive to take their children home. Then the scene shifts in time; night has fallen, and standing outside the theater, alone, the snow getting deeper, are two little children. As the lights in front of the theater flick off, the caption flashes up, reading: "Next time, be sure you've checked the Prestone—before it's too late."

2) The scene is inside a happy home. Everybody is busily scurrying about in joyous preparation for daughter Debby's first ballet recital. Finally, everything is set and all rush into the car. Debby, eyes shining, is radiant with excitement. The general aura is one of warmth and joy, in sharp contrast to the cold, snow-blown outside environment. Debby's dad turns the ignition key and—nothing happens. The frigid motor fails to turn over and the camera pans in on Debby's face, as a tear courses down her cheek. Simultaneously, the caption reads: "When People Depend on You, Don't Forget Prestone."

3) A woman is standing outside her car with the hood up— stranded. For miles ahead of her stretches a single highway through the shimmering desert. Suddenly, in the distance, a low hum of motors is heard and, on the horizon, a cloud of smoke and dust grows larger and larger. As the sound of the motors gets louder, and a large motorcycle gang is seen silhouetted in the cloud, the woman's expression becomes progressively more anxious and upset. Finally, the gang pulls up and surrounds the car. The leader, a mean-looking customer, dismounts and approaches the woman. "What's the problem, lady?" he asks.

Unlike the first two commercials, however, this one turns out to have a lighter message. The leader is only 4 ft. 6 in. tall and has a Mickey-Mouse-like voice. The commercial takes on a slapstick aspect as the entire gang, with the help of a handy gallon of Prestone, quickly cools down the overheated radiator and gets the car running again. As he waves goodbye, leader reminds the woman never to travel without Prestone.

4) As part of a campaign to persuade men to use Prestone to combat corrosion, a number of celebrities were used in testimonial advertisements. For example, one typical advertisement in this campaign has the actor Jack Palance extol the virtues of (1) his fine, mint-condition 1937 Packard and (2) Prestone in helping to maintain this mint condition by retarding corrosion. To make this commercial more memorable, a catchy tune is incorporated into its conclusion which emphasizes the Prestone name.

5) The same tune is used at the end of a commercial designed to promote Prestone as protection against boilovers. However, instead of using a single celebrity to get across this message, the commercial shows a montage of automobiles pulled over to the side of the road on hot summer days, all boilover victims. Copy stresses two points: *you* could be in this picture, Mr. Listener, and Prestone could have prevented all these boilovers. This commercial was scheduled for the April-May pre-summer period.

6) A commercial aimed at generating repeat sales for Prestone shows men dressed in professional white coats emphasizing the point that anti-corrosion products don't last forever—they must be replaced at least once a year. Holding up a pitted piece of metal, one of these "scientists" shows what could happen if this guideline is ignored.

QUESTION

If you were limited to producing two commercials of the six presented here, which two would you choose? Explain why.

32

EASTMAN KODAK

GENERAL BACKGROUND

The Motion Picture & Audio Visual (MPAV) division of Eastman Kodak Company markets motion picture and slide equipment plus a variety of audio-visual aids and accessories. MPAV also promotes the general use of film as a communication medium. Audiences for MPAV advertising include business, education, medicine, government, professional film producers and the entertainment industry.

For this campaign, the specific target audience was "Business Management"—those people who control the operations of medium- to large-sized companies and who determine how much is to be spent for AV programs and equipment.

CAMPAIGN OBJECTIVES

The main purpose of this advertising was to remind business managers that film is a flexible, effective, cost-efficient communication tool and to suggest specific applications for film in business and industry. A second objective was to emphasize the position of Kodak as a dependable source for AV products and advice.

CREATIVE STRATEGY

It was decided that the campaign should deal with five common business communication problems: training, selling, product demonstration, internal corporate communications, and community relations. Each advertisement would pose a specific problem and suggest how film might solve it.

Cartoons were selected as a device to gain interest and impact. Five well-known cartoonists were chosen and each was assigned to interpret

188

Figure 32-1.

If all of your prospects were pushovers, you wouldn't need film.

Film can be your foot in the door.

Whichever format you choose – super 8 movies, 16 mm movies, or 35 mm slides – film can make a tough sales call concise, direct, informative. And interesting.

Film comes with some nice intangibles, too. Like warmth, drama, and memorability. Good things to have on your side in a tight market.

Making a movie or a slide presentation doesn't mean breaking your budget. Film has the versatility that lets you pick the right equipment and the right style for whatever you've got to spend, and whatever you need to accomplish.

For more information, talk with your own AV specialist or an independent producer. (Look in the Yellow Pages under "Audio-Visual" and "Motion Picture.") Or get in touch with us. We've got some products, literature, and ideas that can help.

Version I advertisement. Reprinted with permission from Rumrill-Hoyt, Inc.

Figure 32-2.

Version II advertisement. Reprinted with permission from Rumrill-Hoyt, Inc.

a specific business situation. The cartoonists were given headlines, rough copy, and a list of possible visual approaches, plus a layout that showed the position and size of the cartoon in the advertisement.

The campaign needed an overall theme, something that would tie all five advertisements together and bring the humorous approach down to earth. Of the several ideas that were considered, the simplest seemed best: "Film is good business."

VERSION I vs. VERSION II

The first version of the advertisements followed the traditional style of magazine cartoons—cartoon on top with punch-line (in this case, the headline) underneath, in italics.

The headlines were all structured as "if . . . then . . ." propositions. Examples:

If all your prospects were pushovers, you wouldn't need film.

If reports to the stockholders were all good news, you wouldn't need film.

The body copy outlined the possible applications of film to the particular business problem. It concluded with a call to action and a coupon. "Film is good business" was the tag line.

Version II put the benefit—"Film is good business"—in headline. The headline was set in display type and copy was cut to an absolute minimum. A different type face was used from the one used in Version I.

Both versions were presented to management.

QUESTIONS

1. Should Version I or Version II be accepted by management? Why?
2. Discuss the pros and cons of a humorous approach in this marketing and selling situation.

33

TRANCOL

Technion Pharmaceuticals is an ethical pharmaceutical manufacturer with sales of approximately $110 million. The company's leading product is a "major tranquilizer"* called Trancol that accounts for nearly half of total Technion sales. Although Trancol is the largest selling product in the major tranquilizer market, its clinical spectrum and safety make it suitable for use in a wide variety of emotional disorders and therapeutic settings.

Each type of emotional illness or clinical setting represents a distinct market segment. The demographic characteristics of these segments differ greatly, as do the specific product benefits that serve as "buying motives" for the prescribing physicians in each market. Disturbed and obstreperous geriatric patients tolerate Trancol very well despite their known sensitivity to drug therapy. Young adults with depressive neuroses receive symptomatic relief without undue sedation. Hospitalized psychotic patients can be relieved of serious hallucinatory and delusional episodes due to to the potent effects of Trancol, and upon discharge these same patients can be maintained back in the community with a freedom from side effects unusual for such potent medications. Psychiatrists often use low doses of Trancol to effectively treat disturbed children as well.

With the expansion of community treatment centers during the 1970s, most patients with psychiatric problems are now receiving some form of treatment, usually supplemented by major tranquilizer therapy. Essentially the market has matured. However, a number of "late entries" have begun substantial nonpersonal and personal promotion in order to carve out a market share for themselves. This

---

* "Major tranquilizers" can effectively treat psychotic symptoms, whereas "minor tranquilizers" cannot.

Figure 33-1.

A consideration beyond efficacy alone

for the discharged patient who needs an antipsychotic agent

The rapidly rising readmission rate among discharged patients is mainly due to noncompliance with antipsychotic drug therapy. And this, in turn, may be largely attributed to disabling extrapyramidal side effects, notable akathisia.[1]

Although extrapyramidal effects are characteristic of antipsychotic agents in general, with TRANCOL such effects are infrequent. Adding an antiparkinsonian agent—which can cause its own side effects—can usually be avoided. TRANCOL is contraindicated in patients with severe hypotensive or hypertensive heart disease.

Extrapyramidal Effects of
Selected Antipsychotic Agents*

DRUG	EXTRAPYRAMIDAL EFFECTS
Chlorpromazine	Moderate
Perphenazine	High
Prochlorperazine	High
Fluphenazine	High
Acetophenazine	Moderate
Trifluoperazine	High
Chlorprothixene	Moderate
Thiothixene	Moderate
Haloperidol	High
Trancol	Low

*Based on antipsychotic dosage ranges.

References
1. Van Putten T: The rising rehospitalization rate of psychiatric patients. Scientific Exhibit, American Psychiatric Association, 130th Annual Meeting, Toronto, Canada, May 2-6, 1977.

2. Byck R: Drugs and the treatment of psychiatric disorders, in Goodman LS, Gilman A (eds): The Pharmacological Basis of Therapeutics, ed 5. New York, Macmillan Publishing Co, Inc, 1975, pp 170-171.

TRANCOL

helps provide effective control of psychotic symptoms

TECHNION PHARMACEUTICALS

"Umbrella" campaign. Outpatient psychiatric-segment advertisement. This product is intended for psychotic patients. Reprinted with permission from Herbert Weinstein.

Figure 33-2.

A consideration beyond efficacy alone
for the elderly patient at home who needs a neuroleptic

Significant neuroleptic side effects can seriously undermine the elderly patient's ability to function independently at home. Two of the more disabling effects—hypotension and sedation—occur infrequently with TRANCOL. However, patients should be cautioned about participating in activities that require complete mental alertness, e.g., driving. Although old age lowers the tolerance for this class of drug and the most common neurologic side effects in geriatric patients are extrapyramidal manifestations, with TRANCOL there is minimal extrapyramidal stimulation. There appears to be an increased risk of agranulocytosis and leukopenia with phenothiazines in the geriatric population. In geriatric patients with organic mental syndrome (dementia), dosage should not exceed 200 mg per day.

TRANCOL

effective for the symptoms of agitation, depressed mood, and anxiety in the elderly with organic mental syndrome

TECHNION PHARMACEUTICALS

"Umbrella" campaign. Outpatient geriatric advertisement. This product is intended for the patient with a neurosis. Reprinted with permission from Herbert Weinstein.

tactic has greatly enlarged the total promotional dollar market, and the established products have had to meet these efforts with similar spending.

For the management of Technion the task of creating an adequate promotional program was further complicated by the fact that in several segments "minor tranquilizers" also were competitors. Minor tranquilizers represent a market several times the size of the major tranquilizer market, and the leading products have correspondingly large promotional budgets.

While pharmaceutical market leaders often command as much as 20 to 25 percent of promotional dollars, in the case of the tranquilizer market the large spending level of the total market made this type of strategy far too costly for Trancol. Some manufacturers have handled this problem by abandoning certain segments and concentrating promotion on a single segment, such as treatment of hospitalized psychotics, to get more promotional "punch" from each dollar spent.

Technion product management found themselves with several market segments to maintain, while several competitors each concentrated their efforts on a single segment. The product manager had to decide how to maintain Trancol as market leader in several segments within the confines of a moderate promotional budget. It was important to spell and reinforce specific product benefits for each specific segment—but how could this be done without fragmenting the message and reducing impact in each segment and as a whole?

To compete effectively the product manager decided to implement what he termed an "umbrella" campaign. The strategy was to zero in on product benefits that held throughout most market segments and use these benefits as the central promotional theme of the entire personal and nonpersonal selling effort for Trancol. At the same time each advertisement would address its target segment and show how the central theme yielded special benefits keyed directly to the target segment.

Because of Trancol's very favorable ratio of therapeutic benefits to side effects, a strong image of product safety existed in all segments. Consequently the product manager chose an "umbrella" theme of ". . . beyond efficacy alone," aimed at distinguishing the specific array of Trancol safety benefits from those of competitors in each specific market segment. Each advertisement prominently repeated the "umbrella" theme, reinforcing the primary message that Trancol offered special safety benefits not shared by its competitors. The individual advertisements each carried one of several "segment themes" that translated the "umbrella" theme into precise benefits that Trancol therapy offered the specific segment. For instance, in geriatric care Trancol "goes beyond efficacy alone" by offering low levels of sedation that allow the anxious patient to be alert and to function without the need for institutional care. In hospital psychiatry Trancol "goes beyond efficacy alone" by delivering potent treatment without neurological side effects that characteristically accompany this treatment with other drugs. In treating the young depressive neurotic the added benefit might be a low incidence of sedation where alertness is a real benefit "on the job."

QUESTION

Suppose, as the advertising manager for Trancol, you were asked to defend the advertising strategy proposed. What would you say?

34

IRVING TRUST COMPANY

When the Irving Trust Company of New York City began planning a retail-oriented advertising campaign designed to persuade prospective customers to ask for a loan or open a checking or savings account at Irving Trust, it faced formidable image and competitive problems.

THE IMAGE PROBLEM

The public image of commercial banks has historically been that they are aloof and impersonal. They are seen as big businesses that would rather deal with corporations than with people. Typical attitudes: "They're so spread out and have so many branches, I don't know who to talk to," and "They're all computers and I'm just another number to them."

THE COMPETITIVE PROBLEM

Irving Trust's main competition for retail customers' dollars came from both commercial banks and savings banks.

Among commercial banks, Irving Trust ranked a distant seventh in size in New York City, as shown by this listing:

Bank	U.S. Rank	Assets (billions)
Citicorp	2	$64.2
Chase Manhattan Corp.	3	45.6
Mfrs. Hanover Corp.	4	31.4
J.P. Morgan & Co.	5	28.7
Chemical New York Corp.	6	26.6
Bankers Trust New York Corp.	7	22.2
Irving Trust Company	15	10.8

Savings bank competition emerged from such large banks as The Bowery, Dime, and Lincoln savings banks, as well as dozens of savings and loan associations. All the larger commercial banks, as well as many of the savings banks, outspent Irving Trust in advertising, some by as much as five to one.

Most of this competitive advertising aimed to project a friendly, helpful, "homey" attitude, and offered multiservice benefits including personal checking and savings accounts, personal loans, safety deposit boxes, and various types of money management services. Most bank advertising also attempted to establish a separate identity or "brand image" to make the individual bank stand out from its competitors.

In creating these campaigns, all banks consider some, if not all, of these areas for emphasis:

1) Different types of checking or savings accounts or certificates of deposit with special names and descriptions.
2) Saving for future goals, such as college education for children, retirement, the down payment on a home, or dream vacation.
3) Easy, low-interest, low-collateral loans.
4) Convenient offices "near where you work or live." This benefit is available to banks with many branches, of which Irving Trust had 142 offering a full range of commercial banking services.
5) Early, late, or Saturday open hours.
6) Free checking with a no-or-low-minimum-balance requirement.
7) "Give-away" programs to attract new accounts, featuring such premiums as small appliances, sets of dishes, lawn chairs, and barbeque sets, all offered for a limited time.
8) Reducing the time customers have to wait in line for a teller.

While all of these appeals had been successfully used to attract new retail customers, each was also accompanied by difficulties and disadvantages. For example, sophisticated potential customers recognized that most bank policies pertaining to interest charged on loans and offered on deposits were established by various government agencies, and hence didn't differ much from bank to bank. Extra services such as longer open hours or short lines require additional employees, overtime payment, or even more computers. And the excitement created by premiums must usually be sustained by another campaign when the "give-away" advertising blitz is over.

As a result of many banks facing many practical difficulties in building many campaigns using many different appeals, the overall noise level is high, many individual bank identities are indistinct, the values of their offerings are blurred, and many consumers are baffled.

THE CREATIVE STRATEGY

In the face of this feverish competitive environment, and working with their account team at the J. Walter Thompson advertising agency, management at Irving Trust decided on a campaign creative strategy based on what they believed was a unique program: a special 90-hour course that trained selected Irving Trust personnel to become consultants for retail banking customers. During this training program, selected staff members learned about every service the bank provided, how to meet people face-to-face, how to counsel them about individual banking needs, and how to develop an ongoing relationship conducive to consumer loyalty.

Using this program as its point of departure, a creative strategy was devised designed to demonstrate Irving Trust Company differences through the eyes of its customers. This was accomplished by showing customer-recall of his or her Personal Banker by name and his or her favorable experience with the Personal Banker (see fig. 34-1). Contrast was also shown between fortunate Irving Trust Company customers who know their Personal Bankers well and less fortunate customers of other banks who cannot identify anyone where they do business (fig. 34-2).

In one typical advertisement, the Personal Banker service was described this way:

When you open an account at the Irving, you get your own Personal Banker assigned to you. An actual, living, breathing human being ... with a face, and a name, and a phone number and a brain. Someone whose job it is to know about your account and take care of any problems you have.

Figure 34-1.

"I call my Personal Banker if I have any kind of problem.

Whether it's running out of checks or wanting some advice about an IRA account or a loan. Just before I left on vacation I spoke to her about a loan to furnish my new apartment. The day I came back she called me to say it was all taken care of."

—Marilyn Moore

"I guess Billie Jeanne Warnock knows more about my finances than my wife does.

I can call her on the phone and say I need a loan, a car loan or whatever, and the next thing I know she'll call me and tell me it's all ready to be deposited."

—Ros Sturm

"My Personal Banker handles anything I want.

I don't have to see 12 people to get one problem solved. If I want a loan application or a check approved, or if I want to open a savings account, or cash bonds or increase the line of credit on my Charter Check Credit Account, I just see Dan, or call him on the phone, and he takes care of it."

—Barbara Sayar

"I have somebody to talk to here— my Personal Banker.

He's arranged a lot of things for me: direct deposit of my paycheck by my company, a safe deposit box, an Executive Credit Account with a line of credit, and a savings account where I don't have to bother with a passbook. He takes care of me personally and I can always find him if I need something."

—Brian Sherwood

A Personal Banker. That's what makes the Irving different.

Irving Trust Company   A Charter New York Bank

34-1

Member F.D.I.C.

Figure 34-2.

Video	Audio
1. CU of smiling woman.	1st woman: What's my banker look like?
2. CU of another woman.	2nd woman: You're kidding. I don't have a banker. Just have a bunch of tellers.
3. CU of young man.	1st man: I never see the same face twice.
4. CU of somewhat older man.	2nd man: What does my banker look like?
5. CU of woman.	3rd woman: My banker?
6. CU of man scratching head perplexedly.	3rd man: My banker?
7. CU of young, smart-looking man.	4th man: My banker? Don? Five eight. Grey hair. He's my personal banker. That's what makes Irving different. I get one guy to call about checking, savings, loans,
8. CU of same young man gesturing toward camera with hand.	whatever, with his name and phone number on every statement. I call Don. He takes care of things.
9. Black screen with words superimposed: Get a Personal Banker the Irving. Irving Trust Member FDIC	Announcer: A personal banker. That's what makes the Irving different.

30-second television script. Reprinted with permission from American Association of Advertising Agencies.

The target market for this campaign comprised, in the main, middle-to upper-income adults; specifically:

50% in the $15,000 to $25,000 group, and
50% in the $25,000 and above group.

QUESTIONS

1. In view of the fact that the general public thinks that banks and bankers are all alike (and governmental regulations require banks very largely to offer similar services and similar rates), assess the chance for Irving Trust Company to cause a significant portion of the public to think that the bank is different from other banks.
2. For the campaign devised for Irving Trust, how would you divide the budget between newspapers and television? Explain.

35

SHERMAN TOYOTA

To supplement the national advertising campaign for Toyota Motor Sales, U.S.A., Sherman Toyota of Freehold, New Jersey, asked its agency, Mark Advertising of Union, New Jersey, to develop an advertising campaign in tune with the nature and needs of its local market.

The ensuing campaign, built around the "Wizard of Wheels" theme, featured characters from the "Wizard of Oz" movie (including Dorothy, the Scarecrow, the Tin Man, and the Munchkins) in various situations involving the purchase or servicing of a new or used automobile. In addition to eight 60-second radio commercials featuring the Oz characters, and three 30-second commercials featuring Bob Sherman, Sherman's new-car sales manager, the campaign also featured newspaper advertisements using the "Wizard of Wheels" theme (fig. 35-1) and, as a publicity stunt, in-person visits to Sherman Toyota by members of the cast of the Broadway play "The Wiz."

Discussing the rationale behind the "Wizard of Wheels" concept, John Cowpher of the Mark Agency stated that, since most people had seen the "Wizard of Oz" movie or read the book, they could readily identify with the characters in the commercials. Furthermore, he noted, these characters lent themselves to a light, humorous touch, in refreshing contrast to the "hard sell" boilerplate characteristic of most automobile dealer advertising.

Following are two sample commercials from this campaign:

Commercial #1: *Cowardly Lion*

(Cheerful introductory music)

Lion:	Oh, what am I going to do?
Dorothy:	Hi, Lion. What's the matter?
Lion:	Well, that old car of mine has about had it, and I'll never get to the land of Shazam if I don't get a new one!

Figure 35-1.

Newspaper advertisement. Hard-sell characterizes this newspaper advertisement, unlike the approach in the radio commercials. Reprinted with permission from Mark Advertising Agency, Inc.

Dorothy:	The lion needs help. We've got to find the Wizard!
	("Byoinng" sound introduces Wizard)
Lion:	Who are you?
Wizard:	I'm the Wizard of savings; the Wizard appeals; At Sherman Toyota, I'm the Wizard of Wheels.
Lion:	But a car is only one of my worries. I'm so cowardly, especially with these car dealers.
Wizard:	Well, buying a new Toyota at Sherman Toyota will make you smile. Because we take the fear out of every trouble-free mile.
Lion:	Oh, I'm so excited—I may get to the land of Shazam after all! I'm off to see the Wizard!
Announcer:	Anyone can sell a car, but Sherman Toyota would like to help you buy one. See the Wizard of Wheels. Sherman Toyota, route nine in Freehold. 500 feet North of the circle.
Singers:	He's the wonderful Wizard of Wheels at Sherman Toyota.

Commercial #2: *Scarecrow*

(Cheerful introductory music)

Dorothy:	Scarecrow, what are you doing?
Scarecrow:	I'm building a car to take me to the land of Shazam.
Dorothy:	Building a car out of wood?
Scarecrow:	No, the wood is for the wheels. I'm making the car out of straw.
Dorothy:	Aw, scarecrow, you can't make the car out of straw. Scarecrow needs some help. I wish the Wizard was here!
	Byoinng!
Scarecrow:	Who are you?
Wizard:	I'm the Wizard of Wheels. At Sherman Toyota, the Toyotas are the finest you'll ever see. And the prices are fairer than fair can be.
Scarecrow:	But I don't know what kind of car I want. That's why I'm building one out of straw. Besides, the price is right.
Wizard:	Well, when it comes to a great buy, the Wizard will treat you fair. At Sherman Toyota, we've got the sharpest prices—just see and compare.
Scarecrow:	If it wasn't for you and the Wiz, I don't know what I'd have done.
Announcer:	Before you take your next drive, see the Wizard of Wheels for Toyotas that are priced with you in mind—That's Sherman Toyota, route 9 in Freehold. 500 feet North of the circle.
Singers:	He's the wonderful Wizard at Sherman Toyota.

QUESTION

If you were in charge of Sherman Toyota, would you approve the campaign proposed by the advertising agency?

PART V
THE MEDIA
DECISION

The cases in this section have a common focus on important "where" and "when" decisions needed to implement "who," "what," and "why" decisions arrived at during previous phases of the campaign-planning process.

To appreciate the importance of these "where-when" media decisions, consider a situation where a persuasively ingenious appeal for, say, a potent cup of tea or a misunderstood soft drink is devised for a product on the basis of a studied understanding of *who* comprises the market for this product, *what* competitors are also aiming at members of this market, and *why* your product might be preferred by these market members.

Now consider just three from an infinite number of possible media strategies designed to carry your persuasively ingenious appeal about your uniquely attractive product to your well-defined market segment.

1) Nine out of ten members of this market will be exposed to your message an average of two times over a two month period, at a cost of one million dollars.
2) Five out of ten members of this market will be exposed to your message an average of four times over a four-month period, at a cost of half-a-million dollars.
3) Three out of ten members of your market will be exposed to your message an average of ten times each over a period of a year, also at a cost of half-a-million dollars.

The first observation one might make regarding these strategies is that even the cheapest of them adds up to heavy expense, and indeed the media function is, almost invariably, the most costly of all the functions performed during the campaign-planning process. Another observation might be that the best way for an advertiser to invest media dollars is in strategy #3, which gives more total "impressions" per dollar or, put another way, costs less per impression.

REACH/FREQUENCY/CONTINUITY TRADEOFFS

While it is certainly conceivable that #3 might be the best message-carrying media strategy, there are many reasons why it might also be the *worst* of all possible media strategies. For example:

1) It is possible that the three-in-ten reached by this option are not the heavy users of the product, or are not in the group that will be most influenced by your appeal, or are already being saturated with competitive advertising.

2) It is also possible that the average of ten times to which each of these three-in-ten people will be exposed to your message is five times too many, so you're paying for wasted exposures.

3) It is also possible that a year is just too long a period to continue this campaign; perhaps, by that time, the product will have become obsolescent.

All these reasons why strategy #3 might (or might not) be the worst of all possible media strategies for a particular product in a particular market can be categorized in three broad areas: *reach* (or the total number of people to whom a message is delivered), *frequency* (or the number of times a message is delivered), and *continuity* (or the period of time over which the campaign runs).

Additionally, all the cases in this section can be interpreted and appraised in terms of these concepts. United Airlines, for example, was concerned with a broad, mass-market reach in its media planning, but devised a strategy for achieving this reach while avoiding competition-cluttered media outlets. Message frequency timed, to an extent, to reflect vacation schedules, and campaign continuity, as with all competing airlines, were key considerations, with many appeals (such as United's "Friendly Skies") remaining unchanged for years.

Campaign continuity was also a key factor in media planning for DeBeers since, presumably, people are going to keep getting married and buying diamond rings. As a virtual monopoly, however, DeBeers does not have quite the media selection problems faced by United, with literally dozens of competitors selling the same message over the same media. Like United, DeBeers must design its *reach* strategy for a mass market of people who will buy or influence the purchase of diamond wedding rings, and must think in seasonal terms in developing *frequency* strategy.

COMPETITION AFFECTS MEDIA DECISIONS

Continuity is also a primary consideration in two other campaigns in this section. Certainly, as long as couples continue to invest in DeBeers diamonds, they will also invest in insurance policies and, possibly, second mortgages, which is where the Money Store and Prudential Insurance might enter the picture. In effect, then, the market for these two advertisers is the DeBeers market, at later stages of the human life cycle. Unlike the DeBeers campaign, however, both the Money Store and Prudential campaigns must be planned in highly competitive markets—a strong consideration in determining what their advertising message will say, and where and when it will be placed. Another strong influence on the media decision of these advertisers, particularly in the *frequency* and *reach* areas, is the "unsought" nature of their products, and the fact that these products are complex and difficult to explain.

SELECTIVE REACH STRATEGIES

Two other cases—Jack Daniel's and Thru-Mov—illustrate media strategies where the reach emphasis is highly selective, focusing on affluent, "reassured" males. The fact that these advertisers can save dollars through selective reach policies means more dollars to achieve desired frequency and continuity goals. Jack Daniel's, however, has a homey, leisurely marketing philosophy that doesn't countenance media-blitz frequency, so its emphasis is on long-pull continuity, with creative and media strategies that have not changed a whit in 30 years.

SHORT-TERM MEDIA STRATEGIES

In contrast to Daniel's leisurely, long-pull philosophy, the SCORE and "SportsMonday" media strategies are vitally concerned with short-run, here-and-now promotional benefits—in the case of both SCORE and "SportsMonday," to introduce new products into fiercely competitive markets. What these campaigns save on continuity is invested in reach and frequency.

Two other cases, Slater & Associates and Berger Chemical (Part B) have in common media strategies affected mainly by budgetary constraints, and a common desire to get the most media "bang" for the dollars spent.

And, finally, the last two cases in this section, Bermuda and Fram, illustrate media strategies strongly affected by, and directed to, distribution networks, with many opportunities for cooperative efforts.

WHAT AFFECTS MEDIA DECISIONS?

Generalizing from all the cases in this section, here are some of the factors that most affect media selection and reach-frequency-continuity decisions:

1) What is the nature of the target market for the product? (DeBeers diamond rings, for example.)
2) Where, and how, is the product distributed? (Such as the feature articles in "SportsMonday," or a vacation in Bermuda.)

3) How about tie-ins with other media and merchandising plans? (Such as those offered by Fram's distributors.)

4) What can we afford? (Not too much in the Berger and Slater cases.)

5) What media are competitors using? (United avoided competition-cluttered media in favor of competition-free network television.)

6) What is the basic appeal? (The Money Store and Prudential media decisions were strongly affected by this consideration.)

7) What are the best *times* to carry our message (of the day, month, season, year)? (A strong factor in the United, DeBeers, and Berger campaigns.)

36

UNITED AIRLINES' ADVERTISING PROGRAM

Assume brand "A" and brand "B" are identical in all significant respects. Also assume the customer has equal access to each brand. Question: how do you persuade this customer to reach for brand "A" instead of brand "B"?

That is the question facing marketing management of almost any commercial airline in the United States. These days, all jets are fast and smooth, all airlines have well-trained flight personnel, and practically all provide good service, food, and personal attention. Additionally, the routes traveled by any one airline are paralleled by other airlines, so the traveler almost always has a choice.

UNITED'S ADVERTISING PROGRAM

At United Airlines, a comprehensive advertising program, featuring clearly defined target audiences, theme campaigns, and an unusually heavy investment in television, has been the major vehicle for creating this "brand preference" among travelers. Following are some of the important components of this program, for which the Leo Burnett Company in Chicago is United's advertising agency.

Advertising Objectives

According to William Alenson, United's director of advertising and promotion, "share of mind" is the beginning of "share of market," and "if we can get people thinking United, we'll get them flying United." Here are four advertising objectives designed to get people "thinking United":

1) United should have the look of a leader.
2) United should look like a friendly airline to fly, an airline whose people are warm, helpful, interested in customer problems.
3) United's advertising should express excitement and sophistication. People should become aware that United is "with it," that United knows how to serve people *today*.
4) United should continue to build on its excellent reputation for efficiency and technical advances.

The Target Audience

Advertising for United has several target audiences, varying by age, income, sex, life-style, and trip purpose (business, pleasure, to visit friends and relatives, etc.). In earlier years, most air travel was done by businessmen. Today, about half of all air travel is for such non-business reasons as sightseeing and taking resort vacations. In addition to representing a smaller total slice of the overall travel segment, the business travel segment is changing in another significant way: today almost 25 percent of business travelers are women, and that proportion is continuing to grow.

Airline passengers also cover a broad range of age and income levels. The majority of travel is among people between 30 and 50 years of age and in the $20,000-to-$35,000 income range, but substantial numbers of passengers have begun to come from outside these categories. This trend, spurred in 1978 by discount and economy fares, continued in 1980 as a significant change in air travel demographics.

Advertising Campaigns

Over the years, United has developed numerous advertising campaigns in TV, radio, and print media. Typically, each campaign is developed around a simple dominant idea, of which the following are typical:

4 Star Service—This advertising features pre-flight and in-flight services on trips between mid-American cities and both Coasts. Included are special food services, in-flight entertainment, and one-call reservations, which combine a ticket, hotel reservation, and car rental with one phone call.

Vacations—United's spring and summer advertising usually focuses on the subject of vacations. The advertising encourages the consumer to visit other cities and resort areas or to get together with friends and relatives in other parts of the country. Travelers are also made aware of discount fares available.

Fares—Since the late 1970s a major portion of all airlines' advertising has been directed to discount fares. United and other domestic carriers offer savings of 15 to 45 percent off normal coach fares. Fares such as Super Saver, Super Coach, Night Coach, and Freedom Fare offer big savings and have stimulated travel. They will probably continue to be a key element in inter-carrier competition.

Other ideas around which United campaigns are built include wide-body aircraft (of which United has the largest fleet in the world); Hawaii (the only specific destination which United's advertising focuses on); and Ocean-to-Ocean Service (special entrees, wine, linen napkins, and in-flight entertainment on transcontinental flights).

Although United campaigns differ as to the dominant idea conveyed in each, all bear a family resemblance through use of music and a campaign theme line which, since the mid-1960s, has been the cornerstone of United advertising—"Fly the Friendly Skies of United."

Another common characteristic of most United campaigns is a focus on people—both United employees and the people they serve. Thus, a typical campaign will show business people relaxing in-flight, families off together on a vacation, or baggage handlers, reservations people, flight attendants, and pilots serving United customers. Figures 36-1 and 36-2 illustrate this emphasis on people: the first is a TV script from United's "You're the Boss" campaign (directed initially toward the business traveler, then extended to family pleasure travel), and the second an advertisement from its "United We Fly" campaign (intended to communicate that "United built the largest airline in the free world around the needs of the individual traveler").

Figure 36-1.

Video	Audio
1. MCU of smiling woman.	(Music under) WOMAN: United Airlines makes me feel like the boss.
2. MCU woman getting serious	They know I'm a busy woman,...
3. CU woman, super words: "On 727's and DC-5's."	...so now they've given me more carry on space then any other airline.
4. CU woman's profile as she reaches for her case.	Which I prefer to think of as carry-off space.
5. CU woman reaching for case	I grab my case...
6. CU woman and hat.	...and hat from above.
7. CU woman reaching for hat.	Completely unsquashed.
8. MCU woman and suitcase.	I get my clothes...free of wrinkles...
9. MCU woman getting clothes from closet.	...from the closet.
10. MCU woman unloading suitcase.	I whisk my suitcase from United's brand new luggage racks...
11. MCU woman leaving plane.	...and the boss is on her way.
12. MCU plane and super words: Call United or your Travel Agent."	(Singers VO) Fly the friendly skies of United.
13. CU woman and super words: "You're the boss."	(Anncr VO) Where you're the boss.

30-second television script, Leo Burnett Company, Inc. Reprinted with permission from United Airlines.

Figure 36-2.

We built the largest airline in the free world.

Around you.

And you...   **and you...**   **and you...**   **and you...**

United Airlines wasn't born big. But we were born dedicated to a big idea: To give you the very best service we could. And we grew.

As your need to travel increased, we grew to more and more cities. Building a reputation for friendly service from the ground up.

Today, United covers more of this land than any other airline. And we continue to give the service you've come to expect in the friendly skies. From curb to curb, take off to touchdown.

Yes, we've grown. Because we've never forgotten where it all began. We built the largest airline in the free world. Around you.

"You wouldn't be spoilin' me now, would you?"

"We're gonna try."

Fly the friendly skies of United.

SPENDING AND MEDIA

Network and local television, radio, newspapers, consumer and trade magazines, and outdoor are all used to tell the "friendly skies" story.

Of total advertising expenditures of $154 million for the top 11 airlines in 1976 (roughly double the amount spent ten years earlier), United's total of $22 million places it second on the list, well behind TWA and just ahead of American Airlines.

The chart below details where these major carriers spend their advertising dollars.

	Total	Net TV	Spot TV	Spot Radio	Maga-zines	Local Nspr.	Out-door
United	$ 22,837	$6,090	$ 6,760	$ 2,513	$ 958	$ 6,486	$ 30
TWA	27,814	——	8,024	3,730	679	15,345	36
American	21,640	108	2,407	4,433	2,193	12,188	311
Delta	20,623	——	1,320	3,835	908	13,547	1,013
Eastern	20,612	1,107	5,174	1,987	1,946	9,478	920
National	11,143	——	2,491	1,652	28	6,550	422
Continental	7,552	——	2,275	2,620	106	2,191	360
Western	6,676	——	1,917	873	368	3,214	304
Northwest	6,502	——	383	1,296	882	3,932	9
Braniff	6,420	——	5	482	1,035	4,762	136
Pacific S.W.	2,077	——	446	575	120	668	268
TOTAL	$153,896	$7,305	$31,202	$23,996	$9,223	$78,361	$3,809
	100%	5%	20%	16%	6%	50%	3%

Note that, among all the competitors, the majority of spending is in local media, particularly newspapers. This is because the route structure of most carriers makes national advertising somewhat wasteful. United, however, can make more effective use of national media because it serves 110 cities, more than any airline of the 11 listed.

QUESTION

Suppose, as advertising manager of United Airlines, you were asked by top management to prepare a *brief* assessment of the various local media as vehicles for the airline's advertising. Give briefly only the major pros and cons of each. Consider the following local media: spot television, radio, newspapers, outdoor, collateral material (such as direct mail letters, promotional folders, window displays). In discussing collateral material tell what specific targets you would have in mind when using such material.

37

DᴇBEERS CONSOLIDATED MINES LTD.

Annual diamond engagement ring sales in the United States amount to $900 million. DeBeers Consolidated Mines Ltd., which produces about 40 percent of the world's diamonds from mines in South Africa and Nambia, controls about 80 percent of this domestic engagement ring market.

DeBeer's business is to mine, and then trade uncut diamonds to processors who cut, polish, and set them into rings, pins, and necklaces. The types of dealers who sell diamond engagement rings, in order of importance, are chain stores, independent retailers, discount stores, and department stores.

These dealers expect strong advertising and merchandising support for products they stock, and they get this support from DeBeers, which is unique in its activity of promoting the sale of diamonds after they become jewelry.

A UNIQUE MARKET

Also unique are some of the characteristics of the diamond engagement ring market to which a large share of the DeBeers marketing budget is directed. For example, in preparing a campaign with N.W. Ayer, its advertising agency, the DeBeers marketing team had to take these factors into account:

Purchase Frequency—Practically all mass-merchandised products are in demand daily, weekly, monthly, or annually. Pre-wedding items, however, are purchased only once in a lifetime by about 70 percent of all buyers, and rarely more than twice in a lifetime. The period of purchase susceptibility lasts for only a few weeks or months before the engagement, after which the potential usefulness of the advertising has ended or at least is dormant.

Alternate Purchase Possibilities—In the engagement ring market, a premarriage couple is faced with more purchase demands in one short period than ever before in their lives. Some short-range alternatives to the diamond ring are no ring at all, fancy luggage, an expensive honeymoon, and another gem (only 5 percent select this option). Some longer-range objectives include a place to live, appliances, a television set, audio equipment, and a new car.

Cost—Because the price of rings has climbed more slowly than the increase in diamond stone costs, the size and grade of diamonds used in most diamond engagement rings has been stabilized at a point that will maintain an attractive retail price for consumers.

In addition to these market characteristics, the DeBeers marketing team also had these demographic and usage statistics to account for:

1) The target market for diamond rings comprises single men and women between the ages of 18 and 24. However, advertising is aimed at all young people because most will become prospects in time.
2) Seventy-eight percent of all first-time brides and nearly 50 percent of all repeat brides in the United States receive an engagement ring. Nearly half of all brides select a matched set of engagement and wedding rings. Seventy-seven percent prefer a solitaire diamond. Brides between 25 and 29 years of age receive the largest diamonds—an average of .78 points or slightly more than three-quarters of a carat.

A CAMPAIGN EMERGES

Based largely on these market and consumer characteristics, the following campaign strategy devised by N.W. Ayer Advertising Agency emerged.

Creative Strategy—The *goal* of this creative strategy: to maintain the diamond engagement ring as the most appropriate symbolic expression of betrothal. The *slogan*: "A diamond is forever."

Creative Tactics—The campaign will be divided into two classifications with these percentages for each: romantic campaign, 75 percent; informational campaign, 25 percent. Romantic advertising will emphasize the symbolic, emotional aspects of diamonds and engagement rings (fig. 37-1). Informative messages will be instructional and help young people become familiar with the terminology and standards that contribute to the value of diamonds (fig. 37-2).

Figure 37-1.

Romantic campaign advertisement. Reprinted with permission from American Association of Advertising Agencies.

Figure 37-2.

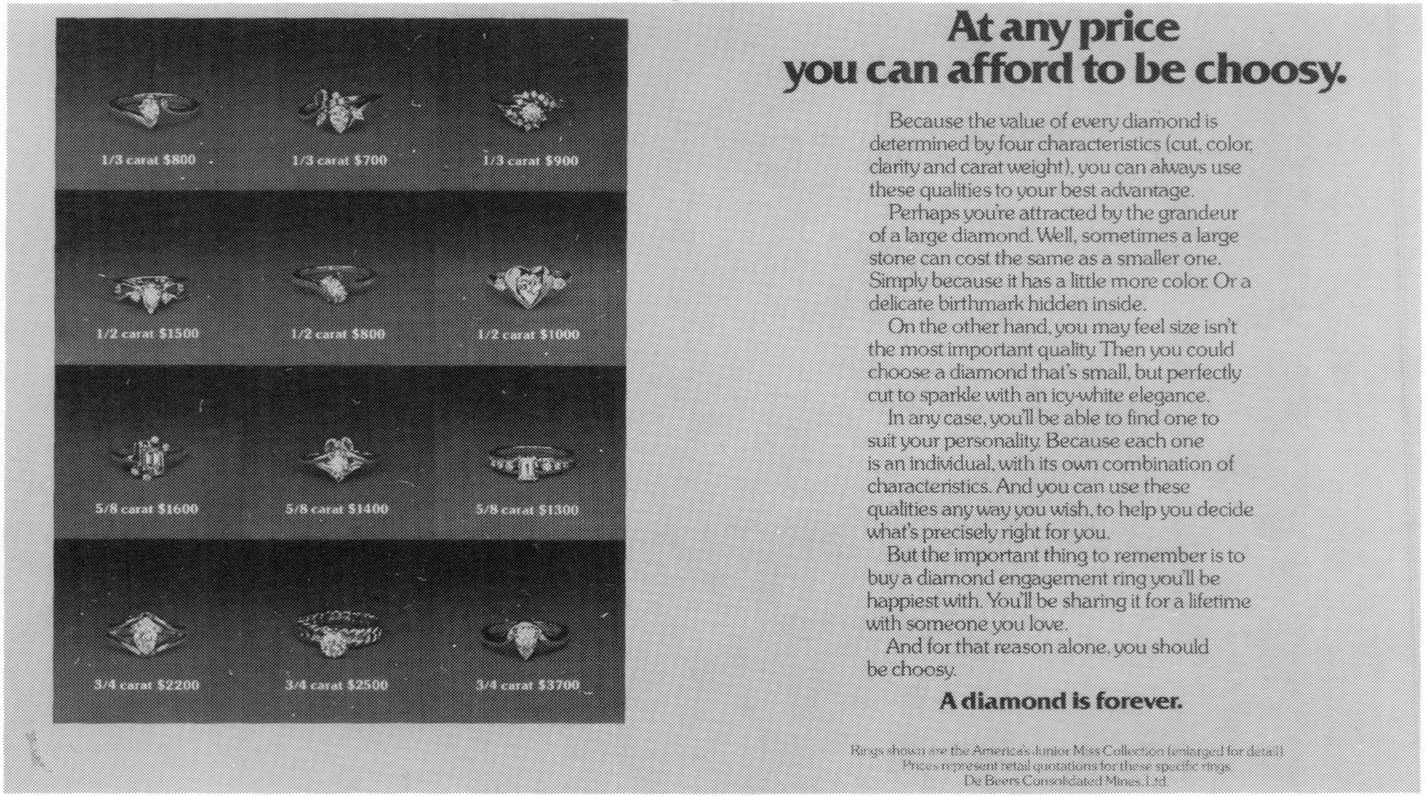
1/3 carat $800
1/3 carat $700
1/3 carat $900
1/2 carat $1500
1/2 carat $800
1/2 carat $1000
5/8 carat $1600
5/8 carat $1400
5/8 carat $1300
3/4 carat $2200
3/4 carat $2500
3/4 carat $3700
At any price
you can afford to be choosy.
Because the value of every diamond is determined by four characteristics (cut, color, clarity and carat weight), you can always use these qualities to your best advantage.
Perhaps you're attracted by the grandeur of a large diamond. Well, sometimes a large stone can cost the same as a smaller one. Simply because it has a little more color. Or a delicate birthmark hidden inside.
On the other hand, you may feel size isn't the most important quality. Then you could choose a diamond that's small, but perfectly cut to sparkle with an icy-white elegance.
In any case, you'll be able to find one to suit your personality. Because each one is an individual, with its own combination of characteristics. And you can use these qualities any way you wish, to help you decide what's precisely right for you.
But the important thing to remember is to buy a diamond engagement ring you'll be happiest with. You'll be sharing it for a lifetime with someone you love.
And for that reason alone, you should be choosy.
A diamond is forever.
Rings shown are the America's Junior Miss Collection (enlarged for detail)
Prices represent retail quotations for these specific rings.
De Beers Consolidated Mines, Ltd.

Informational campaign advertisement. Reprinted with permission from American Association of Advertising Agencies.

QUESTION

Indicate by percentages how much you would allocate to the different media if you were the DeBeers advertising manager. Explain why you have made the allocations you have. (Assume that the budget is $2 million.)

38

THE MONEY STORE

"The Money Store" is a registered trademark that serves as an umbrella name for a group of finance companies which specialize in making secondary mortgage loans to homeowners. Headquartered in Springfield, New Jersey, the finance house currently has 25 branch offices in New Jersey, New Hampshire, Rhode Island, Connecticut, Massachusetts, Pennsylvania, Virginia, Maryland, and Washington, D.C.

Here's how a short article in *Forbes* magazine (August 1, 1977) describes the background and operations of The Money Store:

Last year The Money Store, formerly Modern Acceptance Corp., grossed more than $5 million in income from the sale of second mortgage loans, plus finance income, insurance commissions and appraisal fees. Founded in the mid-sixties with $100,000 capital by Alan Turtletaub and Ben Minkoff, former mortgage and personal loan lenders, it has grown into the largest second-mortgage company in New Jersey, with some $120 million in loans made since then. Using the second mortgages as collateral, TMS turns around and borrows most of the money to finance its loans from banks and other large-scale lenders. Clearly, TMS is a substantially leveraged operation, since its own capital is only about $5 million. How profitable this leverage has been can be seen from the fact that its $5 million in capital is almost entirely reinvested capital; initial capital was only $100,000 and there have been significant withdrawals.

The key to TMS's well-leveraged profitability was summed up by Mr. Turtletaub during a consumer credit management seminar sponsored by Columbia University in June 1978.

Many people ask me what's behind this boom in second mortgages. My one-word answer is "inflation."

Twenty years ago you almost never heard of second mortgages. They were insignificant compared to other financial programs, but in the last ten years we've had a lot of inflation. *U.S. News and World Report* says the median price of an existing home has doubled in the last ten years. And every month the homeowner pays off some of the principal on his loan, reducing his indebtedness.

Salaries have doubled too. So inflation reduces the burden of paying off the first mortgage by reducing the portion of income that must be devoted to the fixed monthly charges.

But alas, all the other things we need, and particularly the luxuries we want, have doubled in price too . . . so inflation is a two-edged sword to the homeowner. While it increases his equity, it also creates the need to borrow against it.

In substance, then, borrowing against the inflated equity in homes is what second mortgages (and The Money Store) are all about.

This trend toward borrowing on home equity, and its consequences, was described as follows in *The New York Times* (December 18, 1977):

For homeowners across the country, borrowing has become a way of getting some cash out of their most successful investment—the single-family house, typically the most substantial asset a family owns. Without selling their homes, Americans are renegotiating and extending their mortgages, shouldering greater debt at higher interest rates, and in some cases taking out second mortgages.

The increased borrowing by homeowners has caused an explosion in mortgage debt on existing homes, which has tripled in magnitude in less than three years. By putting cash in homeowners' pockets, the mortgage borrowings have provided a novel source of consumer credit, fueled consumer spending, and helped the United States climb out of the 1975 recession faster than any other nation.

HOW TMS PROMOTES ITSELF

At TMS, the job of promoting the inflation-induced benefits of second-mortgage borrowing in general, and TMS services in particular, is the responsibility of Joseph Costa, the firm's marketing manager. In his previous capacity, Costa was an advertising consultant, specializing in the preparation of radio and television commercials for a diversity of clients, including a number of Republican congressmen. In his present capacity, Costa presides over TMS's wholly owned advertising agency, called Dyna-Mark Inc., and is responsible for all campaign planning, implementing, and control activities. (He also writes most of the copy used in these campaigns.)

Before discussing the specifics of TMS's campaign strategy, Costa emphasizes two major "image" problems with which the strategy must cope. The first of these problems is the image that many consumers have of mortgages in general.

People tend to think a mortgage is just something you take out to buy a house—now we're telling them that it's also a good way to cash in on your gains; to turn your house into money. Although second mortgages are old, this concept was new to most borrowers when we first started up in the mid-sixties.

The second image problem pertains to second mortgages in particular. Says Costa:

When we first started out, and still today to a large extent, "second mortgage" was a dirty word that people associated with the villain who forecloses on the poor old widow. Actually, defaults are so rare as to be practically nonexistent, and laws have been stiffened to drive clandestine operators out of the business, but the image lingers on.

Following are some of the components of the campaign strategy designed to promote TMS's features and benefits in the face of these image problems:

The Target Market—As defined by Costa, the "average" Money Store borrower is a mature male, 42 years old, who paid $25,000 for a home seven years ago (with $5,000 down), and has since seen the value of that home skyrocket to $45,000. This person has been married for ten years, has an income of $17,000 per year, and will probably use the borrowed money for one of these purposes: home improvements, tuition, debt consolidation, taxes, business investment, or the purchase of another home.

The Appeal—According to Costa, the main message TMS's advertising is designed to convey to its market is one of honesty and integrity. "We're not in business to foreclose on properties, nor do we want to be in the collection business," he says. "So we have high standards for granting loans, and grant them only to about 25 percent of the people who apply for them, when we're convinced they have sufficient income and equity to pay them back." The major secondary appeal of TMS's advertising, says Costa, is "ease and availability" of loans for those who qualify, with many offices and a minimum of paperwork.

The Approach—Central to TMS's promotional approach to conveying its appeals is the "Money Store" name, which Costa describes as "our most important differential—simple, dramatic, easy-to-remember, and strongly associated with our product. It explains complex money matters in three words that can be easily understood by the unsophisticated consumers: We sell cash."

Also central to TMS's promotional approach is the name of Phil Rizzuto, the ex-New York Yankee shortstop who broadcasts New York Yankees games. According to Costa, Rizzuto is in an age category with which members of TMS's target market would be familiar, and projects a "good, clean, friendly, sincere image." Rizzuto appears in all media carrying the Money Store name and message, including television, radio, newspapers, direct mail, and advertising specialties, such as matchbook covers and sugar packages.

Each of the half-dozen or so television commercials he produces each year for The Money Store features what Costa calls the "billboard approach," with Rizzuto making his presentation in front of a Money Store storefront prop. In addition to dramatizing the Money Store concept, this prop also solves the problem of presenting all the information about the company required by law. "Instead of a hodgepodge of superimpositions, we just print everything on the store window," says Costa.

Although the content of Rizzuto's message will vary from commercial to commercial, the basic tone and format of each does not change. Thus, each commercial begins with the line "I'm Phil Rizzuto for The Money Store," the same storefront prop is used, and Mr. Rizzuto delivers the message in the same way.

This sameness is consistent with Costa's penetrate-motivate philosophy, which he explains this way:

> You know, people don't pay much attention to television commercials, but if you keep repeating the same message over again in the same format, it's going to sink in after a while, even if the viewer hears it from the other room when he's getting a beer. Then, when he needs a loan from somebody, our name, at least, will be in his mind, and he'll be motivated to visit us. The idea is to develop a forceful image, and then to *sell* that image. Don't change it, and it will get more valuable as the years go by.

Costa contrasts this "billboard" approach to television commercials with the "entertainment" approach (such as the Blue Nun or Alka Seltzer "Speecy Spicey meatball" commercials) and the "slice of life approach" (the sink gets stopped up or the husband can't stand his wife's coffee), noting that each of these other approaches must be continually changed "or the joke gets stale or the situations get dull."

By repeating the Rizzuto name and picture in all the components of the Money Store media mix, Costa aims to create a synergistic effect in which each medium, and each message, reinforces the impact of the others so that they, in effect, function as a single medium. That this approach is working, he says, is indicated by the fact that people calling The Money Store in response to advertising will often say they got the message "through your television commercial," when the number they are calling appeared only in a newspaper advertisement.

The only advertisements for The Money Store that do not feature Rizzuto are the "reader-type" advertisements which are written by Costa, look like newspaper stories, and are designed to educate readers as to the second mortgage concept and Money Store services. Admitting that these advertisements contain more words that most people care to read, Costa also states that "if a person wants to borrow

Figure 38-1.

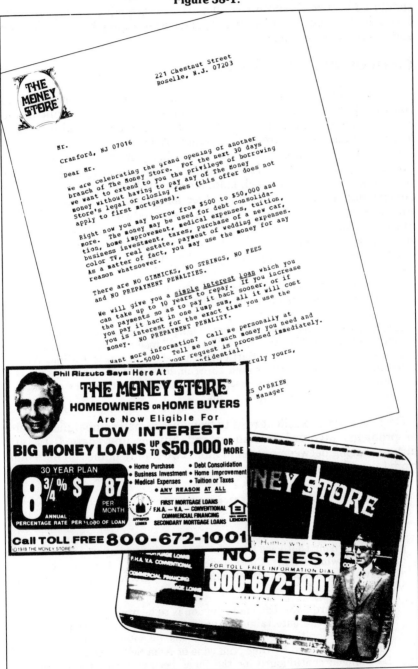

The Money Store uses former baseball star Phil Rizzuto to promote loans, through the mail and on television. The store also uses personalized letters as shown. Reprinted with permission from Dyna-Mark, Inc.

money, he'll be interested enough to read them, and if he's not, why should he bother?" An important part of these advertisements, says Costa, is the headline, which must perform the dual job of preselecting and interesting the reader.

CONTROLLING THE CAMPAIGN

Overall effectiveness of TMS advertising strategy is measured and controlled through procedures for (1) numerically coding print media advertisements and (2) asking each applicant for a second mortgage loan where he or she heard of The Money Store.

From this data, Costa receives a monthly printout from the Dyna-Mark computer for each TMS branch, listing number of loans made, total of all loans, size of each loan, sources of loan leads, total cost of advertising in each medium, and advertising cost per $1000 in loans in each medium. Out of these figures is measured the relative efficiency of each medium in generating inquiries and loans. "We keep our advertising expenditures aimed at the most productive media, and simply don't schedule advertising in media that don't produce business," he says.

To date, local television is far and away the most productive medium, while radio is generally ineffective.

A television message appeals to both sight and hearing, and stays in the mind a lot longer. Also, it's not an "habitual" medium like radio is, where people tend to zero-in on a particular talk show or music station. With television, they'll usually watch three or four different channels. This means that our television message reaches a greater diversity of target market people at the appropriate time.

Costa also gets excellent results from direct-mail campaigns, in spite of problems involved in finding and buying up-to-date lists, and differentiating between one-family and two-family homes on lists built from telephone book listings.

QUESTIONS

Mr. Costa expresses viewpoints about television advertising and newspaper advertising that vary from the viewpoints of many who use these two media. Following are Mr. Costa's viewpoints about television advertising and newspaper advertising. Tell whether you agree or disagree with what Mr. Costa has said.

1. The "billboard" approach in television is to be preferred for Mr. Costa's situation to the entertainment approach because (a) people don't pay much attention to television commercials, (b) entertainment approaches such as those used by Blue Nun wine or Alka Seltzer commercials must be changed continuously or the jokes become stale or the situations become dull.
2. Long-copy, "reader-type" advertisements in newspapers are effective because people wanting to borrow money will be interested enough to read and the others will not, so in their case nothing is lost.

39

PRUDENTIAL INSURANCE

In 1896, Mortimer Remington, then with the J. Walter Thompson advertising agency, noted, on his daily New Jersey commute, a strong resemblance between Laurel Hill, a rocky elevation rising from the New Jersey meadowlands, and the Rock of Gibraltar. The resemblance triggered an association in his mind and, later, copying a picture of Gibraltar from a book in the Astor Library in New York, Remington lettered beneath it this now legendary slogan for the Prudential Insurance Company, then a Thompson client:

"The Prudential Has the Strength of Gibraltar."

Three-quarters of a century later, the Ted Bates Agency, after acquiring the Prudential account and researching the company's competitive situation, gave this traditional slogan a modern twist:

"Own a Piece of the Rock."

Between slogan #1 and slogan #2, knowledge of the insurance business, and how insurance policies should be packaged and promoted, grew at Prudential to the point where the company today is the largest insurer on the North American continent. From this knowledge emerged a group of considerations and guidelines that played an important role in Bates's search for an up-to-date version of the Prudential slogan. These considerations and guidelines pertained to the nature of life insurance as a consumer product, the name of competitive marketing campaigns, and the nature of Prudential's marketing goals.

LIFE INSURANCE: UNSOUGHT

One aspect of life insurance that had a strong influence on Bates in its slogan search was the fact that, in consumer markets at least, life insurance is usually a highly unsought-after commodity. And understandably so. For one thing, a life insurance policy represents, usually, a considerable outlay of money over a long period of time before any kind of "payoff," no matter how generous, is realized. For another, this payoff usually occurs under unhappy circumstances of which people would rather not be reminded, i.e., the death of a loved one. For still *another*, the deceased is often the breadwinner who pays the premiums, so he will not be around to see the return on his investment.

Recognizing these realities, the Prudential Insurance Company has always held that advertising alone cannot sell an unsought product such as life insurance. Rather, it is the task of advertising to create a favorable environment for its 25 thousand agents when they seek sales interviews. In creating this favorable environment, advertising must perform a broad public relations function in addition to its selling function. For example, it must relate to the needs of agents as well as prospective insureds.

COMPETITIVE ADVERTISING: UNDIFFERENTIATED

After analyzing competitive advertising strategies in its slogan search, the Bates account team came to these general conclusions:

1) There was a great amount of "sameness" in life insurance advertising, making it difficult for the public to distinguish between the advertising campaigns of different life insurance companies.
2) In general, life insurance was underadvertised, particularly in light of its unsought-after nature. Given the limited advertising budgets, and the sameness of most campaigns, it was usually difficult for an insurer to be heard over the din of more appealing product and service advertising.

CAMPAIGN GOALS: PROMOTE, PROJECT, MOTIVATE

Other considerations guiding Bates's slogan search pertained to Prudential's broad-based marketing objectives, which included the following goals relating to advertising and sales promotion activities.

1) Promote an awareness on the part of the public of the financial security needs which the Prudential's insurance and equity products help satisfy.
2) Create a preference for Prudential and its representatives when a buying decision is reached.
3) Provide a strong, positive motivation for the field force to help overcome the negative environment in which salesmen must operate because of the public's psychological resistance to life insurance.
4) Project a unique personality for Prudential as a sensitive and socially conscious institution that serves the public interest well beyond its insurance and investment operations.

CAMPAIGN PLANNING: HOLD ONTO "THE ROCK"

With these considerations in mind, Bates created the "Piece of the Rock" slogan and a series of campaigns using this slogan, designed to be memorable and motivating to both prospects and agents, while maintaining the warm, human touch that had long been a feature of Prudential advertising. Figure 39-1 is a storyboard from one such campaign, based on the general theme of interdependence among people ("they need me").

Four media objectives were established to carry out this campaign theme:

1) Prudential prospects and agents were defined as men and women 18 to 49 having incomes of $10,000 and up, and affluent adults (top prospects) regardless of age.
2) The reach objective was seven out of ten target men and women in an average four-week period.
3) The frequency objective was one Prudential advertising message per target adult per average week.
4) It was decided that network television would offer the best means to achieve these objectives because of its ability to reach the broadly-defined audience efficiently, and also because of the theatrical impact it provided in the delivery of the message. Here, one important decision ran counter to a current trend in television—the decision to use 60-second commercials rather than 30-second commercials.

RESEARCH OVERVIEW

Several marketing research studies provided the public affairs department with an assessment of the effectiveness of Prudential's advertising. Among them were:

1) Public Attitude Surveys
2) Caravan Tracking Studies
3) Prudential Field Management and Agent Surveys
4) Nielsen National Television Index

Highlights from each are presented below.

Public Attitude Surveys

This survey last conducted in 1975, was based on a national probability sample of over 2,000 respondents interviewed in person. The results of the study were, therefore, projectable to the total United

Figure 39-1.

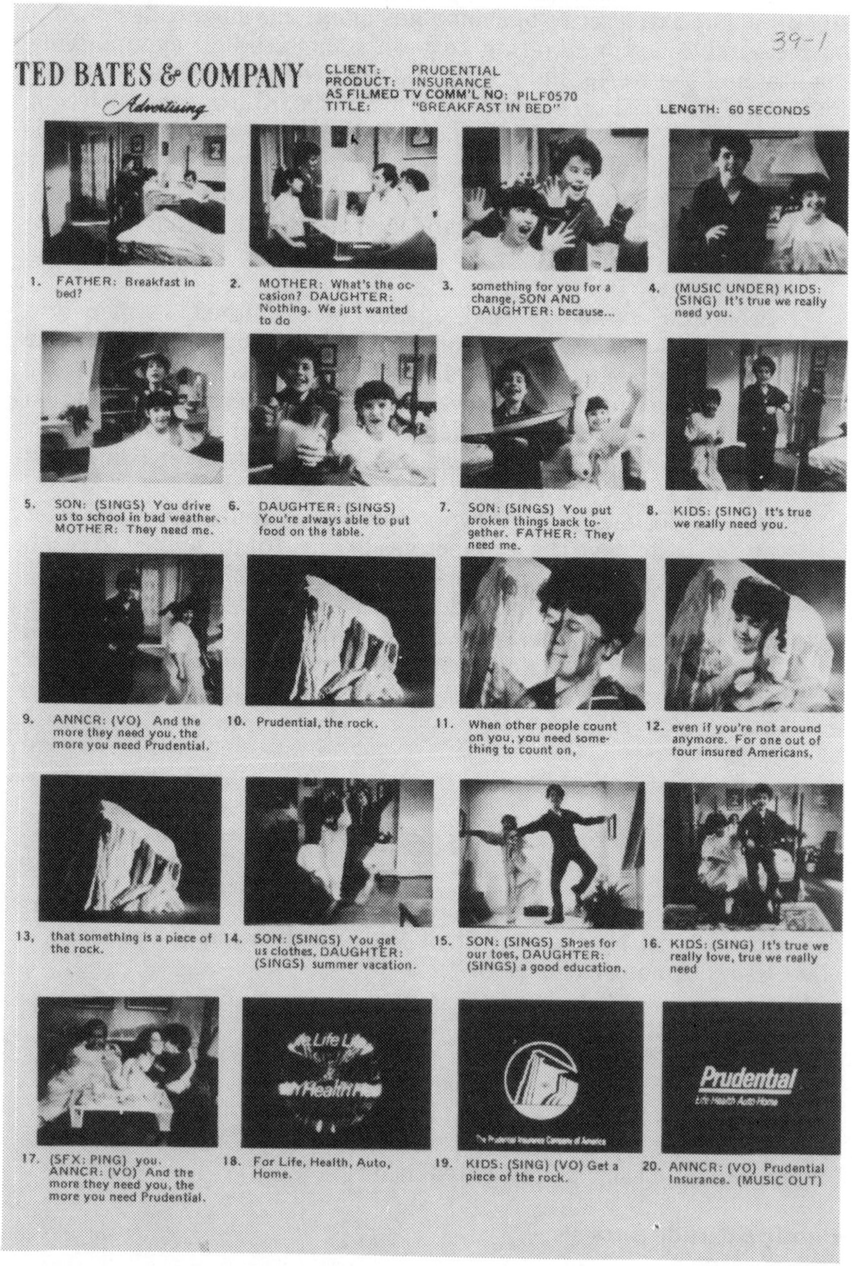

Storyboard for 60-second television commercial. Reprinted with permission from Prudential Insurance Company.

States. Its basic purpose was to determine and probe consumer attitudes on insurance in general, and specific awareness of and attitudes toward insurance companies. Thus, the study showed where Prudential stood absolutely as well as relatively against competition.

The major findings of this study, pertaining to Prudential specifically:

1) Prudential received top mention when people were asked to name life insurance companies.
2) Prudential was mentioned most frequently as the best life insurance company with which to do business.
3) Allstate, Prudential, and State Farm were the best known insurance companies of any type.
4) Prudential ranked highest on favorability among those people who knew something about the company. Three-quarters of those familiar with Prudential were favorably inclined toward the company, a figure higher than that achieved by other insurers among their "public."
5) Television was the major source of information about Prudential.

Caravan Tracking Studies

Once a year, Prudential participates in Opinion Research Corporation's Caravan study to track consumers' awareness of Prudential as an insurer and as an advertiser and their willingness to recommend Prudential to their friends. Conducted in person among 2,000 adults selected by probability methods on a national basis, the study has been used by Prudential since 1970 and has shown dramatic upward movement in the penetration of Prudential advertising.

Here are some highlights:

Unaided awareness of our advertising rose to a new high of 53 percent in 1977—nearly three times as great as that of the next four largest life companies combined.

Total recall (unaided and aided) of Prudential advertising among the entire public stood at 72 percent in 1977.

Unaided awareness of Prudential as a life insurance company rose among adult men from 41 percent in 1970 to 54 percent in 1977.

Prudential continues to receive *top mention* as the best life insurance company with which to do business. About two people in ten (21 percent) say Prudential is the best company for life insurance.

The "Piece of the Rock" slogan continued to be a highly memorable part of Prudential advertising. Among those who recall seeing Prudential advertising, 83 percent play back comments relating to the rock slogan or logo. (By comparison 59 percent mention the main theme or slogan of Allstate, "You're in good hands.")

The Caravan study has also been used—since 1975—to track the progress of the advertising. Since advertising on a national scale did not begin until after the 1975 study, the first study serves as a benchmark. Highlights are:

Total recall of Prudential advertising for homeowners insurance, at 64 percent in 1977, was up nine points from 55 percent in 1976 (unaided recall rose ten points—from 23 percent to 33 percent).

Total recall of Prudential auto insurance advertising rose six points (from 44 percent in 1976 to 50 percent in 1977). Unaided recall rose slightly (16 percent to 19 percent) over the same period.

Among those who recall seeing any kind of Prudential advertising, over eight in ten can play back a correct copy or visual element of the commercials.

Awareness of Prudential as a home insurer rose from 23 percent in 1975 to 29 percent in 1977.

Awareness as an automobile insurer rose substantially—from 8 percent in 1975 to 14 percent in 1977.

Prudential Field Management and Agent Surveys

Another important "audience" is the field sales force. There Prudential's national advertising efforts receive consistently favorable opinions. The two most recent surveys (1976) showed the following:

Ninety-one percent of the District managers and 84 percent of the sales managers gave good ratings to Prudential's national advertising program.

Sixty-five percent of the Ordinary agents were satisfied with Prudential national advertising. An equal number also said national advertising was of "great importance" to them.

Eighty-six percent of the Ordinary agents were satisfied with "the public attitude toward Prudential" and 85 percent considered "the public attitude toward Prudential to be a factor of great importance."

TV Commercial Studies

The evaluation of Prudential TV advertising among people known to have been exposed to it, i.e. among viewers of the TV programs carrying the message, is done via two systems. One is the Opinion Research Corporation's on-air testing system, which provides evaluation of what viewers remember about Prudential advertising the day after they see it. About 300 adult program viewers in 10 cities are interviewed by telephone to obtain advertising awareness, recall, and attitudinal measures.

Figure 39-2.

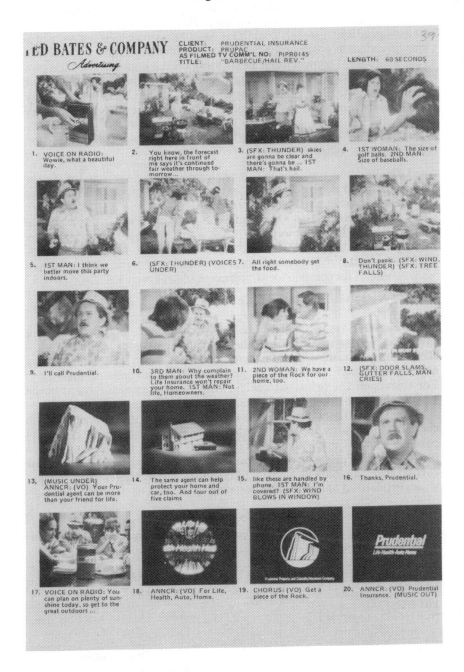

Storyboard for 60-second television commercial. Reprinted with permission from Prudential Insurance Company.

Because no information on the performance of competitive TV commercials is available through ORC's on-air testing system, the syndicated service offered by Gallup & Robinson was recently added as an evaluation research tool. This telephone-interview system provides day-after exposure recall data for Prudential commercials as well as for Prudential competitors. Depending on the popularity of the program, about 300 to 500 adult respondents form the sample base for each evaluation. Each respondent must prove that he or she actually saw the commercial through correct recall of at least one visual or copy point.

In the 1976-77 season five Prudential commercials were studied by G&R, with the following results:

1) On balance, four of the five performed above average for viewer recall and copy point registration; one commercial was closer to the norms but still above average.
2) The "Piece of the Rock" and the fact that Prudential now sold auto and homeowners insurance were the most memorable copy points of the commercials.
3) Prudential's 60-second commercials, in general, outperformed those of its competitors in terms of viewer recall.

Nielson National Television Index

The research reported thus far is of a qualitative nature, assessing the effectiveness and memorability of the advertising. Another vital advertising measurement is that concerned with the quantitative aspects—the numbers of people exposed to the advertising messages. For television the principal vehicle used for such measurement is the Nielsen National Television Index, the famous "Nielsen Ratings."

Since the 1970-71 season, Prudential has had unusual success in choosing programs that have delivered high ratings, averaging a 34 percent share of audience for all its shows, versus a 29 percent share for the average prime-time program over that period. That success has carried into the current season. (All figures are averages per program when Prudential has been the sponsor.)

Company Awareness

Response to the question "When you think of life insurance companies, which three do you think of first?"

	Total Mentions			
	1978	**1977**	**1976**	**1975**
PRUDENTIAL	59%	55%	50%	47%
Next closest competitor	29%	28%	31%	31%

	First mention			
	1978	**1977**	**1976**	**1975**
PRUDENTIAL	31%	29%	23%	21%
Next closest competitor	13%	13%	15%	15%

The following is an assessment provided, at the time, of the ratings and success of television shows carrying Prudential commercials.

	Total mentions for Prudential Men only*
January 1978	58%
January 1977	54%
January 1976	52%
January 1975	48%
January 1974	45%
January 1973	42%
January 1972	40%
January 1971	44%
July 1970	41%

* In 1970-1974 the question was asked of men only

Source: Opinion Research Corporation's Caravan Surveys, January 1978

All four programs delivered at pre-season estimates.

A special word about "Lou Grant." The show has received rave reviews from TV critics. Despite extremely strong competition in the form of one-time specials the show has demonstrated vitality, producing shares of 39 and 40 percent and occasionally ranking near the top 10. Prudential-sponsored episodes have averaged a 38 percent share. It has continued to generate a great deal of favorable notice in the press and is generally considered to be a hit show.

QUESTION

Comment on (a) the use of television as the major medium for Prudential, (b) the use of 60-second commercials instead of the usual 30-second commercials, (c) the research techniques used by Prudential to ascertain the success and/or impact of its advertising and the shows that served as vehicles for that advertising.

40

JACK DANIEL'S TENNESSEE WHISKEY CAMPAIGN

Perhaps the best way to understand the Jack Daniel's approach to advertising is to understand, first, something about how and where the product is made, the nature of its target market, and its competitive situation in the cluttered distilled spirits market.

HOW TENNESSEE WHISKEY IS MADE

The process of distilling Jack Daniel's Tennessee whiskey begins with a sour corn mash, the same way the process of making bourbon whiskey begins. Here, however, the resemblance stops; instead of being placed in oak aging barrels as for bourbon whiskey, the mash goes through a very important intervening process. Specifically, the mash is slowly introduced into tall vats, filled to a height of ten feet with hard-packed charcoal, through which the mash slowly seeps. (The charcoal is made from sugar maples that grow on the site of Daniel's Lynchburg, Tennessee, distillery. Trees are cut down when the sap is low, aged for a year, sawed and carefully stacked in ricks, then burned in open air to a fine charcoal.)

After about ten days, the first drops trickle out, and continue thereafter until the vat empties. Technically called "leaching," this process of filtering corn mash through charcoal had its name changed to "mellowing" by the Gardner Advertising Company of St. Louis, Daniel's agency since 1954. By whatever name, however, it's a process said to remove much of the corn taste from the finished product while giving it a taste usually described as "smoother." It also gives Jack Daniel's whiskey a significant differential over competing bourbon whiskeys—so much so that the government lets the company call it Tennessee whiskey instead.

The final product is bottled and labeled in a distinctive fashion which has not changed in 80 years. For 30 years before *that*, Jack Daniel's Tennessee whiskey was sold by the barrel and jug.

WHERE TENNESSEE WHISKEY IS MADE

Jack Daniel's second significant differential is the place where it is distilled—and the people who work at this distillery.

Here is how an article in the *Wall Street Journal* ("Jack Daniel's Bets That You Can't Tell Black from Green," February 8, 1977) describes this differential:

Yes, there really is a Lynchburg, Tenn., just like it says in the Jack Daniel's whiskey ads, and yes, it has a population of just under 400, same as always.

Most of the men here really do wear bib overalls and talk like Slim Pickens. The distillery is right over yonder in the hollow, alongside the spring where that good, fresh water comes from. Out back, they're burning maple wood for the charcoal mellowing process (pronounced "mellerin" locally) that gives the whiskey its distinctive flavor.

Viewed from a historical perspective (the distillery was listed in the National Registry of Historic Places in 1972), the Jack Daniel's distillery is the oldest licensed distillery in the United States and, except for a modern, brick office building, new production equipment, and some new warehouses, its current buildings conform to its original structures. Its process for making whiskey hasn't changed since then, either.

WHO BUYS TENNESSEE WHISKEY

The people who buy Jack Daniel's Tennessee whiskey are described by company president Martin Brown this way:

We cater to men who value consistency and loyalty in a changing world. We want to reassure them that we're the one thing they can depend on.

Demographically, members of this reassured male population live in urban centers, have an average annual income in excess of $20,000, and are college educated. (One place where none of them lives is Lynchburg, Tennessee, which has been dry since 1909.) This group counts among its ranks such past and present celebrities as Ernest Hemingway, William Faulkner, Henry Kissinger, Carl Sandburg, and Vice President John Nance Garner. (The skimpy female contingent is perhaps best represented by Elizabeth Taylor.)

THE COMPETITIVE SITUATION

Together, these Tennessee whiskey devotees have elevated Jack Daniel's, if not to cult status, certainly to a level of euphoric brand loyalty and insistence, as evidenced by a study of American drinking preferences conducted by Barton Brands Ltd., a Chicago-based distiller, in the early '70s. As reported in the *Wall Street Journal* article mentioned above, here is how a Barton spokesman summarized these findings:

All the answers squared pretty well with actual sales except those that involved Jack Daniel's. About twice as many people said they drank it as possibly could have. Brand loyalty isn't nearly what it used to be in this business, but Daniel's is one brand people want to identify with. It's a product with charisma.

Expressed quantitatively, this charisma translates itself into annual sales increases that averaged 10 percent between 1968 and 1978, at a time when traditional "men's" whiskeys, such as bourbon, were losing market shares to vodka, Scotch, and Canadian whiskey. In 1976, Daniel's case sales growth of 25.6 percent was the largest of any brand among the top 35, and ranked Daniel's thirty-first among all liquor brands.

These dramatic sales increases are in spite of (or possibly because of) an expensive price. For example, in 1977 a bottle of Jack Daniel's black label sold for $7 per fifth in Chicago, compared to $5 for competing bourbon whiskey blends. (Daniel's green label, aged four years, costs one dollar a bottle less than the five-year-old black label.)

THE ADVERTISING AND SALES PROMOTION CAMPAIGN

Jack Daniel's identity with its leisurely past, and unique "mellerin" process, has solved one problem facing most other national advertisers—that of creating a corporate identity or "image" for the product. For this reason, Daniel's advertising can perhaps best be described as "reminder" in nature, designed to tell people about its heritage, its environment, and how it is made, but not designed to position the product among other distilled products in the competitive race. Its advertising seems to say it is above that sort of thing.

Daniel's advertisements, all part of a campaign that has been running continuously since 1954, reflect this low-key, soft-sell, homespun philosophy. Each usually consists of a picture of a "down home" scene at the distillery, while accompanying copy presents facts about how Tennessee whiskey is made, the people who make it, the distillery's heritage, or even a cow that drinks leftover mash (fig. 40-1).

Also low key is the layout of each advertisement—neatly balanced between visual and copy, using traditional typefaces and always in black and white (fig. 40-2). Another characteristic of Daniel's advertisements is wide borders, usually occupying 20 percent of available space.

Figure 40-1.

SOME OF AMERICA'S happiest cows live just down the road from Jack Daniel's Distillery.

We distill our whiskey from a mash of America's choicest grain. Then, after distilling, we sell what's left over to neighboring farmers. And they use it in liquid form to fatten up their cows. Thanks to our choice grain, we've got some highly contented cattle here in Moore County. And, we believe, some highly contented customers most everyplace else.

CHARCOAL
MELLOWED
DROP
BY DROP

Tennessee Whiskey • 90 Proof • Distilled and Bottled by Jack Daniel Distillery
Lem Motlow, Prop., Inc., Lynchburg (Pop. 361), Tennessee 37352
Placed in the National Register of Historic Places by the United States Government

Reprinted with permission from Jack Daniel Distillery, Inc.

Figure 40-2.

Jack Daniel's Tennessee Whiskey. Made with only the choicest grain, hand-picked by our own miller.

CHARCOAL
MELLOWED
DROP
BY DROP

Tennessee Whiskey • 90 Proof • Distilled and Bottled by Jack Daniel Distillery • Lem Motlow, Prop., Inc., Lynchburg (Pop. 361), Tenn. 37352
Placed in the National Register of Historic Places by the United States Government

Reprinted with permission from Jack Daniel Distillery, Inc.

QUESTION

Consider the demographic profile of the Jack Daniel's market furnished in the case material. What media would you suggest for an advertising campaign aimed at this market? Be specific. Also, tell *why* the media selected are suitable.

41

THRU-MOV, INC.

Thousands of classified advertisements appear yearly in the nation's daily newspapers that seek men willing to work in other parts of the country than their present locations. A typical advertisement of this type reads:

Wanted—an executive for responsible position with a major corporation. Must be willing to relocate.

Other employment advertisements, fewer in number, offer positions overseas. In almost all such instances, employers will pay a mover to transport the successful job candidate, or to relocate an executive in his new home base.

Paying such expenses has been estimated to cost corporations more than $8 billion annually. Thru-Mov, a new and little-known moving company, felt that there were strong possibilities in this employee and executive moving market for a moving firm that could find a way to reach the market through promotion and advertising. Since the entire moving market amounts to only $20 billion a year, the $8 billion represented by the corporate moving segment offered an especially tempting target for movers such as Thru-Mov.

Located in New York, the Thru-Mov company had specialized since its beginning in moving households, effects, and installations for military customers. The military market itself was substantial, totaling an estimated $4 billion in moving expenses yearly.

Despite the fact that Thru-Mov had been successful in the military moving market and planned to continue serving the market, the potential in the corporate moving market was strong enough to cause them to set up a special division for this kind of business.

In assessing their plan of attack, Thru-Mov decided that their first objective was to establish their identity among corporations by stressing two of the company's featured services. One was their single charge covering all phases of a move. Two was containerization, or the movement of effects in sealed containers. Based on their experience, Thru-Mov executives decided that traffic managers, purchasing agents, and industrial relations managers were the proper targets for an advertising campaign they had decided to conduct.

Selecting an advertising agency, the company next devised an advertising program. It was decided to use a number of media and to utilize a central theme. A business magazine advertisement was written by the advertising agency that carried a headline conveying the chief thrust of the campaign. The headline read:

New way to move personnel
without headaches

A subhead explained:

Move their effects door to door
in sealed containers
for one charge

The one-charge appeal was considered the key factor in appealing to readers for the advertisement, since the user of the service would have to pay only one bill, regardless of how many carriers or warehousing facilities were used in transporting the effects. In discussing the impact of this copy claim, the advertising agency account supervisor said: "If you don't think this is a godsend to any purchasing agent or traffic manager not to have to process a dozen bills for one move, you're mistaken."

The other advantage offered by Thru-Mov—containerization—was, of course, to be emphasized strongly in advertising and promotion. It would be pointed out that because every item in the containers was individually packed and sealed in fresh packing materials, there was no unpacking at warehouses. There was less chance, therefore, for damage and misrouting. Also, pilferage was almost eliminated.

Another headline and subhead combination suggested by the advertising agency creative department read:

Wherever you've got to move them—across the state or around the world—
let experience-proved Thru-Mov containerization relieve you of personnel moving headaches, at no extra cost

In his approval of this creative approach, the sales manager of Thru-Mov explained that the phrase "wherever you've got to move them" was taken quite literally by his company. "For one thing," he said, "about 75 percent of the corporate households we move go overseas."

He added that in their face-to-face contacts with the carrier-selecting influences in industry, businessmen were informed by company salesmen that Thru-Mov had 700 agents around the free world to supervise carefully all phases of the containerized shipments.

Because of the billions of dollars represented in C.O.D. or individual households moved each year, the company and the advertising agency agreed that a strong consumer approach should be included in the campaign. One headline designed to carry out this approach said, "New idea for people on the move." The accompanying copy asserted that Thru-Mov made moving easy, possibly even pleasant.

Promotions for Thru-Mov were also aimed at freight forwarders, who would, it was hoped, recommend the company's service to their clients in other areas of the country. Considered as a tie-in possibility with this promotion was the development of co-op arrangements whereby the company's agents could put their imprints on Thru-Mov advertisements and brochures.

One attribute of the company's operation that was viewed as important by its management was its flexibility in shipping methods. This was evidenced by the fact that it maintained as little rolling stock as possible. As the sales manager explained—

> We are not a van line. Although we do own some trucks for use in the New York area, we ship the most efficient way possible, regardless of the carrier. We also make it clear that we keep track of the movement every step of the way, and the fact that we don't have assets tied up in trucks lets us do the best possible job for the customer.

It was hoped that Thru-Mov's flexibility in its business operation could be matched in its advertising methods and plans. The advertising campaign was laid out in such a way, for example, that it could be extended to other areas such as commodities shipping. In the words of the sales manager:

> When we step up our drive for the commodities shipping business, probably in six months, we'll have our media already selected and our identity will, hopefully, have been established.

One of the considerations in the promotional plans was the place of origination of the bulk of the company's business. For instance, 75 percent of the company's business was signed in the New York City area, but 95 percent of the corporate moves originated outside of New York.

QUESTIONS

1. What media plan would you suggest for Thru-Mov? Consider the different markets in devising the plan. Make specific media recommendations and indicate the weight to be assigned to the corporate campaign and the consumer campaign.
2. What feature, or features, of the company's service do you think should be stressed in the corporate campaign?

42

SCORE*
HAIR CREAM (A) –
The Media Strategy

The Product

SCORE is a clear, greaseless hair cream for men manufactured by the Bristol-Myers Company. "Creams" are the leading hair preparation for men, and before SCORE Bristol-Myers did not have a major entry in this sizable market.

The Overall Marketing Goal

The goal was to become a leader in the "cream" segment of the men's hair preparation market, primarily by switching current users of other cream products to SCORE rather than by bringing non-users of cream hair tonics (or hair tonics in general) into the fold. More specifically, Bristol-Myers anticipated a 10 percent share of the cream market segment within the first year after SCORE was introduced.

Proposed Creative Strategy

The proposed creative strategy for SCORE would position the product as a new, superior hair grooming preparation that offers the good grooming of white hair creams without the "greasiness" often associated with these creams. This strategy would be implemented through newsy, masculine, straightforward commercials dramatizing the product's main difference—i.e., its transparency in application.

* SCORE is a registered trademark of Bristol-Myers Company.

Research Base

Bristol-Myers's advertising agency uncovered the following demographics (among other research findings) pertaining to general characteristics of the cream hair preparation market.

1) While all men with hair are potential users of hair creams, the "younger male audience (15 to 39 years) purchases three-fourths of the total output, with the "under 19" segment purchasing almost half of the total output.
2) Consumer usage of hair creams is relatively constant during the year.
3) Geographically, the hair cream market shows a slightly higher per-capita usage in the Western and Southwestern sections of the United States.

Competitive Product Strategies

The following data pertain to creative and media strategies of other hair cream formulations which would be competing with SCORE for market shares.

Code 10 (Colgate-Palmolive) is a white opaque cream with a 50 percent oil base. Creative strategy stresses the product's grooming qualities ("grooms a man's hair all day"), while claiming that the product is not greasy ("disappears into your hair") and, on a strong macho note, "gives hair the clean, manly look that inflames women, infuriates inferior men."

The media strategy for Code 10 relies heavily on a network TV schedule consisting mainly of 30-second commercials on two "action-adventure" programs, supplemented by (1) heavy couponing, sampling, and trade advertisements; (2) spot TV schedules in major markets; and (3) half-page advertisements in *Playboy* magazine.

Groom and Clean (Cheesebrough-Ponds) is a transparent cream product with a 30 percent oil formulation. Creative strategy emphasizes the cleansing nature of the product ("actually cleans your hair with every combing") as well as its grooming ability ("leaves hair neatly in place all day") and its nongreasy composition ("for the man who can't stand the feel of grease in his hair and the women who can't stand grease on a man's hair"). In the test market stage, Groom and Clean relied mainly on network and spot TV in its media mix.

Radar (Procter & Gamble) is a clear, alcohol-and-water-base hairdressing that supplements its nongreasy, good-grooming claims with an anti-dandruff claim.

Also in the test market stage, Radar spent $79,000 in measurable media during its initial three months in test, of which $60,000 was spent on TV advertising and $19,000 on print advertising. During its latest three-month test period, this 3:1 ratio of TV-to-print media expenditures changed to better than 9:1, with $56,000 of a total of $59,400 spent on TV advertising, mostly of the "spot" variety.

THE SCORE MEDIA STRATEGY

With the foregoing product, market, research, and competitive considerations in mind, the SCORE advertising team devised a media strategy having the following key features.

The target market for SCORE would comprise the 15-to-39 year male age group with special emphasis on the below-19 group.

Consistent with its marketing goal of quickly becoming a major competitive factor nationally (with a planned first-year share of market goal of 10 percent), media emphasis for SCORE would be on *reach* instead of *frequency* or *continuity*. Thus, it was decided that a disproportionate amount of its annual budget would be invested during the first few months after the debut of SCORE. Such concentration would bring the SCORE message before as many potential users as possible. It was thought that repeat purchases and word-of-mouth advertising would compensate for budget cutbacks during the initial, "media blitz" stage of the campaign.

Until (and if) a specific geographic purchasing pattern emerged, the major focus of the initial media effort would be in highly populated areas nationwide.

Supplementing the media effort, special trade and consumer promotions (cents-off couponing, sampling, price discounts, etc.) would aim to maximize the distribution of all sizes of SCORE and encourage consumer trials of the product.

Because it was felt that visual media would most effectively demonstrate and dramatize unique product differentials of SCORE (and since *reach* was the primary goal of the media strategy), it was decided to invest the largest share of the media budget in network and spot TV, in the following manner:

1) *Network TV*: To reach the younger male audience, a total of 33 minutes per month was purchased for programs known to have high viewing among younger males, such as "The Saturday Night Movie," and two other shows appealing to young males. The estimated four-week reach and frequency of this combined network TV effort would be, respectively, 44 and 1.6.

2) *Spot TV*: Supplementing the nighttime network TV effort, evening spot TV commercials would be scheduled in 55 major markets. Surveys showed that these 55 markets, selected on the basis of population density and competitive activity, covered 70 percent of all U.S. households. When added to the network TV schedule, this spot TV effort increased reach from 44 percent to 78 percent during the first few months of the campaign. Additionally, the average frequency of contact increased from 1.6 to 4.1, all at an average cost of $2.60 per thousand households.

To summarize, here is the combination night network and spot TV schedule recommended to introduce SCORE:

Coverage	Medium	Cost (M$)
National	**Night Network TV**	$1,207
	1 min/week, 23 weeks	
	1 min/end-of-week, 24 weeks	
55 markets	**Night Spot TV**	2,181
	5 min/week, 7 weeks	
	4 min/week, 18 weeks	
	3 min/week, 7 weeks	
	2 min/week, 13 weeks	
	Total Media	$3,388

QUESTIONS

1. Assume that you decide to supplement the television advertising with magazine advertising. What magazines would you put on your list?
2. What information sources would you consult in order to determine your competitive strategies, and to obtain statistical data that would be useful?

43

NEW YORK TIMES "SPORTSMONDAY"

When the *New York Times* introduced its "SportsMonday pullout section, it did so in the face of these competitive pressures:

Dramatic circulation gains by suburban newspapers, brought on largely by the exodus of the better-educated, affluent, white population from the central cities over a 30-year period. At the time "SportsMonday" was introduced, 55 suburban dailies were ringing New York City, all in competition with the *New York Times* and all providing local coverage of considerably more interest to suburban readers than the central-city issues that preoccupied the *Times*. A vexing problem brought on by this flight to the suburbs: large non-reader populations in vacated city zones.

Other New York City dailies competing with the *Times* for readers and advertisers' dollars. The *New York Daily News*, with daily circulation of almost two million readers (compared to the *Times's* average circulation of about 900,000), has the highest circulation of any newspaper in the United States and is the *Times's* major competitor. The *New York Post*, with a circulation just over 600,000, is the only afternoon newspaper of the three, and is hence at a disadvantage in that there is less fresh news that can be included. Like the *Times*, both of these newspapers have undertaken editorial initiatives to broaden the scope of their market. The *News*, for example, publishes suburban editions covering New Jersey and Fairfield and Westchester counties, and has added special sections on food, travel, weekend activities, and gardening. Although the *Post* has not explored suburban editions as yet, it does have an established travel section and recently introduced a new food section.

The *Post* lost almost 20 percent of its circulation in two years before it was bought by Rupert Murdoch, an Australian publishing magnate, who injected new life into the paper with gossip, human interest, and sensational stories. Under Murdoch, the *Post* has experienced a rapid circulation climb, in contrast to the *News,* whose circulation continues to decline slowly. Between 1970 and 1975, average weekly circulation of the *Times* also declined from 885,000 to 828,000; Sunday circulation dropped from 1,455,000 to 1,440,000; and advertising linage dropped from $77 million to $69 million. Various stratagems initiated since 1975 have increased daily circulation 3 percent, arrested the decline of the Sunday paper, and built advertising linage to previous high levels.

Other marketers in the "News and Features" field, including television, radio, and magazines. Although, in newspaper terms, broadcast media usually provide only a headline and "first paragraph," this is often enough for many consumers of news and features materials. Additionally, the increased emphasis on television specials and "depth" news programs such as "60 Minutes" and "The MacNeil-Lehrer Report" represents a growing competitive threat to the depth news and editorial coverage of newspapers. Another threat to this depth of coverage has been the proliferation of hobby or "buff" magazines, in addition to the established news magazines (*Time, Newsweek,* etc.), usually published in New York.

In addition to these competitive pressures, the *Times* also faced an image problem which had dogged it for more than a century; that of the "old gray lady" of journalism—dull, hard to read, and rather pedantic. (It is also regarded as the newspaper of record for the United States, and the standard of excellence by other newspapers throughout the world.)

THE RESPONSE: ZONED EDITIONS, "SOFT" SECTIONS

In response to these pressures, the New York Times management had, during the '60s and '70s, taken a number of initiatives to counter the circulation decline and make their paper more attractive to readers in general and suburban residents and advertisers in particular. Among these initiatives:

Zoned or regional editions, usually comprising an insert of a page or two carrying news and advertising from a specific suburb, and often identified as a "local edition" on the masthead. Although these editions tend to suffer in comparison to most suburban papers in the depth of local news coverage, they have generally proved to be a moderately successful solution to the problem of circulation and advertising losses from the 30 percent of the *Times* readers residing outside of its urban market.

"Soft News" sections in separate pullout sections, to augment the "hard news" sections. Typically, these sections include material found in regular editorial columns which is recharged and expanded into bright, interesting magazines in a newspaper format. These sections, covering such topics as entertainment, cooking, home decoration, and travel, relate to reader life-styles and are designed to attract their own enthusiasts and advertisers. Beginning in April 1976 with "Weekend," a Friday guide to entertainment and the arts, the *Times* had introduced, successively, "The Living Section" (devoted to food and cul-

ture; published on Wednesday), "The Home Section" (covering design, decoration, and furnishings; published on Thursday), and "Business Day," a separate Business/Finance section issued Monday through Saturday.

All of these special sections, it should be noted, were introduced in the context of a *Times* repositioning campaign under the slogan "The New *New York Times* . . . it's a lot more than the news." And supplementing this repositioning campaign were two circulation promotion campaigns, the first designed to develop consumer awareness of the paper's expanded content and the second designed to present *Times* readers as likable young New Yorkers whose needs are uniquely satisfied by the information in the paper ("It's what keeps us New Yorkers a little more interesting . . . more beautiful . . . smarter . . . fascinating").

INTRODUCING "SPORTSMONDAY"

Published as the latest in its sequence of "soft news" sections, "SportsMonday" was based on the following research and creative rationales.

Pre-campaign Research

The *Times* conducts an ongoing reader panel study to track reader attitudes toward the newspaper and its contents. From these interviews, it was determined that the paper had existing strengths as a source of information and news about finance, food, culture, home furnishings, decoration, entertainment, and other topics in the pullout sections. However, the reactions to sports were negative: respondents would definitely *not* turn to the *Times* for news about athletic events, the big games, or backgrounds on players. Thus, according to reader perception, "SportsMonday" would be starting from scratch in a news area for which the *Times* did not have an established reputation.

Initial research also identified the target market for the new pullout as, simply, "sports enthusiasts." This group tends to encompass men and women of all ages, incomes, educations, and occupations, selected on the basis of a psychographic or life-style interest, rather than on any combination of demographic characteristics.

Creative Strategy

The creative strategy closely followed the marketing strategy goal of positioning the *New York Times* as having the best coverage of any medium about what happened in sports during the weekend. This would be done using a subtle form of testimonials and with information about the contents of each section, with emphasis on television and radio commercials ending with the phrase: "SportsMonday" . . . for people who take their sports seriously."

A typical television commercial in the "SportsMonday" campaign featured six well-known sports figures, each reading a copy of "Sports-Monday." All were in street clothes with a limbo setting or seamless curtain behind them. The voice-over announcer, Phil Rizzuto, a baseball celebrity in his own right, described the values of "Sports-Monday." Finally, the last man, Tom Seaver (who left the Mets to join the Cincinnati Reds), said: "And I had to go to Cincinnati."

Two forms of production were used for radio commercials—recorded and live. Pre-recorded copy expressed sympathy for the "enduring sports nut" who dreads Monday because all it ever means is "the end of a weekend of fun and big games." That was true "before 'SportsMonday' " came along to recreate all of the weekend action. The celebrities used in television were not carried over into radio.

QUESTIONS

1. What reasons can you offer for not using a carryover of the celebrities featured in television to radio?
2. In addition to television and radio, what other media might be used in the New York City market?

44

SLATER & ASSOCIATES, INC.

As a regional advertiser in the Pacific Northwest states chiefly (although it services clients throughout the West) the insurance company Slater & Associates, Inc., of Portland, Oregon, was one of millions of small-budget advertisers avoiding the use of television advertising. Its avoidance of the medium was typical of the majority of advertisers in the United States, who do not use television because of budgetary reasons.

These advertisers are likely to offer such reasons as—

We'd love to be on television but we simply can't afford it.

If we advertised on television we couldn't afford to pay for our advertisements in newspapers and magazines.

Even if we could afford the time charges for television advertising, we couldn't afford the production charges.

Only the big advertisers can afford television these days and the situation's getting worse as time goes on.

When Groves & Lee, a Portland-based advertising agency handling the Slater & Associates account, considered these traditional objections, they granted that on the surface the reasons offered by small advertisers for not using television advertising made sense. As an agency spokesman pointed out, however—

You *can* advertise on television without spending a fortune. And you don't have to resort to a few quick videotape stand-up commercials to do it. If you're careful, you can make every one of the dollars you spend look like five. Most small advertisers are afraid of TV, and mostly for the wrong reasons.

The size of Slater's media budget reflected the regional character of its advertising. The company, in fact, concentrated on Oregon, its home state, even though it obtained substantial business from other western states. Thus, the money assigned to advertising media was small compared to that allotted by such national competitors as New York Life, Prudential, and Metropolitan. Despite the company's recognition of the power of television advertising, its consciousness of the cost factors caused it to avoid the medium until Groves & Lee presented a proposal that persuaded the company that the use of television advertising could be compatible with the size of the advertising budget.

Explaining its objectives for the client, the agency said:

First, we wanted to give Slater a brand-new look in the market place. Second, we wanted to help them gain some important new business. Third, we wanted to help improve the morale of the Slater salesmen.

To accomplish these objectives, the agency's proposal required a media expenditure of less than $44,000.

The agency's proposal, which dramatically increased Slater's market exposure and allowed it to reach an entirely new audience, was rooted in an offer of one-quarter television sponsorship of the professional basketball games for the impending season. These were to be telecast in Oregon over KPTV-TV in Portland. A package deal that the client and agency felt was too good to turn down consisted of 52 minutes of commercial time during the regular season games, plus a free spin-out package of commercials that were telecast during prime-time viewing hours.

Additionally, because of a late-date cancellation by one of the other sponsors, the station also offered another 30-second spot per game at a 12-game cost of only $4,500. As a public service, Slater donated these commercials to any interested local public-service organization.

In assessing the impact of the purchase of this television time, the agency media department presented the following figures to the client.

11,752,560: Total audience reached
1,607: Gross rating points total
$2.70: Cost per thousand
$67,282: Normal cost of the schedule on KPTV-TV
$43,500: Actual cost
$21,782: Saving to Slater & Associates on the buy

Once the time purchase had been negotiated, it was decided that the subject matter for the first commercial would be group insurance. Slater proposed to tell television listeners that it had established group policies with a number of the most important companies in Oregon.

An obvious creative direction would be for the agency to produce the commercial by arranging a four-day schedule of location shots in Oregon and show on film the various companies insured by Slater. A commercial utilizing this approach might have been effective, but it would also be expensive and would undoubtedly cause the agency to go over budget, always a serious matter and especially so for a newcomer to television who had been assured of its low cost.

Instead of the potentially high-cost location shooting the agency settled upon an inexpensive, but effective, creative approach. Building around the idea of a "Blue Chip" commercial, the creative team called for silk-screening the names and logotypes of a number of Slater's biggest "blue chip" clients on the face of blue poker chips. On the back of each chip was silk-screened the name *Slater Insurance*. The commercial consisted simply of a man's hands turning over the blue chips on a desk top to reveal company names. In one of them, for example, the voice-over began with:

> If you work for Portland General Utility Company, you're lucky. You're covered by one of the best group life-insurance plans there is.

After all the chips had been revealed one at a time, each was subsequently turned over to show that all the companies were covered by Slater's. No background set was needed because the commercial was filmed very tightly. Elimination of the set cut costs, but the agency insisted the lighting be first rate; no economies were to be attempted in this area of production.

Two objectives were planned for the second commercial.

1) The agency wanted to make people aware that Slater's sells more life insurance in Oregon than any company in America. This was important because very often residents within a state or region are unaware of the scope of a local enterprise, so impressed do they become with the messages of national advertisers.
2) The agency wanted to demonstrate that Slater's had a greater commitment to the people of Oregon than any other life insurance company.

Once again the creative technique was simple. The video situation required that a spokesman walk through a beautiful park in Oregon. As he did so, he made appropriate copy points about Slater's Insurance. Since on-camera talent was being used, it was vitally important to use first-rate talent. Thus, rather than economize by using a local actor, a Hollywood actor was brought in. Because of his professional skill and the pre-shooting preparations, the entire spot was filmed in a local park in one day.

Although the agency cut corners in every possible way, they did not attempt to shave expenses in the important matter of talent because, in the long run, it may be expensive not to use top talent, just as it might have been expensive not to use the best of lighting.

In the pre-shooting planning for the third commercial, the agency decided to try another direction. This commercial was to be aimed directly at the interest of the program audience—basketball.

Accordingly, Bruce Gans, a star of the city's professional basketball team, was hired to do the commercial. For the video portion, Gans did what the audience wanted to see him do—play basketball. This was simple footage to obtain.

For the audio portion, Gans did a voice-over in a direct and honest message. This was the message:

> Let's face it. I know a lot more about playing basketball than I do about life insurance, but I can tell you this—if you want to talk to an expert, call the man from Slater's. Believe me, he knows what he's talking about.

A $5,000 production budget covered the three commercials. This was a fraction of the media expenditure. Yet many comments were received from people remarking on the "network quality." Other viewers, in fact, believed the spots were high-budget syndicated commercials which Slater's had merely tagged with its super.

QUESTIONS

1. Based on the facts presented in this case, formulate two generalizations for small-budget advertisers who are planning to use television.
2. Of what significance are the gross rating points that were mentioned in connection with the media schedule proposed by Groves & Lee?
3. How does the $2.70 per thousand figure for the program compare with CPM figures for national programs? Discuss.

45

BERGER CHEMICAL COMPANY (B)
II. Putting Together
The Media Mix

The first part of this case (page 165) focused on the problems faced by Kurt Berger in developing a successful swimming pool service and supply company. His major problem was the building of a list of customers willing to contract for a package of products and services. Berger's initial promotional efforts to build such a list consisted of calling cards and advertising flyers that supported his personal selling efforts. First was a flyer promoting Berger Chemical's season-end pool-closing services.

BUILDING FOR THE FUTURE

Although the close of its first full season found Berger Chemical producing a steady income for Kurt Berger, he began to plan additional promotional approaches to help assure that this income would continue to grow in future seasons.

As a first step in this business-building effort, Berger developed a customer map that pinpointed the location of his current customers (fig. 45-1). After studying this map, Berger made his first important decision in his new promotional drive: he decided that he would center the drive on prospects in Kenilworth township (from which 60 percent of his present business derived), and from townships touching Kenilworth, such as Springfield, Union, Roselle Park, and Cranford.

This decision was based on two considerations. First, logistically it was much cheaper and easier to service customers in areas close to his Kenilworth home base. This was especially true with heavier equipment, including entire swimming pools, which would have to be transported to on-site locations.

The second consideration related to the fact that there were many pool-owning prospects in the Kenilworth area. In fact, according to data he received from the New York office of a large association of

Figure 45-1.

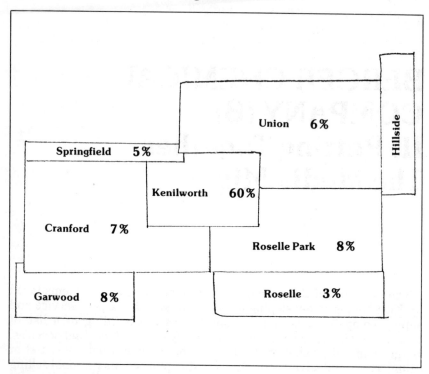

Map showing locations of 98% of Berger's customers. Outside areas making up other 2% included Irvington, Elizabeth, Linden, Westfield, and Scotch Plains.

swimming pool dealers, Berger estimated that there were more than 800 prospective customers for his services in Kenilworth alone. This figure was based on association figures that showed a ratio of one swimming pool per five families in residential areas where average per-family income was over $20,000, and this income figure applied in all of Berger's "target" townships.

Furthermore, even local families that didn't currently own swimming pools could be considered prospective customers for Berger's pools and pool services, since the association research also indicated that, if past trends continued, pool ownership would more than double in the decade ahead.

In this relatively affluent territory, a larger percentage of present and future prospects would purchase sunken and year-round swimming pools, instead of the relatively inexpensive "upright" variety, thus providing a profitable, expanding, year-round business base.

REACHING HOT PROSPECTS

Having made the preliminary decision to focus promotional efforts in his own backyard, Berger next faced the problem of converting prospects into customers. Flyer and word-of-mouth advertising, while effective in the past, would no longer be sufficient in the future, he decided. They would have to be supplemented with a more comprehensive, integrated campaign. Berger next did some research into the nature, scope, and cost of some of the alternative promotional possibilities to support his personal selling efforts.

The Yellow Pages seemed a likely possibility because many prospects, looking for a "Berger Chemical," would automatically check there first. And the fact that his company's name began with a "B," and would hence be close to the beginning of the listings under "Swimming Pool Service," should be helpful.

A proposed three-line Yellow Pages layout looked like this:

Berger Chemical
Pools, Filters, Chemicals, Service
Kenilworth, New Jersey 245-8200

This message was placed in the classified sections of two telephone books, covering Berger's target territory, for $13 per month and, for an extra two dollars, could be included in bold type on the white pages of these phone books. However, it occurred to Berger that this bold-type listing in the white pages might not be necessary since, when people consult the white pages, they presumably already know whom they are looking for.

Another possible component in his new promotion mix that Berger considered was advertisements in church bulletins. For example, a "double box" advertisement in the Saint Joseph's Church bulletin in adjacent Roselle Park, which drew most of its parishioners from Berger's target territory, would cost $48.75 for a 13-week period. This period would include the three busiest months of the Berger Chemical season (June, July, and August). A "small box" size was also available for two dollars per week, but Berger decided that he would need at least the double-box size to say all he wanted to say about his company. He made the following notes on church bulletin advertising.

Church Bulletin—St. Joseph's Church, E. 3rd Ave. Roselle 241-1250. Referred to private publisher who prints the church bulletin at the following rates. 3 sizes available, small box $2.00 per week. Double box $3.75. Large box also offered but not available presently. Ads run for a 13 week minimum, with a 2 week notice required for cancellations. Double box is closest to 4 lines with 13 week price being $48.75.

For example, the following layout would fit nicely into the double-box size:

Swimming Pool Service

- Sales
- Repairs
- Openings/closings
- Liquid chlorine
- Filters
- Pumps
- Liners
- Free delivery to all customers

Berger Chemical   245-8200

This layout or one similar to it, might also be appropriate for advertisements in local newspapers, and Berger, after a few phone calls and a trip to the library, gathered the information given below on newspaper advertising and its costs.

Spectator—112 E. 2nd Ave. Roselle 686-7700. 4-line ad for $3.60 appears in all 8 community papers besides Roselle. Roselle Park Spectator also includes Springfield, Mountainside, Irvington, Union, Kenilworth, Vailsburg. The ad will appear in all these papers once. The papers are town weeklies.

Suburban News—822 South Ave. W. Westfield 232-3800. 4 lines $1.05 a line with a 3-line minimum. $4.20 for 4 lines. Weekly paper ad is printed once. About half the circulation is outside the Kenilworth target area.

Daily Journal—295 N. Broad, Elizabeth 355-1212. 4 lines, $4.50 per day or $13.12 for 4 days is the special rate. Largest circulation of all in Kenilworth target area.

He also gathered information on an outdoor advertising agency.

Seymour Chas Advertising—1155 W. Chestnut St. Union. A corp. such as American Advertiser owns numerous bill boards across country. You have to contract with them for the use of the board. Seymour Chas Agency has a 5 yr. contract with the Bill Board Co. and will rent you a bill board for $116.00 per month with a 6 month minimum. This does not include furnishing, art work, etc. That must be put on the board, another firm must be hired to do this work.

QUESTIONS

1. If you were Berger, which of the various media would you use if you had to limit your budget to $150, or less?
2. Devise a rough media plan and supply figures.

46

THE BERMUDA DEPARTMENT OF TOURISM

Here are facts and figures pertaining to a campaign developed by the Foote, Cone & Belding advertising agency for the Bermuda Department of Tourism.

The Product

A member of Bermuda's Department of Tourism describes his homeland:

> The Island of Bermuda, located 568 miles East of Cape Hatteras, has played host to kings, queens, presidents, prime ministers, and famous people the world over. This was not a chance happening but rather a design of the people of the island who have created such a congenial atmosphere that many visitors find it irresistible. It is not surprising to hear many visitors echo the sentiments of Mark Twain after his Bermuda visit: "You can take heaven, I'll take Bermuda."

The specifics comprising Bermuda's "congenial atmosphere" at the time the campaign was being planned included the following:

1) A unique location, close to mainland U.S.A.
2) A consistently pleasant climate, and beaches, people, and shops reflective of the fact that tourism had been the Island's chief industry for more than 40 years.
3) A ten-month-long tourist season.
4) A low-key, blue-chip image as a vacation resort which differentiated it from other, more commercialized resorts awash in gambling, gaudiness, or governmental instability.

The Market

Because of the limited size of the Island, and a conscious decision not to jeopardize its blue-chip image by catering to hordes of tourists, Bermuda's tourist bed capacity was limited to the 10 thousand visitors who could be comfortably lodged in hotel accommodations. In addition, no more than five ships could be berthed in any 24-hour period.

More than 80 percent of this total number of visitors come from the geographic triangle formed by Washington, Boston, and Chicago. Here is a breakdown showing the number, and percentage, of visitors from various areas within this triangle.

Metropolitan Market Areas (ADI) 1975

ADI	RANK	VISITORS	PERCENT
New York	1	121,475	35.58
Boston	2	66,366	19.44
Philadelphia	3	30,865	9.04
Hartford-New Haven	4	15,738	4.61
Providence	5	14,892	4.36
Washington, D.C.	6	12,184	3.57
Baltimore	7	6,633	1.94
Chicago	8	4,437	1.30
Harrisburg-York	9	3,816	1.12
Portland-Poland Springs	10	3,702	1.08

Of this total, the largest group (31 percent) was in the 20-29 year age bracket, with both the 40-49 and 50-59 year brackets each accounting for about 20 percent of total visitors, followed by the 30-39 year bracket with 15 percent.

Viewed from the income perspective, approximately 50 percent of these visitors earned incomes in excess of $20,000, and only 8 percent earned less than $10,000. In terms of occupational status, 60 percent were of professional or managerial status, 19 percent were white collar workers, and 15 percent were blue collar workers. One interesting statistic: 59 percent of visitors were women, 41 percent men.

The Message

Most of the advertisements in FC&B's campaign for Bermuda focused on "typical" tourists (as defined by the demographic and geographic profiles) enjoying, and commenting on, experiences unique to Bermuda, and were reflective of the "unspoiled, unhurried, uncommon" charm of the Island.

Figures 46-1 and 46-2 are typical advertisements in this campaign. The first shows a honeymoon couple being serenaded by the Band of the Bermuda Regiment; the second a couple returning to the Island for the eighth time.

Depending on when it was scheduled, each advertisement featured an event characteristic of one of Bermuda's three tourist seasons, i.e.,

Figure 46-1.

Reprinted with permission from the Bermuda Department of Tourism.

Figure 46-2.

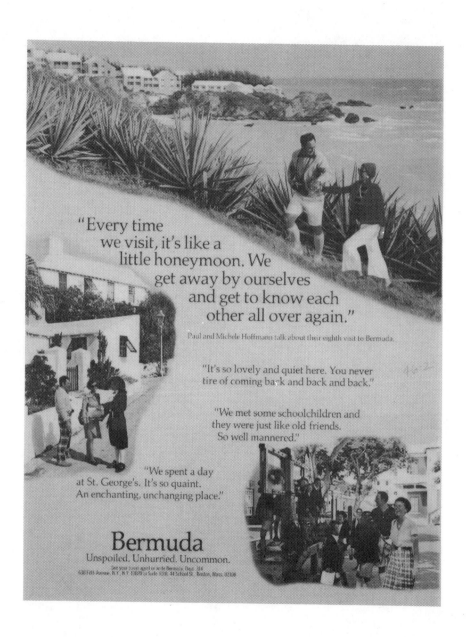

Reprinted with permission from the Bermuda Department of Tourism.

Rendezvous Season (December 1 to February 28), Shoulder Season (September 1 to November 30), and the peak Summer-Spring Season (March 1 to August 31).

Other Information

Other information that might help you appraise FC&B's media decisions includes the following:

1) Most reservations for Bermuda vacations must be booked well in advance, as airline seats, ship berths, and hotel accommodations are limited. Thus, Bermuda vacations are hardly "spur of the moment" decisions.
2) Advertisements for Bermuda vacations do not provide information on rates, advance booking, or the advantages of midweek travel or off-and-on peak period rates. Most of these advertisements do advise readers to "see your travel agent" for such information.

FC&B'S MEDIA DECISIONS

The key decision made by FC&B's media department was to concentrate most of its $2.4 million advertising budget in 22 local and regional magazines and 10 national magazines. Supplementing this schedule were:

1) Advertisements in specialized music magazines promoting the Bermuda Music Festival.
2) Trade advertisements in four travel agent journals.
3) A "miscellaneous media" scheduled aimed at small, but important, target market tourist groups, such as saltwater sportsmen and dog handlers.

Supplementing this schedule of trade and consumer magazine advertisements were occasional radio spots, but television was not used, primarily because it was not considered "sufficiently selective," or because it might encourage a greater influx of tourists than Bermuda was prepared to cope with.

Newspaper advertising was placed mostly by cruise ship companies or major hotel chains and hence was not included in FC&B's budget.

The Bermuda Department of Tourism also sponsors a briefing tour for approximately 1,200 travel agents from mid-Atlantic states to give them a first-hand view of the product they might be promoting.

QUESTIONS

1. On the basis of the facts given, design a media schedule for the forthcoming year that will (a) provide the right amount and frequency of media cover-

age, (b) reach the market desired, (c) provide the proper vehicles for the advertising messages of the Bermuda Department of Tourism.
2. Provide a general rationale defending your media selections. In this, include an explanation of the frequency with which you have used the media and the weight of the dollars assigned. This explanation does not have to be applied to every medium used but should be applied to media receiving very heavy or very light use.

47

THE FRAM CORPORATION

To promote its products, the Fram Corporation, a large manufacturer of automobile filters and pollution control valves, engaged in an advertising and sales promotion campaign (A&SP). In the following are facts and figures pertaining directly, or indirectly, to the campaign.

Fram sells most of its products through automotive parts distributors. It spends 6 to 8 percent of net distributor sales on A&SP campaigns. The filters it manufactures and sells are for oil, air, and fuel.

Most of Fram's advertising falls into three categories: (1) trade advertising directed to existing and prospective distributors of Fram products, (2) cooperative advertising with distributors directed to consumers through newspapers and radio, and (3) a heavy television advertising schedule in programs of championship sports events throughout the year.

Fram's trade advertising utilizes advertisements that appear three or four times a month in such publications as *Discount Store News*, *Hardware Age*, and *Jobber Topics*. Figure 47-1 shows an example of such an advertisement.

Two advertising agencies create and distribute Fram's newspaper advertising. These are James Symon Inc. for creative services, and SFM Media for media services. Much of this advertising is placed by wholesale distributors and jobber customers to take advantage of lower local rates. To encourage participation among its distributor customers, Fram contributes 1 percent of total net distributor sales to a cooperative advertising fund, from which each distributor receives a percentage based on sales volume.

In general, newspapers are considered by Fram marketing management to have the following advantages over other media: (1) customers

Figure 47-1.

Servicing transmission filters isn't like performing brain surgery

47-1

and with Fram it's a fast operation

Replacing an automatic transmission filter is as easy as it is profitable. No special tools are required, nor any intensive specialized training. You can do it by simply following the step by step instructions printed on every Fram box. A Fram easy-to-follow transmission wall chart makes it simple to find the right filter.

Fram offers the most complete line available.

FRAM
Automotive Division
Fram Corporation, Providence, R.I. 02916

Please send me information on transmission filters and modulators and a FREE wall chart.
☐ Have a Fram Representative Contact Me
☐ Please add my name to your mailing list

NAME_____

COMPANY_____

STREET_____

CITY_____ STATE _____ ZIP _____

Reprinted with permission from Fram Corporation.

in local markets are better oriented to newspaper advertising, typically combing newspaper advertisements for sales before going shopping; (2) newspapers offer greater flexibility in placing and changing advertisements; (3) newspapers offer greater penetration of local markets. Figure 47-2 shows typical newspaper advertisements prepared by Fram for its distributors.

Figure 47-2.

Reprinted with permission from Fram Corporation.

Fram's radio advertising, consisting of 30- and 60-second spot commercials, is also placed through the firm's distributor and jobber customers on a co-op basis. In general, radio is considered to be an effective medium to reach the suburban market, where metropolitan newspaper circulation normally falls off. Figure 47-3 shows sample 30- and 60-second radio commercials prepared by Fram.

The Fram marketing team is responsible for most of the firm's television advertising, with distributors making use of the medium only for special occasions or situations. To determine which stations will carry its advertising messages, Fram's primary concerns are listener-

Figure 47-3.

RADIO ADVERTISING

60 SECOND RADIO SPOTS

AUTOMATIC TRANSMISSIONS NORMALLY OPERATE SO SMOOTHLY THAT MOST
OF US TAKE THEM FOR GRANTED. UNTIL SOMETHING GOES WRONG, THAT
IS. THEN WE FIND OUT THAT MERELY CHANGING THE TRANSMISSION FLUID
PERIODICALLY WAS NOT ENOUGH. WE ALSO FIND OUT THAT IT WAS A
COSTLY LESSON, AND IT MIGHT HAVE BEEN AVOIDED IF WE HAD CHANGED
THE TRANSMISSION FILTER EVERY TIME WE CHANGED THE TRANSMISSION
FLUID. THE REASON IS THAT, IN ORDER TO PROPERLY PERFORM ITS JOB
OF COOLING AND LUBRICATING, TRANSMISSION FLUID MUST BE KEPT FREE
FROM HARMFUL FOREIGN PARTICLES. AND THAT'S EXACTLY WHAT A FRAM
TRANSMISSION FILTER DOES. YOUR NEARBY FRAM DEALER, (Dealer Name and
Address) RECOMMENDS THAT YOU KEEP YOUR AUTOMATIC TRANSMISSION
OPERATING SMOOTHLY BY CHANGING THE FLUID AND INSTALLING A NEW
FRAM FILTER EVERY TWELVE MONTHS OR EVERY TWELVE THOUSAND
MILES. SEE HIM TODAY. (Dealer Name and Address.)

47-3

FRAM CORPORATION, MANUFACTURERS OF AMERICA'S MOST COMPLETE
LINE OF QUALITY GUARANTEED AUTOMOBILE FILTERS, AND YOUR
NEARBY FRAM DEALER, (Dealer Name and Address), HAVE A QUESTION FOR
YOU ABOUT CAR CARE. YOU'VE BEEN DRIVING FOR SOME TIME AND YOUR
CAR SEEMS TO BE OPERATING PERFECTLY. SUDDENLY, THE OIL PRESSURE
INDICATOR LIGHTS UP AND THE ENGINE BEGINS TO MAKE STRANGE
NOISES. IS IT TRUE OR FALSE THAT THE SAFEST THING TO DO IS TO DRIVE
TO THE NEAREST GAS STATION? FALSE. THE OIL PRESSURE INDICATOR
LIGHT AND ENGINE NOISE ARE SIGNS OF SEVERE LOSS OF OIL PRESSURE.
WITHOUT ADEQUATE OIL PRESSURE, THE ENGINE'S VITAL PARTS GET NO
LUBRICATION. AND DRIVING EVEN ONE MILE WITH AN UNLUBRICATED
ENGINE COULD CAUSE SERIOUS, EXPENSIVE DAMAGE, AND PERHAPS EVEN
DESTROY THE ENGINE COMPLETELY. IF IT HAPPENS TO YOU, STOP IMME-
DIATELY, AND CALL FOR PROFESSIONAL HELP. AND REMEMBER, REGULAR
CHECK-UPS AT YOUR NEAREST FRAM DEALER, (Dealer Name and Address),
CAN HELP PREVENT THIS KIND OF PROBLEM BEFORE IT STARTS. STOP
IN TODAY.

ship in the station's market area, cost per spot, and quality of spot availabilities at the time of purchase. In evaluating this "quality" factor, Fram typically purchases spots adjacent to highly rated programs and nationally known personalities.

Fram supplements its dealer and consumer advertising with publicity campaigns, usually consisting of company-produced press releases placed in local newspapers by Fram dealers at the urging and coaching of Fram salesmen and placed nationally by a public relations firm. Figure 47-4 shows a sample of the press releases prepared by Fram for use by dealers at the local level.

A TYPICAL CAMPAIGN

To illustrate how these media are integrated and coordinated during a typical campaign, here is an outline of the sequence of events involved in a recent annual advertising and sales promotion program for Fram's entire product line.

First, the annual television schedule was proposed by Fram's media agency, SFM Media in New York City. Research conducted by SFM had confirmed that most potential Fram customers were males between the ages of 18 and 40, hence the emphasis on sponsoring sports events such as the World Series, the Kentucky Derby, and the professional tennis finals.

In developing commercials for these sponsored events, James & Symon Inc. devised the basic creative appeals, auditioned talent, and paid performers residual fees. Symon also created magazine advertisements that tied in with television commercials, as well as one-minute radio commercials on the World Series and other sports events.

A test market for radio advertising was run at the local radio station in Providence, Rhode Island. The station's special feature was helicopter traffic reports, which were followed by a Fram commercial. Fram purchased 180 spots keyed to specific traffic and weather conditions. For example, if it was raining, a Fram wiper commercial would follow the report; if the forecast was for fair weather, Fram's commercial would urge people to change oil filters before taking a long trip. This campaign was supplemented with tie-in newspaper advertisements and point-of-purchase posters, and local distributors were offered spots at half price in order that they could get their names on the commercials.

After eight weeks, research on this campaign indicated that it would probably not be a wise idea to run it nationwide, since distributors found it impossible to relate actual sales to campaign effectiveness.

Another campaign had run nationally. During this campaign, five truck driver commercials ran nationally between 1:00 and 3:00 in the morning on country/western stations. To supplement the radio campaign, direct mail was sent to members of various truck driver associations.

Figure 47-4.

for immediate release...

John Hall, Fountain View Automotive Company executive, addressed the
Old Valley P.T.A. at the Park School Auditorium last night. His subject
was "Pollution and What the Automotive Industry is Doing About it." Hall
placed much of the blame for auto induced air pollution on the car owner
and cited numerous examples of industry progress toward reasonable reme-
dies. "If car owners would get regular tune-ups and filter changes, and
have their pollution control valves changed regularly, our battle would
be half won," he said. Hall credited FRAM with being a leader in positive
action toward automotive air pollution control. FRAM is a manufacturer of
air, oil, and fuel filters, and pollution control valves.

for immediate release...

John J. Lutz, owner of the Main Street Garage in Sanson, attended a FRAM
Dealer Workshop last week in Chicago. The workshop session, one of eleven
scheduled throughout the nation this year, was attended by twenty-two other
Mid-Western FRAM dealers. Purpose of the session is to familiarize dealers
with new techniques for detecting trouble spots in faulty engines and to
educate the dealers on the need for and installation of various FRAM filters.
Lutz has been a FRAM dealer for the last three years.

for immediate release...
(photo caption)

DUNDEE LITTLE LEAGUERS FETED. Bob Dundee, President, is shown here with
General Manager, George Hopkins and the entire Dundee Garage Little League
baseball team at the annual outing yesterday at Mountain Park. Dundee Garage
has sponsored a team for the past four years and the outing for the last three.

for immediate release...

Bob Marriott has been promoted to assistant sales manager of the Loac Automotive Sales Co., of Seabrook. According to Loac President, Dave Mills, who
made the announcement, Marriott will assume direct responsibility for dealer
sales of engine parts. He has been in the automotive industry for seventeen
years, the last nine as a Loac salesman covering the Northeast. Loac Automotive Sales Co. is an automotive jobber representing numerous major national
firms. They have recently acquired the FRAM Line of oil, air, and fuel filters.

FRAM

QUESTIONS

1. Do you agree, or disagree, with Fram Corporation's omission of national magazines as the major consumer medium for its products? Explain.
2. In view of the changes in the status of women and the great numbers of women drivers, do you agree with Fram's directing its advertising and promotion at a male audience?

PART VI
CONTROLLING
CAMPAIGN
EFFECTIVENESS

With the cases in this section, the campaign-planning process comes full circle: what began with research to identify and define strong internal and external positions now ends with research to control campaign effectiveness in solidifying these positions.

In general, and as illustrated by the cases in this section, the "control" process involves four steps: (1) the establishment of performance goals; (2) the establishment of standards, or "yardsticks," against which to measure progress toward these goals; (3) the establishment of feedback mechanisms for reporting the extent to which standards are being achieved; and (4) provision for action when performance doesn't measure up to expectations.

Here is how the cases in this section illustrate this sequence of steps involved in the control function.

In the SCORE Hair Cream campaign, performance standards pointing toward broad profit and share-of-market goals were embodied in a projected budget (page 00). Represented was a plan for the campaign and a yardstick against which to measure campaign performance. During the first year of SCORE'S introductory campaign, actual results, in terms of sales and costs, were quite close to these budgeted figures, although advertising and promotion costs were about 12 percent higher than expected. Action to bring performance in line with expected performance began with a series of additional studies of various components of the promotion mix (advertising copy, direct mail, couponing, media effectiveness) to identify areas needing strengthening.

In the St. Regis Paper Company case, a series of goals and subgoals pertaining to awareness, understanding, and attitude changes were established for a series of four advertisements promoting "product superiority." A number of feedback studies (such as Idea Communication and Proved Name Registration tests) then measured the extent to which each advertisement achieved campaign goals and subgoals.

For the ITT campaign, a "results-minded management" wanted proof of effectiveness of an advertising campaign designed to "demonstrate, dramatically, the company's concern with, and involvement in, improving the quality of life." This objective was measured against standards pertaining to "awareness" and "improved attitude" among people in the $15,000-plus income bracket.

The Vulcan, Inc., campaign made use of inquiries from keyed coupons and other sources as feedback to measure the comparative effectiveness of various business publications carrying its campaign for a new type of materials handling hopper. The "average cost per inquiry" figure that emerged from an analysis of this feedback then became the benchmark against which to measure the performance of publications carrying this campaign.

The Johnson Controls campaign illustrates the use of the campaign control process in an experimental as well as a functional sense. In this campaign, innovative, relatively untried approaches were employed which tended to violate advertising "conventional wisdom," including attempting to interest managers and other generalists with lengthy, highly specialized engineering copy. A number of feedback sources, including measures of awareness and action, were used to measure performance in such areas as copy and media effectiveness, as well as to build a data base for future campaign plans.

The two cases pertaining to the Mobil Oil campaign view the control process from a somewhat different perspective, in contrast to the cases discussed in the foregoing. In the first case, the process is viewed as applied by the *media* toward advertisers, and the reader is invited to judge whether (1) the *standards* applied by two television networks toward Mobil's campaign content were fair and reasonable, (2) Mobil was fairly judged against these standards, and (3) the actions taken by the networks after applying these standards were appropriate.

The second case in this series turns the tables, and the reader is invited to judge *Mobil's* actions after applying its own standards to the performance of the media, or, at least, one television news show characterized by Mobil as "inaccurate, unfair, and a disservice to the people."

48

SCORE* HAIR CREAM (B)
Controlling the Campaign

The first part of this case focused on decisions made by a marketing team comprising people at the Grey Advertising agency and the Bristol-Myers Company in devising a media strategy for a new men's hair cream called SCORE.

This final portion of the case focuses on recommendations made after the first phase of the introductory campaign had been completed. In general, the recommendations aimed at improving the media mix for the subsequent campaign phases, and at integrating this mix into the overall campaign promotion mix.

For a better understanding of the context in which these recommendations were made, tables 48-1 and 48-2 summarize financial results following the first phases of the campaign. Table 48-1 shows actual vs. projected sales of SCORE after six months, with the "actual" figure reaching 91.5 percent of projected results. Table 48-2 shows various key ratios and totals relating to costs and sales during the first year of the SCORE campaign. Note that in general, most costs (with the exceptions of costs for "sampling" and "talent and production") exceeded expectations. This cost overrun, combined with the fact that total sales were slightly below expectations, pushed the advertising/sales ratios higher than originally anticipated.

With these summary statements as background, then, here are some of the recommendations made for research studies designed to improve the overall promotion mix supporting the SCORE introduction so that the ratio of expenditures to sales could be reduced during the second year of the campaign.

    1) *Copy testing:* Commercials would be tested to determine the degree of product awareness engendered by present commercials

---

* SCORE is a registered trademark of Bristol-Myers Company.

Table 48-1.

Actual vs. projected sales of SCORE during first six months.

	Projected	Cum. Projection	Actual	Cum. Actual	% Cum. Actual vs. Projection
		Millions of Dollars			
September	1,100	1,100	861	861	78.2
October	450	1,550	399	1,260	81.3
November	100	1,650	67	1,327	80.4
December	100	1,750	146	1,573	89.9
January	400	2,150	336	1,909	89.0
February	750	2,900	740	2,649	91.5

Table 48-2a.

Projected vs. actual cash flow figures for first year of SCORE introduction.

	Projected Budget (Millions)	Actual (Millions)
Factory Sales	7,553	7,435
Estimated Variable, Fixed and General Expenses	3,248	3,155
Available	4,305	4,280
Advertising	3,389	3,989
Sampling	129	12
Talent and Production	150	133
Merchandising	384	418
Total Advertising and Promotion	4,052	4,552
Profit/Loss	+253	−272

Table 48-2b.

Ratios of A&SP costs to sales after the first year of the SCORE introduction.

	Projected	Actual
Advertising /Sales Ratio	47%	55%
Advertising and Promotion/Sales	54%	60%

as compared to (a) competitive appeals and (b) alternate appeals for SCORE.

2) *Campaign-change experiment*: To be conducted in a small sample of 55 major target markets covered by both network and spot TV, this experiment would aim at determining at what point during the life cycle of a campaign schedule the campaign theme should be changed.

3) *Advertising expenditures study:* In the Buffalo and Syracuse major market areas—the original advertising-only markets for SCORE—the first year's advertising expenditure level would be tested to arrive at a second-year level. In general, the approach would involve decreasing advertising expenditures in one of the two areas, and measuring the result on sales in this area as compared to the other, "control" area.

4) *Advertising and sales promotion expenditures:* In Rochester, the original advertising-and-sampling market area for SCORE, a test of the promotional effectiveness of advertising and mail couponing would be made. During this test, expenditures for advertising and couponing would be increased 50 percent over first-year levels, and the result of this increase would be measured in terms of differences in advertising and promotion/sales ratios.

5) *Double weight test:* A test was proposed to supplement and validate the Buffalo-Syracuse and Rochester tests. The objective was to measure the effect on SCORE's share-of-market if the advertising expenditure was twice as large as the first-year level. Results of this test, combined with the results of the other tests, would be applied nationally during the second year.

6) *New product test:* In Baltimore, a test market was proposed for the new Barber-Size SCORE. If results indicated success for this product, it would be introduced nationally during the Barber Supply convention in July and August.

7) *Market potential test:* This proposed test would analyze the 55 major market areas receiving both spot and network TV coverage to determine if and how the spot market budget should be changed during the second-year effort. In general, the approach would involve applying a number of criteria to each market (i.e., competitive activity, advertising/sales ratios, advertising awareness, etc.) to identify markets that are most, and least, responsive to the SCORE campaign, and making budget modifications accordingly.

8) *Promotion-mix tests:* These proposed tests would measure the impact on sales and profits of various modifications in the promotion mix in order to identify the "best" mix. Typical tests would involve:
   - Price-off promotions on the 79- and 98-cent sizes of SCORE.
   - SCORE coupons enclosed with BAN deodorant.
   - Magazine pop-up coupons for SCORE.
   - SCORE sold with other Bristol-Myers products.

QUESTION

Comment on the efforts of the company to determine the effectiveness of advertising, and the effectiveness of certain other elements in the marketing mix. "Effectiveness" refers to the influencing of sales.

49

THE ST. REGIS
PAPER COMPANY

In 1977, the St. Regis Paper Company and its advertising agency, Cunningham & Walsh, launched an advertising campaign which was described as follows in a brochure sent out to St. Regis sales personnel.

To support your selling effort in 1977—to give you that competitive edge—St. Regis provides a broad program of print and television advertising directed to decision-makers . . . the markets *you* want to reach, with applications-oriented themes that make *your* points.

Graphic demonstrations of St. Regis product superiority in action will be seen by up to 35 million people a week on one of the nation's top-rated, award-winning programs, "ABC's Wide World of Sports."

Millions more will have these commercials reinforced in blue-chip, special interest issues of the magazines we know they read. These are your commercials and print ads . . . Tell your friends and family . . . customers and prospects, that this is St. Regis . . . Serving Man and Nature to the Benefit of Both.

In addition to this generalized objective of pre-selling "decision makers" on St. Regis "product superiority," the campaign also had a number of more specific goals pertaining to its impact on awareness, understanding, and attitudes of readers and viewers.

Included in both print and TV schedules during this campaign were four advertisements entitled "Paper Bridge," "24," "Bag of Pearls," and "Bull Fight." The first two of these are shown in figures 49-1 and 49-2. After these advertisements had appeared, the Gallup and

Figure 49-1.

How St. Regis made a two-by-four that's 32 ft. longer than the world's tallest tree.

The world's tallest tree is a 368 ft. redwood in a national park near Eureka, California.

And yet we made a two-by-four that's 400 feet long – 32 feet longer than the world's tallest tree. Forty stories of continuous two-by-four.

How did we do it? Simple. We glued 60 off-sized pieces of two-by-four together with hot-glued finger joints. And then got fifty men and women to carry it out into the field above and intentionally break it against a tree.

Our tests show that the joints are stronger than the surrounding wood.

Of course, our speciality is not 400 footers but eight footers—the so called stud, the main support of the home building industry. We're one of the largest makers of eight foot two-by-fours.

And, as in any operation where the raw material is non-uniform, there's a certain amount of waste. That's why we go out of our way to use the short leftover pieces. It's our policy to use the resource wisely. So we're out to use all the log—100%.

What's the future of wood building products? Are they being replaced by synthetics?

Pound for pound wood has greater compression strength than steel. And it's certainly more workable.

But also we make a lot more building products than two-by-fours and dimension lumber.

We make prestressed concrete walls and floors. Insulation and vapor barrier papers. And even culverts.

All this reflects the marketing stance of St. Regis toward all our packaging, paper, lumber and construction products. To use the full weight of our technology in serving our markets and in renewing the forest resource our products come from.

St. Regis—serving Man and Nature.

Reprinted with permission from American Association of Advertising Agencies.

Figure 49-2.

We drove this 2½ ton Rolls Royce over a bridge made entirely of St. Regis paper to prove a point.

The point is that paper can be stronger than you think. Especially if it's in the form of corrugated box material.

The roadbed of this bridge was made out of six layers of St. Regis triple-wall corrugated–a material we supply a lot of to the U.S. The verticals were made of five layers, and the triangles of four.

Triplewall is made up of three layers of the corrugated "medium" and four layers of linerboard. And it can withstand 1,100 lbs. per square inch of puncture pressure on its side. And on its edge, a 12 x 12 in. piece can take 930 lbs. A mere seven layers of paper!

The strength of corrugated isn't only in the paper itself. It's the structure. The shape of the medium is one of the strongest structures known. In Colonial Virginia walls were built in the corrugated, or serpentine form. And they're still standing today, although they're only one brick thick.

Corrugated box material is a sandwich. A wavy corrugated medium is squeezed between two rollers with meshing teeth. That's the meat of the sandwich. The bread is two layers of heavy paper called linerboard.

Since it was patented in 1871, corrugated has been one of the mainstays of the American distribution system. In fact, the corrugated box is one reason we have the most efficient distribution system in the world.

And St. Regis has had its share of innovations in the field. Partly because we're one of the largest makers of linerboard in the world. And partly because of our technology and marketing thrust.

All this reflects the marketing stance of St. Regis toward all our packaging, paper, lumber and construction products. To use the full weight of our technology in serving our markets and in renewing the forest resource our products come from.

St. Regis—serving Man and Nature.

Reprinted with permission from American Association of Advertising Agencies.

Robinson research organization presented a report to St. Regis marketing management which summarized the results and significance of copy tests this organization had made on the impact of these four advertisements.

Included among these copy tests were:

Proved Name Registration (PNR) tests to estimate the *awareness* impact of each of the four advertisements. This test uses an index of percent of respondents who can recall and accurately describe the advertisement, aided by company or brand/product cues.

Idea Communication tests to estimate the extent to which key ideas about St. Regis were *understood* by readers following exposure to each of the four advertisements. Included were tests to measure *Registration of Main Ideas* (RMI) and *Average Number of Copy Points Recalled* (ANPR).

Favorability to Company tests to measure the nature and direction of attitude changes toward St. Regis based on exposure to each of the four advertisements.

Although these tests were limited to single- and double-page versions of each advertisement appearing in such publications as *Business Week* and *Forbes,* it was assumed the test results could also be generally applied to the versions of each advertisement appearing on TV.

QUESTIONS

1. Examine the two St. Regis advertisements shown and give each a rating of from one to three (above average, average, below average) in each of the following categories. Explain why you have rated as you have.
   (a) *Awareness* (the relative ability of each advertisement to attract readers).
   (b) *Understanding* (the relative ability of each advertisement to communicate ideas).
   (c) *Attitudes* (the relative ability of each advertisement to persuade).

2. Rate* the two advertisements on a scale of 0 to 100 for:
   (a) *Proved name registration.*
   (b) *Registration of main idea.*

   Rate* the two advertisements for:
   (c) *Average number of points scored* (in this instance, don't use the 0-100 scale but simply indicate the number of points).

   Explain why you have rated as you have.

---

* Think in terms of the readers of *Business Week* and *Forbes,* and viewers of ABC's "Wide World of Sports."

50

INTERNATIONAL TELEPHONE AND TELEGRAPH CORPORATION

At one time corporate advertising had relatively little interest for most corporations. This was reflected in the small budgets assigned to such advertising as contrasted with promotional budgets for such products as a new mouthwash, a detergent, or a refrigerator.

Times have changed. Vast new pressures have been directed against virtually all institutions. Business organizations, as one of these, have become a major target. Corporations have frequently found themselves facing hostile communities.

Despite what seems, under the circumstances, to be an obvious need for remedial action, corporate managements have been reluctant to assign substantial advertising funds to corporate advertising. One reason for this is the lack of tangible returns from a corporate campaign. When a company, in contrast, invests in the advertising of packaged goods or hard goods, there are marketplace indicators of success or failure such as factory sales or high Nielsen index figures showing movement of goods in markets or drugstores.

Thus, the question arises, how can those who believe in corporate advertising provide proof of its effectiveness to results-minded management?

Here is how International Telephone and Telegraph Corporation (hereinafter referred to as ITT) approached the problem from its world headquarters in New York City.

ITT had been concerned about the antagonistic drift in public opinion. This hostile climate that has beset corporations in the recent troubled years would certainly embrace a company big enough to be rated as the ninth largest industrial company in the *Fortune 500*. In short, ITT is a major corporation among major corporations.

Anxious to discover what the public knew about ITT, the company engaged the well-known research firm of Yankelovich, Skelly & White.

A major discovery was that most Americans knew very little about ITT. The company was known to fewer than one out of three adult Americans in households with incomes of $15,000 or more. The lack of knowledge about the giant corporation was considered extraordinary. Furthermore, the knowledge that was being acquired by the public was being furnished by news stories conveying unfavorable allegations about ITT.

Lack of advertising could not be considered a factor. ITT has been using a first-rate advertising agency—Needham, Harper & Steers—for a number of years to conduct what had been considered a successful corporate print campaign. This campaign has been directed at a narrow, carefully defined target—people in business, finance, government, and the campus world. The company felt that its message had been penetrating these important segments of the public.

Research, however, indicated to ITT that this advertising effort, though successful in its limited way, was not enough. A chief conclusion was that the so-called "influentials" reached by ITT's advertising were not communicating downward. Those at lower levels were not obtaining from the influentials the latter's subjective reactions about ITT such as awareness of the corporation, understanding of it, and confidence in it. Instead, there were great numbers of people—prosperous, relatively well-educated people—who did not know what ITT was, or what it did.

These people—voters, potential buyers of ITT stock, college students (the influentials of tomorrow), and others—did not recognize the ITT name. Far more familiar to them were the names of companies making well-advertised consumer goods. Accompanying this lack of knowledge was a readiness to believe almost anything unfavorable that was said about ITT—and, unfortunately, much that was said *was* unfavorable.

At this point, ITT decided to expand its corporate advertising campaign in order to communicate how the company could help improve the quality of life through its continuing program of research and development, through its products, and through its services. The objectives of the campaign were (1) to demonstrate *dramatically* the company's concern with and involvement with improving the quality of life and (2) to reach a much larger, expanded audience *quickly* with this message.

Reaching a bigger audience and changing minds quickly would require a much larger advertising expenditure. It was necessary to demonstrate to management that the added expense was justified, and that a major corporate advertising campaign on the scale projected could fill the identity vacuum while diluting the unfavorable publicity the company had been receiving.

Because, as said earlier, the corporate campaign conducted until this time could not be measured by ratings or sales, the company decided to undertake a major research program that had two objectives:

1) To track changes in awareness, familiarity, and reputation of ITT among people in households with $15,000-plus annual incomes.

Figure 50-1.

Television commercial. This photoboard demonstrates that the company's concern with people is international in scope. Reprinted with permission from International Telephone and Telegraph Corporation.

Figure 50-2.

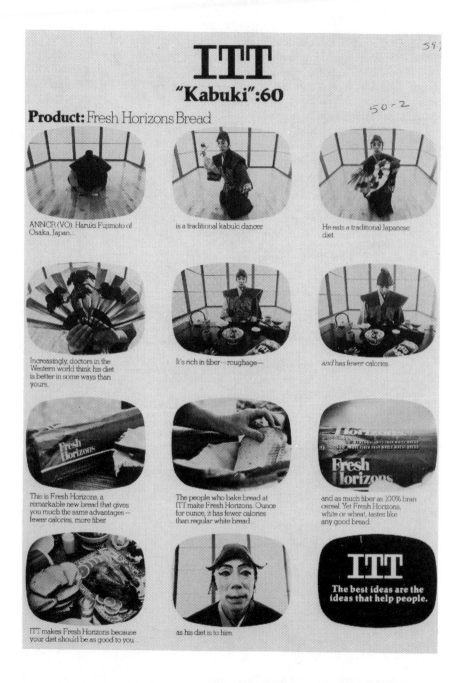

Television commercial. The company's diversification is shown in this photoboard. Reprinted with permission from International Telephone and Telegraph Corporation.

2) To assess the effectiveness of the campaign in improving attitudes among this target audience.

A questionnaire was developed, carefully pre-tested, and then administered before the campaign began. This was done to attain a benchmark (a basis of comparison). Six months later the questions were used again, then again after another six months. In fact, the six-month checkup has been continued in order to chart the company's progress, or lack of it.

In conducting the investigation, the researchers called for a national probability sample of households having $15,000 or more annual income. Each sampling consisted of at least 1,500 telephone interviews.*

---

* The case material given here has been adapted from a talk delivered by John Lowden, director of advertising and sales promotion for ITT, at the 1975 Eastern Conference of the American Association of Advertising Agencies.

QUESTIONS

1. In order to reach quickly the expanded audience desired by ITT, what would be your choice among the following alternatives? Explain your choice fully.
   a. Switch entirely to television advertising.
   b. Greatly expand the magazine coverage with particular emphasis on weekly magazines.
   c. Use television advertising as the chief medium with magazines in a supporting role.
   d. Use magazines on an expanded schedule with television advertising in support.
   e. Use some other medium, or media combination.
2. Develop a set of questions that you think would obtain for ITT the answers that would be helpful to them in finding out what people thought of them and what contributions ITT was making in improving the quality of life.

51

VULCAN, INC.

When Vulcan, Inc., a small industrial firm in Canton, Ohio, began promotion of a new type of materials-handling hopper—the company's second product—the move was another step in the steady progress of the company since it had reevaluated its advertising program eight years before. In that period it had doubled its sales without employing a single salesman.

Vulcan was one of many companies that found their business completely changed by the production requirements resulting from World War II. Although it had been a structural steel shop since its founding in 1915, Vulcan was converted radically in the war period to a plant that stressed the manufacture of materials-handling equipment.

Upon the war's conclusion, company officials were forced to decide whether they would return to their prewar type of business, or whether they would continue in the manufacture of materials-handling equipment. They decided on the latter. Emphasis was to continue on the production of Vulcan's single wartime product, a self-dumping hopper.

This hopper, selling at a wide range of prices depending upon the applications, might be called an industrial wastepaper basket. It can be attached to any forklift truck. A touch of a switch and the hopper turns on end, empties its contents, and then swings back into place.

Vulcan hoppers are used in metal-working plants for handling scrap metal; in foundries and food-processing plants for transporting small items; and, in the case of the company's open-end hopper, for handling long, bulky materials.

For some years after World War II the Vulcan Company achieved moderate success in selling its products. Its advertising was conducted by a small advertising agency in Ohio. The company's president, aiming at a more impressive sales performance, decided that a change of advertising agencies might be beneficial. Such a change occurred soon after the Vulcan Company ran an advertisement for a new agency in the Wall Street Journal.

Gladstone, Inc., a Cleveland-based advertising agency with strong experience in industrial marketing and advertising, was selected from among the agencies responding to the Wall Street Journal advertisement. Vulcan's president, John Schulte, had been the company official most responsible for the search for the new agency. He had feared that an agency of the size and experience of Gladstone would turn down Vulcan's account because of the modest advertising budget. The Gladstone executives, however, decided to add Vulcan to their account list even though some difficult problems faced them. These problems were considered major obstacles by the agency people:

1) A very small advertising budget.
2) A tiny sales force (consisting of John Schulte, the company's president, and Clausen Jenner, the company's only vice president). Potential customers were contacted by telephone by these two men.
3) A company unknown except to a small group of present customers.
4) A product that was unknown compared to those of leading competitors in the industrial field.

In assessing the tasks facing the company, the agency executives pointed out that the efficiency of each advertisement must be great. Because of the limited advertising budget, the company would need to reach the biggest number of potential customers with every advertisement run. Along with such efficiency would be a never-ceasing check on the media to make certain that the target audiences of plant superintendents, maintenance engineers, and purchasing agents were being reached. Appropriate business publications must be used and must be cut from the list if not yielding satisfactory results. There was no "fat" in the budget to allow for publications not doing a maximum job.

Budget limitations affected advertisement size, too. Full pages were a luxury that could not be afforded. It was decided, accordingly, to adopt two advertisement sizes for the campaign: quarter-pages and third-pages. The third-page advertisements ran from the top to the bottom of the page. Their main element would be an illustration of the product in action.

A four-step diagram was designed showing a man releasing the hopper switch, after which the hopper "dumps itself . . . rights itself . . . locks itself." The only color used appeared in arrows that indicated specific hopper actions. In one of the advertisements the diagrammed demonstration was followed by a headline saying "Unload two tons with one hand." The following copy stressed the ease of using the hopper and asserted that the machine "cuts costs of hand unloading by 50 percent."

To stimulate action, a coupon was placed at the bottom of the advertisement. Contained in the coupon copy was the following:

Want details? Clip this coupon . . . attach it to your letterhead . . . sign your name . . . and mail to . . .

Another typical advertisement contained the following:

NEW
SELF-DUMPING
OPEN-SIDE
HOPPER

This headline was followed by illustrations of the unit at work, plus three illustrations accompanied by the captions *Dumps itself, Rights itself, Locks itself.* The body copy came next.

Fastens to lift truck—handles lumber, strip metal, pipe, banana stalks, wire rolls, etc. This hopper may be carried by any lift truck, fork, or platform, with complete safety. A simple latch lets it dump automatically and return when empty. Your lift truck doubles its usefulness and you cut handling costs by fifty-percent and more.

A complete line of closed hoppers are also available for moving all types of materials from metal to glass. Thousands are now working in every industry. For more information, phone us collect, or use the coupon.

Specifications: Open-side hopper—3/16 inch steel plate, seams arc welded, reinforced front and back with angle iron. Widths from 3½ to 8 feet. Mounted on skids or choice of casters, wheels. Heavier plate, galvanized, aluminum and stainless also available. Standard models shipped from stock.

This copy was followed by the company's logotype and the standard coupon for all the company advertisements.

At the start of the campaign there were 75 inquiries monthly. In the following two years the average number of inquiries monthly was 100. This seemed to reflect an almost doubling of the advertising budget. Two years later the inquiries were averaging 150 per month and then, with the budget doubled once again (to $50,000), the inquiries were averaging 225 monthly.

At the beginning, Schulte and Jenner followed up all inquiries by telephone. Since the increase in inquiries made such a procedure impossible, only the larger companies were followed by telephone. The others were sent follow-up letters.

Almost 50 percent of the inquiries were turned into sales, according to a results study made by the company. In the period after Gladstone took the account sales doubled.

During these years of increased advertising and sales only six different advertisements were used. At first three advertisements were put into rotation. Eventually, three more advertisements were worked into the rotation. In discussing the advertising strategy, Jenner, the company's vice president, said, "We felt repetition was more important than having new ads."

As part of the effort to maintain a constant watch over the comparative efficiency of business publications used for the company's advertising, the agency keyed the coupon in each advertisement. Through such keying the company could determine the number of inquiries obtained from each advertisement. The cost per inquiry was also determined through keying. This cost amounted to about $15 per inquiry.

The cost efficiency of the publications on the media schedule was measured by the inquiry cost. Thus, when the average cost of all inquiries from an advertisement in a certain publication became too high, the publication was dropped temporarily until it could be assessed once again. If such an assessment determined that there was little prospect of reducing the inquiry cost, the magazine might be dropped permanently from the media list.

Along with media analysis the company engaged in copy analysis and determined that for both closed and open-end hoppers the copy should shift from a straight product-points story to a stress on specific applications, and to cost savings. As an extra attention-getter, headlines for the third-page advertisements were printed in red.

QUESTIONS

1. What do you consider to be the chief objective of the Vulcan advertisements?
2. Do you consider $15 per inquiry to be a satisfactory rate per inquiry? Explain.
3. Do you agree with the statement "We felt that repetition was more important than having new ads"? Discuss.
4. Discuss the relative merits for Vulcan of using—
   a) a straight product-points copy approach;
   b) an applications approach;
   c) a cost-savings approach.

JOHNSON CONTROLS, INC.

Johnson Controls, Inc., Milwaukee, Wisconsin, is the world's largest producer of building control systems. Annual business of the company averages more than $250 million. Their advertising had been directed almost entirely to the primary sales targets—architects, engineers, and other technical people.

Suddenly, however, with the introduction of a new control system, the company felt that a drastic change of advertising direction was needed. The new system, called by the company "Total Building Automation," made it possible for all automatic building systems to be monitored, coordinated, and operated by a single computer. As a company executive expressed it, "This is not just an improvement in existing systems. It is a whole new method of automated building control."

The introduction of Johnson Controls' total building automation coincided with the emergence of a set of new problems facing building owners. Among these were the energy shortage, strict new fire codes, and rising crime rates. Total building automation was designed to deal specifically with these problems.

Much thought was devoted by the Johnson Controls management to determining the proper target of advertising that featured total building automation. Fred Brengel, the company president, said:

Clearly, opting for this sophisticated new technology demands decisions far beyond the authority of the technical people we usually deal with. We have to reach the men who make the major decisions, building owners and developers, corporate executives, government administrators. We have to tell them who we are. We have to interest them in what we're doing.

The trouble is, an adequate presentation of the Johnson Controls story will have to be both lengthy and technical in nature. This brings us toe to toe with two advertising bugaboos. The first: Long copy doesn't get read. The second: Top management doesn't read technical information.

Despite serious concern about certain aspects of the advertising that was planned, the company decided to proceed with a campaign that met head-on such isues as—

1) long copy advertisements;
2) technical copy in advertisements addressed to top management;
3) image advertisements that frankly aimed at creating awareness of Johnson Controls as much as selling any specific service.

In the following pages appear samples of Johnson Controls advertisements that ran over a period of nine months. All appeared in the Wall Street Journal. Except for a center-spread that began the campaign, all the advertisements were in one-page size. There were 3,000 words in the spread.

Following the advertisements shown here will be a representative cover of the six booklets that were offered in the advertising.

Figure 52-1.

Another in a series of reports to American business: The Wall Street Journal and advertising effectiveness.

"In less than a year our campaign in The Journal debunked 5 advertising bugaboos."

— Fred L. Brengel, President, Johnson Controls, Inc., Milwaukee

"A couple years back, I wouldn't have been talking advertising," said Fred Brengel. "Oh, we spent enough on advertising. Johnson Controls is the world leader in building controls systems, and we do over a quarter-billion dollars worth of business a year. But our advertising was directed almost entirely to the architects, engineers and other technical people we had been selling to for ninety years. Then something happened at Johnson to change all that."

In 1973 Johnson Controls introduced Total Building Automation, a system that allows all automatic building systems to be monitored, coordinated, and operated by a single computer. This was not just an improvement in existing systems. It was a whole new method of automated building control. And its development coincided with a rash of new problems — the energy shortage, strict new fire codes, rising crime rates — facing building owners that total building automation is exceptionally suited to overcome.

**Long copy.
Will busy executives read it?**

"Clearly," continued Brengel, "opting for this sophisticated new technology demanded decisions far beyond the authority of the technical people we usually dealt with. We had to reach the men who made the major decisions, building owners and developers, corporate executives, government administrators. We had to tell them who we were. We had to interest them in what we were doing. The trouble was, an adequate presentation of the Johnson Controls story would have to be both lengthy and technical

in nature. This brought us toe to toe with two advertising bugaboos. The first, *long copy doesn't get read*. The second, *top management doesn't read technical information*.

"Well, we did what we felt we had to do. Our first ad ran last March, with more than 3,000 words in it. It was richly technical. And in three days we had received 153 requests for more information.

"Since then, over 2,000 direct inquiries, many signed by corporation presidents, have proved that long, technical copy does get read if it's interesting and useful to the reader. In fact, we're now convinced that if we had run short copy and left out the technical details we wouldn't have gotten anywhere near the readership we did."

How long does a newspaper ad live?

"Of course, good advertising takes more than just good ads," said Ron Caffrey, Vice President-Marketing at Johnson Controls. "We had to get our ads to the right people, in an important way, at a time when they were prepared to initiate business decisions.

"We looked at all the media. Among The Journal's four million plus readership we found the full range of middle and top executives we wanted to reach. A full page in The Journal certainly gave us an importance commensurate with our position in the industry. And the regularity and constancy of Journal readership during business days of the week assured us that we would be reaching our audience at a time when they were actively doing business.

"Still, we were a little uneasy about another advertising bugaboo that's been touted for years, the one that proclaims that *a newspaper has only a one-day life*. So we built a specific response mechanism into every ad we ran.

"A one-day life," Caffrey chuckled,"we really debunked that one. The first ad we ran in The Journal was still drawing regular responses *two months* after issue date."

Can image ads increase sales?

George Huhnke is Advertising Manager of Johnson Controls. He, too, cited advertising bugaboos. "They say *it takes years to create an awareness for your company*. Well, we didn't want to wait years. We had changed our name from Johnson Service Company to Johnson Controls, and we wanted to register that change fast. To check on progress, we set up a research series to objectively measure the results of our total Journal campaign. What happened? In just six months our advertising in The Journal increased our top-of-mind awareness by 63%!"

There's an award on the wall alongside George Huhnke's desk, a first place won by Johnson Controls in the Business/Professional Advertising Association's 1975 competition. "Obviously, we're delighted with the results of our Journal campaign," said Huhnke. Looking up at the award on his wall he added, "It's nice to have your cake and eat it too."

There's another advertising bugaboo Johnson Controls has debunked,too — the one that says *image ads don't make sales*. In 1975, when new construction was off by 20%, Johnson Controls sales to the construction industry increased by 20%. It's one more reason why you'll find Johnson Controls advertising in The Wall Street Journal again this year.

**THE WALL STREET JOURNAL.
IT WORKS.**
4,559,000 readers every business day.

Reprinted with permission from Johnson Controls, Inc.

300

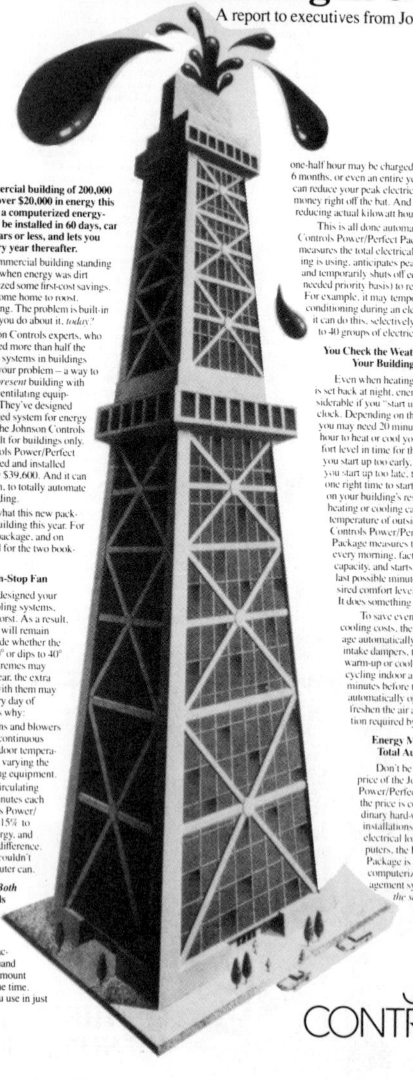

Figure 52-2.

Reprinted with permission from Johnson Controls, Inc.

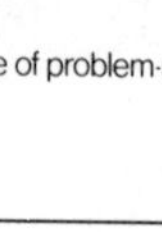

Figure 52-3.

10 Ways to Tell If Your Modern Building Is Squandering Costly Energy.

A report to executives from Johnson Controls.

Fully 90% of today's multi-story buildings are paying up to a 15% premium on their electric bill for electricity they don't need. As many as 90% are heating and cooling at the same time. These are just two of the outrageous energy-wasters commonplace in today's buildings. And you don't have to be an engineer to ferret them out.

The 10 energy trouble spots below have been pinpointed by Johnson Controls, the people who have designed and installed more than half the computerized automation systems in U.S. buildings. To see how your building shapes up, check these trouble spots yourself. Find out if you're actually *wasting* energy in winter by lowering thermostats to the recommended 68°. And if your cooling system, like many, runs merrily on when it's below freezing outside.

You can find out more about how to cut your building's greatest single operating cost with the booklet offered below. It's new, authoritative, written by the experts at Johnson Controls. And it gives you the up-to-date facts and figures you need to make important decisions — and savings — now.

1. Take the temperatures of *interior* rooms or interior areas of your building (buy or borrow an accurate thermometer). If the readings are less than 78° in summer *or in winter*, chances are your heating and cooling system is wasting costly energy.

To conserve energy, the U.S. Government recommends that you set temperatures at 68° during the heating season, 78° during the cooling season. But take a tip from Johnson Controls and be wary. During the heating season, don't try to make interior rooms the same 68° temperature as perimeter rooms. Interior rooms are naturally warmer, and your cooling system would have to operate to *lower* the temperature of these rooms to 68°. You'd waste money by heating (perimeter rooms) and cooling (inside rooms) at the same time.

2. During working hours, listen at any register bringing air into a room. If the rush of air is noisy, you may be distributing more air than is required. This may be wasting energy and over-taxing expensive motors as well.

By simply resetting fans to reduce air flow 10% and deliver this air more gently and continuously, Johnson Controls engineers have been able to save as much as 15% in electrical usage over wasteful, noisy air delivery.

3. Go on a thermostat hunt. If you can't find one in every exterior room, and at least one in every interior open area, you're probably wasting energy.

Without on-the-spot regulation by local thermostat, comfort is sacrificed and full control of energy expenditure is impossible. Fortunately, it is a simple task to add thermostats to most heating and cooling systems. (At Johnson Controls we've been doing it since Professor Warren Johnson invented the thermostat back in the 1880's.)

4. Make a change, any change, in the setting of a thermostat. If you can do it, so can anyone else, raising hob with reasonable energy-saving settings you must maintain to cut energy costs.

Apartment tenants, of course, should be free to adjust temperatures as they see fit. In commercial buildings thermostats must be set to pre-determined temperatures. We have a number of ways to lock thermostats to prevent occupants from fiddling with them.

5. During the winter, take the day and night temperatures of exterior rooms along the outside walls of your building. If these rooms are not 10° cooler when unoccupied at *night*, you're "heating the neighborhood."

By setting back temperatures at 10° at night, when commercial buildings are unoccupied, the running time of heating equipment and heat loss through walls are significantly reduced. Johnson Controls field engineers report calculated savings of 37% in Atlanta, 20% in Chicago, 30% in New York, 32% in Portland, and a whopping 55% in Los Angeles. There are important percentages of *total heating costs*.

6. Hold your hand under running hot water in lavatory sinks. If you can't stand the heat without mixing in cold water, you're wasting energy.

Water for hand-washing should be supplied between 110° and 120°. Use your thermometer to measure the temperature. If it's too hot, have your building engineer lower the heat.

7. In your building control room, look for two outside air measurements. There must be two. One measures the outdoor air temperature. The other measures the humidity — either R.H. (Relative Humidity) or the Dew Point Temperature — and it will say so on the dial. If you don't have this *second* measurement it's likely you're losing up to 10% in needless cooling expenditures.

If your building's system can't measure outside humidity, it can't mix inside and outside air in just the right amounts to save maximum energy. Using damper and controls, our engineers can incorporate this big energy saver into your present air conditioning system.

8. Does your air conditioning equipment run when outdoor temperatures dip below 55°? If so, you're probably wasting energy.

The average commercial building needs cooling instead of heating even when outside temperatures dip to 30° or even 20°. At the very same time your building should be using outside air for "free cooling." For more on "free cooling," see page 5 of the booklet offered below.

9. Ask your building engineer for the following figure: total cubic feet per minute of outside air being introduced into your building at any given time. Divide this figure by the number of people you estimate to be in the building at that time. If the resulting number is more than five (5), chances are you're wasting energy.

Using huge volumes of outside air can be extremely costly when the temperature of that air must be drastically changed. Recognizing this, many codes have been revised to allow use of less outside air. The trend is toward a figure of five cubic feet per minute per person. Find out the current regulations for your city and insist on your usage being pegged at that.

10. Look for the demand meter in your building's control room. It's a graph of your building's electrical consumption, giving the date and time of peak use. Note the time when you're using the most electricity. (For commercial buildings, this will probably be between 11 a.m. and 2 p.m.) Then ask your building engineer what's being done to cut down this costly peak of electrical demand.

You pay *two* electric bills: One for the electricity you actually use, the other a penalty for using too much at one time. The "peak" rate for what you use in just one-half hour may be charged to you for a month, 6 months, or even *an entire year*. By careful control, Johnson Controls engineers can schedule your building systems to selectively shut down during certain key periods, eliminating costly electrical peaks.

These 10 items are a quick check on whether your building is squandering your energy dollars. For a more thorough going-over, you need an *energy analysis* that takes in *all* the factors affecting energy expenditure. It will lay energy waste bare, give you dollar figures on how much you can save, and tell you how to save it.

For a free estimate of the cost of this analysis, call your local Johnson Controls office.

At Johnson Controls our business is control. The automatic control of America's buildings for heating and cooling, ventilating, humidification, firesafety, security, lighting, communications and clock systems, and today more than ever, energy conservation. We've been on top of this business for 90 years. Last year alone we did almost one quarter of a *billion* dollars worth. One-third of all buildings in the United States employ some form of Johnson control.

Find out more about how you can save costly energy in your building without replacing present heating or cooling equipment.

Send for Johnson Controls newest booklet, *"Total Energy Management: an idea book to help you control costs."* Write to Fred L. Brengel, President, Johnson Controls, Inc., P.O. Box 423, Milwaukee, Wisconsin 53201.

JOHNSON CONTROLS

Prime source of problem-solving systems.

JC75P2
Printed in U.S.A.

Reprinted with permission from Johnson Controls, Inc.

Figure 52-4.

Unless Your Building Can Do 40 of these 48 Things, You May End Up with a White Elephant.

A report to executives from Johnson Controls.

Buildings today are in trouble. Demanding tenants, fast-changing firecodes, energy short-falls, soaring crime rates are just some of the problems your building must overcome if it's not to end up in distress.

Listed here are things a modern building can and should do to meet these pressing problems. Prepared by Johnson Controls, the experts who have designed and installed more than half the computerized automation systems in U.S. buildings, this list offers you a quick, easy way to measure a building's obsolescence. Compare and see how your building measures up. To keep abreast of competition, it should do at least 40 of these things.

Your Building Should Have An Automated Firesafety System That:

1. Anticipates fire, sniffing out products of combustion before a fire can start.
2. Detects smoke or heat *or* flame.
3. Gives the alarm in less than 5 seconds.
4. Calls the fire department automatically.
5. Exhausts smoke, heat and deadly gasses from the fire area.
6. Automatically closes fire doors to create safe areas, and pressurizes safe areas to keep smoke and gasses out.
7. Projects a floor plan of the fire floor onto a central illuminated screen.
8. Displays instructions to building operating personnel for evacuation, firefighting.
9. Broadcasts prerecorded and actual voice commands throughout the building, telling people what to do, where to go, when, and why.
10. Listens to what stranded people have to say, and activates 2-way communications.
11. Determines location, extent and progress of fire for firefighters.
12. Masses elevators at ground level to rush firemen to the fire scene.
13. Puts firemen in full command of elevators and communications with a control panel made operative only by fire department key.
14. Protects itself by automatically bypassing burned areas, to keep vital information flowing.
15. Provides a fire case history, including a typewritten stage-by-stage record of alarms and a taped record of all voice communications and replies.

A Failsafe Security System That:

16. Gives the alarm the instant entry is attempted.
17. Identifies the exact point of intrusion by projecting a floor plan of the area on an illuminated screen.
18. Turns on the lights, if required.
19. Zooms in on the intruder with closed circuit television.
20. Calls the police automatically.
21. Permits entry only at specified hours, using unpickable card readers in place of pickable metal key locks.
22. Lets you change locks instantly, electronically.
23. Blocks off-limit areas, main passageways, safes, and confidential files with a cordon of silent electronic sentinels that detect the slightest movement.
24. Listens for screams. If a victim cries out in a laundry room, elevator, stairwell or other isolated place, it gives the alarm instantly.
25. Sounds the alarm if the security system is tampered with, even when it's off.

An Automatic Energy Conservation System That:

26. Plans heating and cooling requirements with programs considering occupancy, sunlight, cloud cover, wind force, humidity, and other variables.
27. "Hunts" for the most economical mixture of outside air and recirculated inside air.
28. Uses 100% outside air for "free cooling" when outside air is at the right temperature.
29. Eliminates unnecessary heating whenever possible, by admitting the barest minimum of outside air to meet codes.
30. Sets temperature higher or lower automatically at night to save heating or cooling costs.
31. Turns non-critical equipment on and off automatically to cut costly peaks in electric demand bills.

A Self-Running Control System That:

32. Centralizes all monitors and controls at a one-man control center.
33. Interfaces all separate building systems to form a single, unified automation system.
34. Computer-manages this system with superhuman efficiency, using a computer built especially for building automation.
35. Monitors, continuously, hundreds of points inside and outside your building.
36. Reads, electronically, *thousands* of incoming reports per minute.
37. Remembers these readings and keeps them on file.
38. Produces filed-away information at the touch of a button.
39. Makes lightning calculations based on information received or on file to arrive at a single intelligent decision.
40. Executes decisions at the right time and in the right sequence for simultaneous, automatic, exacting control of all building systems.
41. Performs innumerable management functions: keeps daily totals, makes efficiency reports on equipment, schedules maintenance programs, maintains a running summary of building operation costs.
42. Takes orders and responds in English (with no codes to memorize, operation can be learned in as little as two days).

A Built-In Service-Maintenance System That:

43. Reports equipment emergencies by both visible and audible alarms.
44. Signals all abnormal equipment *trends* before they become emergencies.
45. Shuts down endangered equipment automatically.
46. Contacts a repairman if an important motor breaks down in the middle of the night.
47. Types and issues, on schedule, work order sheets for maintenance men describing jobs and even listing needed equipment.
48. Operates under the protection of an annual service-maintenance contract made with experts who know computerized building automation.

These are just some of the essential, sometimes mind-boggling tasks a Johnson Controls automated building can perform for itself by positive, exacting control.

At Johnson Controls our business is control. The automatic control of America's buildings for heating and cooling, ventilating, humidification, energy conservation, security, firesafety, lighting, communications and clock systems. We've been on top of this business for 90 years. Last year alone we did almost one-quarter of a *billion* dollars worth, from more than 100 Johnson Controls offices throughout the U.S.

You'll find your local Johnson office listed in the White Pages under Johnson Controls or Johnson Service Company.

Find out how modern building automation systems can be put to work in any building you plan or own. Get this 24-page booklet, "The Big Idea in Building Automation." Write Fred L. Brengel, President, Johnson Controls, Inc., P.O. Box 423, Milwaukee, Wisconsin 53201.

JOHNSON CONTROLS

Prime source of problem-solving systems.

JC75P9

Reprinted with permission from Johnson Controls, Inc.

Figure 52-5.

How to Keep Your Building from Being Branded a Firetrap.

A report to executives from Johnson Controls.

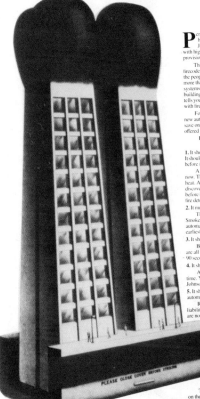

Per capita fire losses in the U.S. are the highest in the world, 5 times greater than Japan. This grim fact, and the fear associated with high-rise fires, has spawned a rash of firecode provisions that are bewildering building executives.

This report on the state of our fast-changing firecodes has been prepared by Johnson Controls, the people who have designed and installed more than half the computerized automation systems in U.S. buildings. It tells you what your building's firesafety system *must* do now. It also tells you what your system *should* do to keep pace with firesafety demands in years ahead.

For information on how you can pay for a new automated firesafety system with money you save on building operation, write for the booklet offered below.

13 Things Your Firesafety System *Must* or *Should* Do

1. It should do more than just ring a bell.

It should *anticipate* a fire so the fire can be *stopped* before it starts.

A fire may be lurking in your building right now. There's no smoke, no flame, no appreciable heat. A products-of-combustion detector can discover this impending fire — hours, even *days* before it inevitably breaks out. For the facts on pre-fire detection, call your Johnson Controls office.*

2. It must detect smoke *or* heat *or* flame.

The manual fire alarm box is not enough. Smoke, heat or flame detectors must give the alarm automatically. Fire must be discovered at the earliest, whether there are people on the scene or not.

3. It should give the alarm in less than 5 seconds.

Because fire feeds itself, the first few minutes are all important. Some installations could take 90 seconds to put an alarm through!

4. It should process simultaneous alarms.

Arsonists often set more than one fire at a time. Your alarm system should handle them all. Johnson Controls systems have a U.L. #1 rating.

5. It should call the fire department immediately, automatically!

Recriminations, and possibly, even legal liabilities fall upon building executives when fires are not reported promptly.

6. It should locate the fire precisely, project a plan of the fire floor onto an illuminated screen, and give sequenced instructions for evacuation.

Pinpointing the fire area and clearing it of people are imperative. An evacuation plan is important to protect lives before the fire department arrives.

7. It must direct elevators to ground floor.

To avoid ghastly accidents (elevators stopping on the fire floor), elevators must automatically descend to ground the instant an alarm is sounded.

8. It must permit the fire department to control vital systems.

Firemen must be put in full command of elevators and communications systems with a fire control panel made operative only by a fire department key.

9. It must provide firesafe islands in the building.

Firesafe islands must be accessible from all locations. They can be formed automatically by fire doors that close when the fire alarm goes off. By adroit control of your building's ventilating system, a slight air pressure can be built up in these islands that will keep them free of smoke and poisonous gasses.

10. It must talk to people on every floor.

It takes 1-1/2 hours to evacuate a 30-story building. To save lives, avert panic, and speed orderly evacuation, people must be told where to go, what to do, when, and why. A Johnson Controls firesafety system can achieve this by broadcasting prerecorded or live voice commands. It also allows people to talk back, giving you first-hand intelligence of what's happening.

11. It must exhaust deadly smoke and gasses.

Smoke, gasses and lack of oxygen are responsible for most fire deaths. Call your Johnson Controls office* to find out how your air conditioning system can be controlled to exhaust smoke from the fire area.

12. It should fight fire locally.

A sprinkler system is one of the most effective ways to nip fires in the bud. Trouble is, it's expensive. To meet firecodes in your area, it may be possible to "trade off" sprinklers for other effective forms of fire protection.

13. It must be able to test itself and resist the onslaught of fire.

A modern Johnson Controls system has a self-testing capability that works *silently* and *continuously*, and it automatically bypasses burned areas to safeguard the flow of vital information.

Learn More About Automated Firesafety

These 13 items include some of the latest demands levied on building owners by firecodes. All can be met by the technology of positive, exacting control.

At Johnson Controls our business is control. The automatic control of America's buildings for heating and cooling, ventilating, humidification, security, lighting, communications and clock systems, and firesafety. We've been on top of this business for 90 years. Last year alone we did almost one-quarter of a *billion* dollars worth, from more than 100 Johnson Controls offices in the U.S.

Your local Johnson office is listed in the White Pages under Johnson Controls or Johnson Service Company. If there's anything you'd like to ask us about, just give us a call.

Find out more about how you can meet new regulations with a firesafety system that pays for itself. Send for Johnson Controls new booklet, "Firesafety Systems: an idea book to help you cope with changing codes." Write Fred L. Brengel, President, Johnson Controls, Inc., Reference M-2, Box 423, Milwaukee, Wis. 53201.

JOHNSON CONTROLS Prime source of problem-solving systems.

JC75P10A

Reprinted with permission from Johnson Controls, Inc.

Figure 52-6.

Reprinted with permission from Johnson Controls, Inc.

Figure 52-7.

Reprinted with permission from Johnson Controls, Inc.

Figure 52-8.

Reprinted with permission from Johnson Controls, Inc.

307

Figure 52-9.

PRIME SOURCE OF PROBLEM-SOLVING SYSTEMS

For progressive, cost-conscious building management. Johnson Controls offers the ultimate in total automation—a single-unit console that monitors and controls all building systems, from security to heating, ventilation and cooling, firesafety and sound systems. And it's all managed by a single operator.

This remarkable control center stores thousands of useful bits of information that make effective security control a reality. It retrieves this information and spells out the answer on the console screen in plain English at the push of a button.

Most important, the JC/80 can pay for itself in a few years, and from then on, actually save you money. How? Because of its flexibility. You may initially install the system for security. Later you may wish to add an automated firesafety system, easily done because you already have the basic computer and building wiring. You can also economically add energy management programs. Programs such as these can cut your energy bills up to 40%, and dramatically reduce personnel payrolls. The JC/80 could be the best investment you ever make.

Johnson Controls, Inc.
Milwaukee, Wisconsin 53201

Publication No. 2052

Computer control

Sound and communications

Security

Printed in U.S.A.

SECURITY SYSTEMS

An ideabook to help you protect your building and its occupants

Cover on booklet that backed up media campaign. Reprinted with permission from Johnson Controls, Inc.

QUESTION

Assess the worth of the Johnson Controls campaign, considering such factors as (a) the use of technical copy addressed to top management, (b) the use of unusually long copy, (c) the use of a newspaper such as the *Wall Street Journal* instead of magazines such as *Business Week* or *Fortune*, and (d) the use of an image campaign to make sales.

53

MOBIL OIL (A)

The following advertisement was run in the *New York Times*. Also shown here is the video and audio material for a Mobil television commercial.

Figure 53-1.

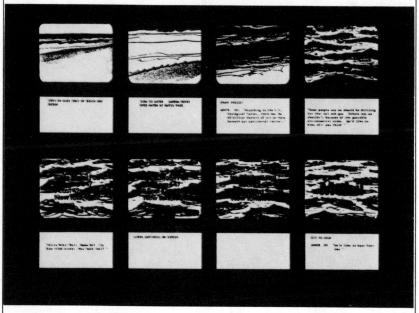

Why do two networks refuse to run this commercial?

CBS:

"We regret that the subject matter of this commercial...deals with a controversial issue of public importance and does not fall within our 'goods and services limitation for commercial acceptance."

ABC:

"This will advise that we have reviewed the above-captioned commercial and are unable to grant an approval for use over our facilities."

NBC:

"Approved as submitted."

As you can see from the storyboard reproduced above, we want to ask the public how it feels about offshore drilling.

But the policies of two national television networks prevent us from asking this question.

This is dangerous, it seems to us. Any restraint on free discussion is dangerous. Any policy that restricts the flow of information or ideas is potentially harmful.

The networks say that the public's need for information is best served in news programs prepared by broadcast journalists.

Behind the networks' rejection of idea advertising may be the fear that demands for equal time will be made. We have a reasonable answer to that. We offer to pay for equal time, when the request is legitimate.

We think *more* discussion, not less, is needed of vital issues such as the issue of America's energy needs. We're willing to buy the time to say what we should be saying. We're willing to buy time so you can hear opposing views.

But two big networks aren't willing to make time available, in this case.

You know the principle at stake here. You've seen it in writing, more than once.

"Congress shall make no law... abridging the freedom of speech."

You've seen it in the First Amendment to the Constitution of the United States. So have we.

We'd like to know what you think about either of these issues. Write Room 647, 150 East 42nd Street, New York, N.Y. 10017.

Mobil®

Reprinted with permission from Mobil Oil Corporation.

Figure 53-2.

Copy and video in television commercial

Video   Audio

1. Open on wide shot of beach
   and ocean.

2. Turn to water. Camera moves
   over water at rapid pace.

3. Frame freezes.   Ann: (VO) According to the

                                     U. S. Geological Survey, there

                                     may be 60 billion barrels of oil

                                     or more beneath our continental

                                     shelves.

4. Scene of open water.   Some people say we should be

                                     drilling for that oil and gas.

                                     Others say we shouldn't because

                                     of the possible environmental

                                     risks. We'd like to know what

                                     you think.

5. Overprint on scene of
   open water.

   Write Mobil Poll
   Room 647
   150 E. 62nd Street
   New York, 10017

6. Super continues on screen.

7. Super continues on screen.

8. Cut to logo: Mobil   Ann: (VO) We'd like to hear

                                     from you.

Reprinted with permission from Mobil Oil Corporation.

QUESTION

If you were head of CBS or ABC, what reasons would you give for refusing to run the commercial that was accepted by NBC?

54

MOBIL OIL (B)

Included in the following material are an advertisement and a news release. Both were written to counteract what the Mobil Oil Corporation felt was an unfavorable and unfair program series presented by Liz Trotta on WNBC-TV (Channel 4), New York City. The series appeared during the period when there was much concern about the possibility of drastic oil shortages, and the concern extended to the present and future high prices for petroleum products.

Figure 54-1 is a half-page newspaper advertisement that ran in the *New York Times,* the *New York Daily News,* and the eastern edition of the *Wall Street Journal.* Figure 54-2 is a news release sent to local media to explain Mobil Oil Corporation's position in the WNBC-TV situation.

Figure 54-1.

What ever happened to fair play?

WNBC-TV's recent series on gasoline prices was inaccurate, unfair, and a disservice to the people.

Like a lot of folks in the New York Channel 4 viewing area, we tuned in the local news show a few days ago to catch Liz Trotta's highly promoted five-part series on the price of gasoline. The show—it was hardly news—left us dismayed, concerned, and angry.

For many years now, we've engaged in a running commentary on how energy news is reported, especially on television. Generally, we've given the media credit for objectively attempting to tell a complicated story, and we've said so publicly on occasion. Sometimes they made mistakes, which we tried to correct. Fair enough.

But what we saw on the Liz Trotta segment of the WNBC-TV Evening News for five nights running really shook our confidence that objectivity is of paramount concern to some journalists. We saw a parade of warmed-over distortions, half-truths, and downright untruths marching across the screen like an army of tired ghosts—ghosts we thought had been laid to rest two years ago. Ghosts that made us wonder whether, in an election year and with various proposals to break up the oil companies rapidly becoming a campaign issue, WNBC-TV hadn't made a conscious decision to actively help those politicians who are busily running against the oil industry.

On a show-by-show basis, let's compare the facts with what Liz Trotta, her script writers, and WNBC-TV sent into your living room.

Monday: *The embargo through a dirty looking glass.*

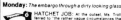

HATCHET JOB: **At the outset, Ms. Trotta referred to "the rather vague circumstances that surrounded the Arab oil embargo back in 1973."**

FACT: There wasn't anything "vague" about the embargo. The Arab nations made a simple, straightforward decision to use oil as a political weapon and they cut off supplies to certain countries, including the U.S. We hope Liz Trotta knew this. If she didn't, her research was shoddy. Apparently she preferred to create an aura of mystery and conspiracy around a straightforward set of circumstances.

HATCHET JOB: **After stock footage of the gasoline lines that followed the embargo, Ms. Trotta asked: "How did we ever get into such a bind?" Her answer: "It all started in October of 1973."**

FACT: Sorry, Ms. Trotta, but it all started well before 1973. On August 7, 1967, for example, Mobil told Interior Secretary Udall, in the context of an oil import program then under discussion, that domestic production would become increasingly important "not only for national security reasons . . . but also as a deterrent against potentially irresponsible price demands on the part of foreign producing governments." On May 11, 1972, in a message in *The New York Times*, Mobil said: "By 1985, Americans will be consuming twice as much energy as they do today, according to government forecasts. . . . The problem is, no one can be sure how the U.S. will be able to get the additional energy needed . . . ."

The oil companies didn't delay the Alaska pipeline, or set the policies that crimped natural gas supply, or prohibit drilling off the East Coast, or decree a moratorium on production off the West Coast. The government did. And all these things happened well before 1973. And the oil companies warned that, taken together, they could prove disastrous.

HATCHET JOB: **One of Ms. Trotta's guests stated that the crisis was a "rip-off," and that the oil companies "taught" the Organization of Petroleum Exporting Countries how to raise their prices.**

FACT: Aside from the fact that no oil company spokesman on the show was asked to rebut this particularly nasty attack, the fact remains that a few years ago, when Mideast oil sold for about \$2.00 a barrel, the oil companies earned about 35 cents on each barrel produced. Today, with Middle East oil selling for over \$11.50 a barrel, industry profits on this oil are averaging just under 20 cents a barrel. Since when is a 15-cent-a-barrel profit reduction a rip-off?

The truth is that OPEC—sovereign nations, not companies—unilaterally raised the price of crude oil.

HATCHET JOB: **"There were reports," said Ms. Trotta, "that tankers loaded with millions of gallons of oil were waiting offshore in New York Harbor." This statement was accompanied by pictures of tankers at sea, leaving the inference that these tankers were among the ones doing the "waiting"—for higher prices, presumably.**

FACT: Of all the embargo-spawned nonsense, the tanker rumor was the most vicious and ridiculous. But it keeps popping up, in spite of the documentation provided by the Coast Guard, the captain of New York Harbor, and William Simon, who was head of the Federal Energy Office at the time. All conducted investigations and stated on the record that tanker traffic was normal for that time of year. WNBC-TV must have been aware that this whole tanker story was false.

HATCHET JOB: **Another of Ms. Trotta's visiting "experts" opined that if the oil industry had produced more gasoline in the first six months of 1972, the embargo could have been avoided.**

FACT: The truth is, there is absolutely no correlation between gasoline production in early 1972 and events a year and a half later. As we've already pointed out, made-in-Washington energy decisions *really* made the embargo as effective as it was.

If the Alaska pipeline had been built on schedule, it would have been moving 1.2 million barrels of oil a day into the American market during the embargo. If we had been allowed to develop the Santa Barbara leases, and if there hadn't been a virtual moratorium on offshore leasing for about two years, U.S. production could have been higher by about 400,000 barrels a day. If nuclear power plants had been built, and if coal hadn't been restrained as a fuel for power plants, there would have been a saving of 700,000 barrels a day of liquid fuels used to generate electricity. These factors, when coupled with the auto emission control devices that increased gasoline consumption by about 300,000 barrels a day, added up to about the number of barrels this country was short during the embargo.

Tuesday: *Confusing the past with the present.*

In her "opening monologue," Ms. Trotta rightly pointed out that a dealer's price reflects his rent, his federal taxes, his local taxes. These factors were never mentioned again, as she went into a pitch about the oil industry's "generous tax benefits and tremendous government influence, not only in Washington but in most capitals of the world."

FACT: The show kept harking back to 1911, and the days of John D. Rockefeller. Even when Ms. Trotta purported to be reporting in the present tense, she came on like ancient history. How can one reconcile "generous tax benefits" with major oil companies' loss of the depletion allowance—still permitted *other* extractive industries? Or with the cutback in foreign tax credits—again, only for oil companies? Moreover, the oil industry is the only one in the nation still under the price controls initiated back in 1971—another fact Ms. Trotta never mentioned. And where's the vaunted political clout of an industry that's had its prices rolled back, is fighting divestiture at home, and watching its properties become nationalized overseas?

HATCHET JOB: **In the same rapid-fire monologue, Ms. Trotta listed the profits earned by Mobil and other companies in the last quarter of 1975.**

FACT: Ms. Trotta didn't even attempt to explain what those numbers represented, either as a rate of return on invested capital, or as a return on the shareholders' investment. She simply implied they were too high. (In Mobil's case, profits represent 1.5 cents on every gallon of petroleum sold in our worldwide operations.) Reciting numbers alone, we submit, is an exercise in deliberate distortion unless they're put into context. She didn't mention that in 1975, the aggregate earnings of 25 leading oil companies fell 23.6 percent from 1974 levels.

HATCHET JOB: **Ms. Trotta said that the seven largest oil companies produce "39.8 percent of all domestic crude oil. They account for 44 percent of the oil refined domestically, and they market 44.8 percent of all gasoline sold in this country. Critics say the consumer pays for all that concentration . . . ."**

FACT: All what concentration, Ms. Trotta? You counted up to seven, and you still didn't reach 50 percent of any single market. Last time we looked, there were only *three* major television networks, and they controlled about 75 percent of their market. However, we would be the first to admit that the television viewer would be worse off if every local station had to produce its own TV shows.

The truth is, there are more than 8,000 companies engaged in oil production, some 130 in refining, and about 15,000 in wholesale marketing.

HATCHET JOB: **Ms. Trotta asked several motorists why gasoline prices varied from place to place. While most of those shown said they didn't know, one asked her if *she* did.**

FACT: Point is, Ms. Trotta *does* know. She herself had cited the big reasons for differing prices when she opened the show: different tax structures in different communities, different rents, and different competitive situations. And, in some cases, distances from a refinery. But Ms. Trotta chose to treat the subject like a deep, wicked conspiracy.

HATCHET JOB: **Asked Ms. Trotta: "If there's a surplus of oil, then why hasn't the price of gasoline gone down?"**

FACT: It has, by about two cents a gallon in recent months. This reflects competition in the marketplace, plus the rollback of the average price of domestic crude, and the disappearance of the \$2 import duty. Besides, gasoline is selling today at below government-set ceiling prices because of competitive conditions in the marketplace.

Interestingly enough, in reeling off the prices, she cited an "independent" as being the lowest of all. Weren't they the fellows the "majors" were driving out of business? If so, how come the independents have substantially *increased* their share of the market over the last eight years, largely at the expense of the majors? And why didn't Ms. Trotta point out that fact? Besides, under federal law, it's impossible to unilaterally stop supplying any independent.

Of course, no discussion of pricing can overlook, as Ms. Trotta did, the fact that almost 40 percent of America's oil comes from foreign sources, at prices set by foreign governments.

HATCHET JOB: **Said Ms. Trotta: "The objective, then, is to sell as much gasoline as possible to keep the high-profit refining operation going."**

FACT: What high profit? Mobil's U.S. refining and marketing operations actually *lost* money in 1974 and only began to break even in 1975.

Wednesday: *Two sides to every story?*

HATCHET JOB: **In this segment, Ms. Trotta attempted to show that the big companies are pushing their dealers around—she calls the gasoline dealer "a small businessman under siege." After talking to two of them, including a Mobil dealer, she concludes that one hears "the same sorry complaints throughout the metropolitan area. Dealers aren't making it. The major oil companies . . . simply won't allow them to make a decent profit. The dealers say they are caught in a vise controlled by the oil companies."**

FACT: There are thousands of dealers in the Channel 4 viewing area. Certainly, some of them must be making a decent living. But there's no way to find out from Liz Trotta's show. She talked to a few dealers with gripes, and from her tiny sampling—apparently hand-fed to her by various dealer "spokesmen"—she came up with a sweeping generalization. Why didn't she interview some of the dealers who are satisfied with their company arrangements? If she can't find any, we can and will.

According to Platt's Pricing Service, the average dealer mark-up in New York City in February 1976 was 12.2 cents a gallon. In March of 1973, it had been 9.8 cents a gallon.

HATCHET JOB: **Ms. Trotta said that a Mobil dealer claimed he was promised \$25,000 to sell Mobil gasoline but the company never came up with the money or signed the contract.**

FACT: Mobil never made such an offer. The money in question was the amount the dealer said competing companies offered him to join them in 1973. (How's that for competition, Ms. Trotta?) In any event, Mobil specifically told him that we had no intention of meeting these offers and that he was free to accept them. The dealer didn't. Moreover, in 1975 he accepted a new Mobil contract, and just recently, that contract was renewed.

Thursday: *More of the same.*

HATCHET JOB: **This one is a beauty, because it involves TV production technique, rather than words alone. Says a dealer: "The only difference between them [oil companies] and the hoodlums in the street is that they don't get caught. They're too big." Then the camera flashes back to an oil company executive, obviously in the midst of a pre-recorded interview, and the first words allowed to come out of his mouth are: "It is true, we're not willing to subsidize an economic loss at a marginal station . . . ."**

FACT: The implication is clear. The oil man is made to appear in agreement with the line about "hoodlums." Frankly, nothing in the show made us as angry as that cheap distortion, because it was so patently contrived.

Friday: *Beating the drum for divestiture.*

HATCHET JOB: **At the start of her grand finale, Ms. Trotta said "reformers are trying to pass laws that would break up the big oil companies into smaller units in hopes of making them more competitive and more responsive to consumers."**

FACT: Sure, they're trying to break up oil companies but to call it "reform" is pure bias. What gives her the idea it would in any way help the consumer to break America's large oil companies into small firms limited to exploration and production, *or* transportation, *or* refining, *or* marketing?

The consumer would end up paying more, not less. Suppose, for example, our refineries had to stand alone, as a separate company. Does Liz Trotta really believe that whoever operates them would be content to lose money, or just break even? Obviously, any such operator would have to raise prices.

Happily, not all TV stations subscribe to this view. KNXT-TV, for example, a CBS-owned station in Los Angeles, had this to say in an editorial—which was labeled as such, by the way: "Several of the biggest campaigners have decided to take on the oil companies and preach the gospel that the companies are monopolistic and ought to be broken up. If they're sincere, they're misguided. . . . The complaint about monopoly is a joke. You can't find much more intense competition anywhere than when the oil companies bid for leases or bid for retail dollars. The customer benefits. The biggest oil company has less than 10% of the market."

HATCHET JOB: **"The decision on divestiture," Ms. Trotta intones, "will be made in Washington. But legislators find it difficult to obtain information, especially since most of it comes from the oil companies themselves." As "proof", the camera showed a hearing conducted by Senator Jackson, in which he roasted an oil company executive who couldn't recite his company's per-share dividends in 1972 and 1973.**

FACT: First, that particular hearing had nothing to do with divestiture. Second, it took place in early 1974 as an outgrowth of the embargo-induced gasoline shortage. Third, many thoughtful people (including some Senators) felt Senator Jackson's inquisitorial grandstanding deplorable, and said so. Fourth, the figures the Senator requested were easily available public information. Moreover, Ms. Trotta didn't see fit to mention the recent hearings held precisely on the divestiture proposals. Mobil's president was just one of many who testified, on all aspects of the issue. But their reasoned words weren't as dramatic, apparently, as Jackson's ancient and unrelated diatribe.

HATCHET JOB: **Said Ms. Trotta: "To several Senate and House committees, the idea of vertical integration has all the earmarks of a conspiracy to monopolize the industry."**

FACT: Never, to our knowledge, has any Senate or House committee stated or claimed what Ms. Trotta alleges. Now, would you believe this: we made several requests to WNBC-TV for documentation as to which committee-adopted reports this charge was supposed to have come from, and we were told by a station spokesperson that it is "official NBC policy *not* to provide any documentation on news items."

HATCHET JOB: **Much of this final segment presented in a most laudatory light a spokesman for a self-styled public interest group, which favors divestiture. Said Ms. Trotta of the group, whose spokesman in a recent Congressional hearing was movie actor Paul Newman: "This is a new and energetic group of young lobbyists, who are determined to take on the powerful oil lobby."**

FACT: Does youthful energy make the difference between a "good" lobbyist and an "evil" one? Come on, Ms. Trotta. Everybody has the right to present his views in Washington, oil companies as well as movie stars. But do Americans *really* want energy policy made in Hollywood?

In fairness to WNBC-TV, we will say that they asked to interview a Mobil spokesman for the Trotta series. In fairness to ourselves, we didn't participate. Experience has shown us how what we say on prerecorded TV, as contrasted to live, is edited out or watered down. And the treatment accorded to the oil people who *did* appear makes us doubly glad we weren't there. We didn't want to be the ones to appear to "agree" we're hoodlums.

We've written to WNBC-TV about our objections to the Liz Trotta energy series, and we've offered to buy 30 minutes of air time in which to present our side of the story, without any editing. So far, we haven't had any reply. Based on the record, we aren't holding our breath.

What official sources have said about us.

In Liz Trotta's words, "some critics" saw "the look of conspiracy" in the companies' dealings with Arab oil-producing nations.

Well, the oil industry's conduct during the Arab embargo has been looked at microscopically by experts, and in our view, it's Liz Trotta who has tunnel vision. Here's what some official sources had to say after examining our business:

- **From a January 2, 1975, report of the Senate Foreign Relations Subcommittee on Multinational Corporations: "While the Arabs provided explicit instructions on the allocation of their production, the consuming nations provided no coordinated guidance . . . Essentially, U.S. companies decided that 'the pain should be evenly spread' to all major consuming regions . . . During the embargo, the international oil companies acted as a buffer between producer and consumer nations."**
- **From a January 27, 1975, report of the Federal Energy Administration: "U.S. companies helped to blunt the edge of the Arab oil weapon by redistributing global supplies so that the constriction of supplies was fairly evenly allocated."**
- **From a report by independent consultants to the FEA: "Although the Arab production cutbacks were eventually increased to 25%, the impact of the embargo was ameliorated by increased production in non-Arab countries and by the skillful and evenly balanced distribution of available supplies by the major petroleum companies."**
- **From a special report of the Commission of the European Communities (The Common Market): "Thanks to the oil companies, neither Denmark nor Holland suffered any serious supply shortage."**

Mobil

Figure 54-2.

FROM: Ken Peterson
(212) 883-3232

Mobil news release

FOR IMMEDIATE RELEASE

MOBIL OIL CORPORATION
150 EAST 42ND STREET
NEW YORK, NEW YORK 10017
TELEPHONE (212) 883-3232

WNBC-TV OFFER TO AIR SHORT MOBIL STATEMENT
TERMED IRRESPONSIBLE FORMAT FOR RESPONSE

NEW YORK, MARCH 9 -- Mobil Oil Corporation today characterized as "irresponsible" the format of a television interview proposed by WNBC-TV to enable the company to respond to a series of television shows on the oil industry. The series, which ran Feb. 23-27, consisted largely of interviews conducted by WNBC-TV reporter Liz Trotta.

Mobil's initial reaction to the WNBC-TV series was a letter submitted March 1, requesting the purchase of one-half hour of time on the New York station in order to "present additional information which we feel is pertinent to the many issues raised by Ms. Trotta." Though that request was rejected yesterday, Mobil renewed it today.

Mobil said the WNBC-TV offer, embodied in a telegram from the station's news director, asked for a company spokesperson to make a short statement and then respond to a series of questions posed by Ms. Trotta.

The oil company branded the format of the WNBC-TV offer as "patently unfair because it would be impossible for Mobil to compress its response into a short statement of a few minutes in reply to five nights of one-sided editorializing totaling some 36 minutes."

In addition, the company had placed full-page advertisements in the New York Times, New York Daily News and Wall Street Journal which corrected, point-by-point, the inaccuracies made on the WNBC-TV series.

Following are the texts of the WNBC-TV wire to Mobil and the oil company's response:

(TELEGRAM FROM WNBC-TV DIRECTOR, TELEVISION NEWS)

"Once again, Newscenter 4 offers Mobil Oil via its authorized spokesperson to appear live on our news broadcast to make known its views concerning the questions of gasoline prices, marketing or gas station ownership. Since you fear editing of your statements, I am offering to allow you to make a short statement followed by questions by Ms. Trotta. Please let me know when you can have a spokesperson available."

(THE MOBIL REPLY)

"This is in reply to your offer to have a Mobil spokesperson appear on WNBC-TV News to make a short statement and respond to questions posed by Ms. Trotta. The format you propose in no way provides Mobil with a reasonable opportunity to respond adequately to the many inaccuracies contained in Liz Trotta's series on the oil industry.

"First, the format you offer is patently unfair because it would be impossible for Mobil to compress its response into a short statement of a few minutes in reply to five nights of one-sided editorializing totaling some 36 minutes.

"Second, the format you offer is irresponsible because it exacerbates the unfairness of the original show, in which WNBC-TV News and Ms. Trotta used their full control over the structure of the show to present a biased report on the complex issues involved. Mobil does not believe it can redress this unfair presentation with WNBC-TV News controlling the agenda of the questions posed by Ms. Trotta.

"Third, the issues related to oil policy are far too important to the future of the United States and too complex to be handled adequately in an unresearched, off-the-cuff, question and answer format. Especially in light of the unfairness of the Trotta series, these issues require fair and balanced analysis in depth.

"Mobil believes that after WNBC-TV's one-sided presentation of these issues, we are entitled to a fair and sufficient amount of time to redress the balance for your viewers. As we pointed out in our Op-Ed message in the March 5 New York Times, 'We recognize that the structure of TV and radio news and documentaries is not satisfactory for handling complex material or long stories. But this is no justification for failing to provide suitable access for correction of errors caused by this structure.'

"It is for these reasons that we delivered to WNBC-TV on Monday, March 1 Mobil's request to be allowed to purchase 30 minutes of time, during which we would present additional information on the energy issues raised by Ms. Trotta with no editing. As you are aware, your management rejected this request yesterday. We are, however, renewing our request for unedited time today in a separate letter to your station manager, based on the reasons listed above. We stand ready to have our program available for airing within two weeks."

Reprinted with permission from Mobil Oil Corporation.

QUESTIONS

1. Comment on the relative effectiveness (in your opinion) of the Mobil Oil advertisement and the Mobil Oil news release, both of which concerned Ms. Trotta's series over WNBC-TV on gasoline prices.
2. What do you think about the merit, or nonmerit, of the fairness issue brought up by Mobil Oil in both the advertisement and the news release?

PART VII
CLIENT-AGENCY
RELATIONS

Advertising is a very personal business. Nowhere does the personal character of the business become more apparent than in the relationship between a client company and its advertising agency. On the client side, one person is usually entrusted with the major portion of the responsibility for directing the work of the advertising agency. This person may be a product manager, a brand manager, an advertising manager, a sales manager, or may have another title.

Whatever the title, the functions are about the same. This person will help the advertising agency in the planning of the media schedule, will work out the budget with or without agency help, will keep the agency informed of marketing and sales objectives, will convey agency ideas and reactions to company management. Probably the most important function of the client contact is to work with the agency in establishing a creative rationale for the advertisements and then to supply opinions, advice, and encouragement in the carrying out of creative assignments.

The client contact may be one of several types.

Passive—In this case, there is little help given. There is no fighting for the agency cause with top management, but neither is there any positive direction that will let the agency know just what is wanted.

Negative—This person fights the agency, almost as if they were viewed as the enemy. Without giving helpful suggestions, the client contact turns down almost all work submitted, or makes drastic, unreasonable changes. The agency is given little time to do its creative work and the result is despair throughout the agency, especially in the creative departments—art and copy.

Positive—A client contact of this type works as a team member with the advertising agency. He lets the agency know what is wanted in its creative approach and then lets the agency work freely within the guidelines suggested. If creative work is not suitable, the client tells the agency exactly why it is unsuitable and makes intelligent suggestions for its improvement. Also, such a client contact has the ear of top management and, once convinced that the agency's work is good, will work hard to sell top management on the worth of that work.

Unfortunately, in the following two cases we have persons who fall in the "negative" class. One exhibits the negative qualities even in the trial period before the agency is engaged—a clear warning to the agency of trying days ahead should the prospect become an actual client.

In the second case—the Matson Trust Company—you will find a classic example of how not to work with an advertising agency. The client's contact person in this instance had no sense for human relations, nor any idea of the inner workings of an advertising agency. Such a person can quickly demoralize an advertising agency. If the agency is very large and the account does not represent a major portion of its business, it will resign the account rather quickly if it is found that the relations are too difficult and the profit picture poor. But if the agency is smaller and the account's billing amounts to a sizable portion of the agency's total revenue, then the resigning of the account is done with great reluctance. Before an agency resigns an account under such circumstances, usually every means of avoiding this action has been taken.

Although there are many personal conflicts in agency-client relationships and many account changes stem back to such conflicts, the preponderance of agency-client relationships are harmonious. Most clients are more enlightened than the ones described in these two cases. Usually agency account executives and other agency personnel are eager to please and will go to great lengths to satisfy a client. If the client will meet them halfway, the relationship can be one of the most satisfactory in the business world. On the contrary, there is no more miserable relationship if the client is determined to make the agency sweat for each dollar it earns and if the client is insensitive and unreasonably demanding and uncommunicative.

If we were to sum up the lessons of these two cases, they would be:
1) Tell the agency clearly what is wanted.
2) Tell the agency clearly what is wrong when work is unsatisfactory, and provide guidance to help the agency achieve the desired results.
3) Have enough knowledge of agency operations to know when requests are realistic or unreasonable.

55

TRU-COPY, INC.

Chartwell Associates, a small advertising agency in a Massachusetts city of 100,000, made considerable use of photocopying machines. After trying different models on a lease basis and having considerable trouble with breakdowns and, subsequently, in getting quick, efficient repair service, the agency finally bought a machine.

This machine, a $5,000 model called the Superba, was distributed by Tru-Copy, Inc., a small firm on the other side of the city from the agency. Unlike other models used by the agency, the Superba did not require the use of special (and expensive) paper. Ordinary bond paper could be used with no lessening of reproduction quality. Agency workers, in fact, agreed that the Superba provided the clearest, sharpest reproductions of any of the numerous machines that had been used by the agency.

Along with excellent reproduction and the use of bond paper, the Superba had a number of other advantages. It seemed to be comparatively trouble-free. Unlike most competitive models it was quiet. Jamming of paper was impossible, a welcome change from some of the competitive models that had jammed frequently. The machine could take several different paper sizes, which could be placed vertically or horizontally, thus offering a useful versatility. Paper trays could be taken out and replaced easily by the least mechanical persons on the agency staff. Lastly, the machine printed rapidly up to 250 copies at one loading.

Because of the substantial sum required for the purchase of the machine, William Wamplur, president of the agency, engaged in several discussions with Stinsen Mellor, sales manager of Tru-Copy, Inc.

Wamplur, impressed by the quality of the Superba, was pleased to learn Tru-Copy had not hired an advertising agency to take care of its admittedly small advertising program.

Despite Mellor's frankness in saying (1) that only a small amount of money would be available for promotional purposes and (2) that he and the president of Tru-Copy, Inc., were skeptical about the ability of advertising agencies to do a good job for them, Wamplur decided to make a pitch for the account. With some reluctance, Mellor agreed. Since it was then December 15, it was decided that the meeting would take place January 2, in the offices of Tru-Copy, Inc.

THE JANUARY 2 MEETING

The meeting, purely exploratory in character, occurred as scheduled. The discussion was reflected in the call report distributed to agency personnel following the meeting. This report was the result of notes taken by Wamplur. Customarily, agency call reports were distributed to clients as well as appropriate agency personnel, but at this stage of the relationship with Tru-Copy, it was considered unsuitable to distribute the report to them.

Informal discussion at the agency found opinions divided. Everyone agreed that the Superba was an outstanding copier and that any machine with all its advantages represented a potential market. On the contrary, the copier field was intensely competitive. It was, of course, dominated by Xerox and International Business Machines. In addition, many other companies were scrambling for the business not acquired by the two giants.

Some pessimism was expressed concerning achieving any success for Tru-Copy, Inc. First of all, the company was so small that the agency was required to think very small in any spending plans. Second, Tru-Copy, Inc., was merely a regional distributor. Thus, account growth was necessarily limited. Third, the agency personnel using the Superba were somewhat concerned about Tru-Copy's service policies. Despite the company's enthusiastic description of the service they rendered, it had been difficult to get a service man to call. Mary Grant recalled that in one of her conversations with Mellor he had admitted, when pressed, that "sometimes" company representatives tended to oversell the company's service capacity. For a small company competing with the giants, it was felt that good service might be a strong point of difference for Tru-Copy. Fourth, and probably most discouraging, was the negative feeling about advertising and advertising agencies expressed by Mellor, the company's sales manager. Despite such reservations, it was agreed that the January 2 exploratory meeting was worth the time it had taken.

CALL REPORT

Date: Friday, 2:30 p.m., Jan. 2

Location of meeting:	Offices of Tru-Copy, Inc.
	835 Almont Plaza
	City
Client:	Tru-Copy, Inc.
Present for client:	Neale Havirfurd, president and general manager
	Stinsen Mellor, sales manager
Present for agency:	Sidney Chartwell, chairman
	Bill Wamplur, president
	Carol Traister, creative director
	Mary Grant, account executive
	Paul Burnes, art director
Subject of meeting:	A discussion to learn more about the company's marketing situation. To offer some possible promotion plans. To examine their product lines.

Comments:

The next meeting is set for 2:30 p.m., Tuesday, Feb. 2, at the agency offices.

At this meeting we need:

(1) Budget proposal showing estimated costs for the types of promotions we propose.
(2) Graphics style for use on letterheads, envelopes, machine name plates, and perhaps newspaper advertisement sig or logo.
(3) Telephone yellow pages ad.

Copier lines

The copier lines handled by Tru-Copy, Inc., are:

- Superba
- Excell-O

Sales points and problems

Superba is the fastest growing bond copier.

Superba gives the best reproduction results—perhaps followed by Excell-O for quality.

Superba and Excell-O cost less than IBM and Xerox (especially on a rental or lease purchase arrangement).

Tru-Copy, Inc., has a broader range of copiers than IBM, and more names and variety of machines than does Xerox.

Tru-Copy, Inc., is the only firm in the area with the knowledge and facilities to recondition machines.

Minuses

One of the biggest problems is finding people who are interested in copy machine purchase at the moment.

Tru-Copy, Inc., as a company name is not known well.

Superba and Excell-O machines are not known well.

When representatives of Tru-Copy, Inc., make cold calls they must have some means of surmounting the handicap of the well-known reputations of Xerox and IBM.

Promotions

1) Ad needed for local telephone book yellow pages. Closing date: Feb. 14.

   Suggestion that ads be considered in outlying directories in three nearby cities when they become due.

2) Photocopy Machine Show to be held in this area to demonstrate new machines. Might generate leads and names of those who might have used Tru-Copy, Inc., machines and speak favorably of them.

   A mailing is being sent to list of 3,500. Attendance at booth usually between 50 and 100. All these should be covered.

3) Direct mail has been used on some occasions in past. One of our suggestions: To use a smaller list with follow-up.

4) Discussed benefits of ads in newspaper business pages and in business publications, as well as radio in drive time. Excell-O Company has an advertising fund available and will go co-op on proof of advertising placed.

5) Excell-O cameras available at reasonable prices for promotion giveaways.

THE FEBRUARY 2 MEETING

No one at the advertising agency had grandiose ideas about the amount Tru-Copy would be willing to spend on advertising. Thus, after much figuring, consisting of more cutting and trimming than adding, a budget proposal was evolved. The total, considered a minimum, was approximately $15,000 for the forthcoming year. It broke down as follows:

$ 6,000	in business sections of newspapers in the region
3,000	in radio, early morning and afternoon drive-time
2,000	in yellow pages in several cities
2,000	in local business magazines published in the city in which Tru-Copy was located, plus business magazines published in other metropolitan areas they served
1,820	production costs, representing 14% of the media costs
$14,820	total advertising budget proposed by Chartwell Associates

The company quickly rejected the budget, declaring that "You're not even close." Yet, in preliminary discussions a figure of $15,000 had been termed a possibility.

When asked "What figure can you live with?" Mellor, the Tru-Copy sales manager, and Neale Havirfurd, president and general manager, excused themselves and left the room to consult with their book-keeper. Upon returning, Havirfurd said, "Five thousand is the very most we're willing to go and we're stretching like hell to spend *that* much."

Mary Grant, speaking for the agency, replied, "Cutting back to $5,000 will require total re-thinking of the approach we had in mind. Point one, this means that the ads necessarily are going to be small and they'll be run infrequently—and that's assuming that we'll use nothing but newspapers." She added that if additional media were used, advertising impact would be even less because the advertising money would be spread so thin.

Breaking in at this point, Wamplur of the advertising agency explained that agency commissions on a $5,000 expenditure—or even on $15,000—would be insufficient to warrant taking on the account. He suggested, therefore, that the agency rebate all media commissions to the client. Agency compensation would, therefore, be derived from a monthly retainer fee, plus a markup of 17.65% on production and other outside costs.

Discussion of the budget was terminated at this point with Wamplur saying that the agency would study the situation and make a new recommendation. Following this statement, the agency presented some graphic material and a small yellow-pages display advertisement. The former was approved; the advertisement was rejected as "simply not suitable."

Then, as a surprise, Mary Grant, the agency's account executive, presented four newspaper advertisements which, she explained "will show you the direction the agency feels Tru-Copy should go."

A few minutes' silent perusal of the advertisements displayed on the corkboard wall resulted in a grunted comment from Mellor, the Tru-Copy sales manager: "You haven't hit it. We want more oomph." When asked what could be done to improve the advertisements, Mellor answered, "I just don't like them. You'll have to take it from there. *You're* the experts."

Another meeting was set up for February 9 at the company offices. New newspaper advertisements were to be presented. Mellor and Mary Grant were to attend.

THE FEBRUARY 9 MEETING

Once more, Mellor said no to all six newspaper advertisements that were shown. These were in 3-column x 8-inch size. All utilized line drawings to hold down production cost. Copy was forceful and offered several approaches.

Mary Grant persisted in her efforts to learn what Mellor did not like about the creative approaches until finally Mellor said in effect that—

1) he'd like something that resembled the Avis approach (the "we try harder" theme);
2) he'd like more hard-sell;
3) he did not want an offer of a demonstration such as two of the advertisements had used.

When Mary Grant returned to the advertising agency with her discouraging news, the creative people questioned whether the account was worth pursuing. As one copywriter said, "This outfit looks like bad news to me. If they're this much trouble before they're clients, what are they going to be like when we're their official agency?" To the creative group, the small budget, the hard-to-please attitude, and Tru-Copy's skepticism about advertising seemed to raise too many obstacles.

Although admitting the negatives, Wamplur, the agency president, said: "Look, there's a lot in what you say. But, still, this product is a knockout and the best way to advertising success is to present a product that has a jump on the market. My feeling is that the product makes it worth a certain amount of speculative investment of agency time and money. I smell a great growth possibility in this product and if the account grows, so will we. I know it's been hard to take so far but let's take another whack at coming up with something they'll buy."

Thus, despite grumbling from the creative staff, layouts and copy were once more prepared for the forthcoming February 16 meeting at the agency offices. This would be attended by Havirfurd and Mellor from Tru-Copy and agency personnel concerned with the account to this point.

THE FEBRUARY 16 MEETING

Once more, six layouts were put up on the wall for everyone to examine. To save art time, these were just a shade better than rough-rough layouts, but they conveyed the message very well. After a quick glance at the layouts and accompanying copy, Tru-Copy's president, Havirfurd, exclaimed, "You're wasting our time. We've had four meetings now and you haven't begun to get the idea."

As in previous meetings, no constructive criticism was offered to amplify the statement "I just don't like them." When pressed, however, Havirfurd and Mellor said that demonstrations weren't mentioned in the advertisements.

Mary Grant rejoined with some vigor that Mellor had objected to the advertisements shown in the February 9 meeting because two of them had contained demonstration offers. Mellor countered with "You must have misunderstood me, Mary. It was the way those ads *made* the demonstration offer that I didn't like."

Both men, once again, said they wanted more hard sell. Carol Traister, the agency creative director, said in a strained voice, "But there *is* hard sell in every one of these ads. Let me ask you directly: What can we *possibly* do to make the approach more hard sell than it is right now?"

After a few moments of silence Havirfurd replied, "Look, we're not advertising men. We expect you to tell *us* what to do, not the other way around."

Because it was obvious that an impasse had been reached in the discussion of the proper creative approach, Mary Grant shifted the discussion to the budget. She said, "Although we feel strongly that

$5,000 is not enough to do the job we'd like to see done, we're willing to work with this on a trial basis. However, this doesn't give us sufficient for a variety of media. We suggest, therefore, that most of the money should be used for small-space newspaper ads and the rest for yellow-pages advertising."

Havirfurd agreed that this use of the budget seemed logical but then added, to the dismay of the agency representatives, "I figure that the first ad should be the tipoff. If this brings in sales and creates a lot of interest, then maybe advertising's an answer for us. If it doesn't, then maybe we'd better stay with straight selling, backed by direct mail."

Repeating what he had said in the first meeting, Havirfurd said that 80 percent of the demonstrations made by him and Mellor resulted in sales. "Now," he said, "if advertising can approach that kind of performance, I'll go along more willingly on a bigger budget."

To this, Mary Grant replied, "I'll be very much surprised if any first ad, no matter how good, will result in a flood of orders. These initial ads will be doing their job if they create enough interest to cause prospects to ask for further information."

Breaking in at this point, Mellor asked agency opinion about a promotional idea he said he'd been considering. "My idea," he explained, "is to give as an extra buying incentive a first-rate camera to anyone who buys an Ex-Cello. As you know, the Ex-Cello company makes a camera, a darned good one. That's the one we'd give. Naturally, our costs on the cameras can be low enough so that we won't cut too deeply into the profits on each sale."

This proposal started a general discussion. Agency opinion was negative. Tru-Copy, it was felt, would not put its products in the Xerox or IBM prestige class by using such a forcing device. In fact, the opposite impression would be created. "Furthermore," Mary Grant argued, "the money represented by these gifts will, in the long run, be better spent on advertising."

Finally, Havirfurd stood up and said, "Although you people have struck out so far we're willing to have you make one more pass at us, but this time you'd better have some ad ideas we can buy."

The next morning the agency creative, account, and management personnel gathered to discuss the Tru-Copy account.

QUESTION

What decision should the agency make? Explain your reasoning carefully.

56

MATSON TRUST COMPANY (PEOPLES BANK)

For ten years the L. M. Plinth Advertising Agency of Hanland, Massachusetts, had handled the account of the Stapleton Bank & Trust Company, Stapleton, Massachusetts. During this period, the bank had seen a steady rise in its business. The number of checking accounts had increased each year, as well as the number of loans negotiated. Likewise, savings account deposits showed steady gains even though competing savings banks offered higher interest rates.

One unusual aspect of the client-agency relationship was the confidence placed in the agency by Frederic N. Belsue, president of the Stapleton Bank & Trust Company. Belsue, a financial man, supervised the advertising but left major decisions to the advertising agency in such matters as creative direction, media usage, and budget. In the ten years that the Plinth Advertising Agency acted in behalf of the bank, Belsue had achieved a close personal relationship with L. M. Plinth, chairman of the agency.

Such was the confidence placed in Plinth's judgment that it was almost unheard of for the bank to turn down a proposal of the agency's. On its part, the agency provided much extra service and continually suggested marketing and creative ideas to the client. There was, in short, the happiest of associations between the agency and the client. Plinth often remarked to his staff that Belsue was the "ideal" client and that if all clients would have the same approach, the advertising agency business would not be the nerve-wracking occupation it so often was.

Although Plinth had turned over various accounts he was handling to agency account executives, he continued to act as the account executive for the Stapleton account. Accordingly, on one of his trips to Stapleton, he was informed by Belsue that the Stapleton Bank & Trust

Company had been approached by the Matson Trust Company, of Linch, Massachusetts, with a proposal that the banks merge. Located about 40 miles from Hanland, the Matson Trust Company had about twice the assets of Stapleton Bank & Trust Company. Once a somewhat conservative institution, Matson Trust had recently acquired a dynamic, 42-year-old president who had been a vice-president of a large bank in Hartford, Connecticut.

This president, Raymond R. Hansun, Jr., in talking to Frederic Belsue of the advantages of the merger, stressed the expanded services made possible through the joining of the banks. Furthermore, he pointed out, the population in the banking area served by the two institutions was growing rapidly, new shopping centers were being established, and a number of plant openings were scheduled for the section. Lastly, he spoke glowingly of the young, vigorous staff he had assembled at Matson Trust.

In relating his negotiations to Plinth, Frederic Belsue said that he was taking up the merger proposal with his board of directors but that meanwhile the advertising program for Stapleton Bank & Trust Company would continue as usual. A week later Belsue telephoned Plinth to inform him that the board of directors had agreed to the proposal and had approved the suggestion of Matson Trust that an application for the merger be filed with the state banking authorities. Such applications usually were not processed in less than a half year and often took longer to conclude.

Hansun, of Matson, had urged that the advertising and promotion for the combined operation be one of the first matters to be settled during the period when approval of the application was pending. Thus, a meeting was set up attended by Hansun, Belsue, Tim Lantz, Matson marketing director, and Plinth, of the advertising agency.

At the outset it was apparent to Plinth that the easy relationship characterizing his association with the Stapleton Bank & Trust was ending. Belsue, president of that organization, was to be a vice-president of the combined operation but was to have nothing to do with advertising and sales promotion. Responsibility for these activities was to be assigned to Tim Lantz, the 25-year-old marketing director of Matson. Lantz, two years out of a graduate school of business, had been in banking since his graduation. Although he had never been directly in advertising, his marketing assignments in his work in banking had given him some contact with the advertising function.

Plinth discovered quickly in talking to the youthful marketing director that the latter had positive ideas about advertising and that he prided himself on being what he described as "a do-it-now guy." He said, "We're fast-moving around Matson and we expect our agency to be fast with ideas and fast in getting work done." Lantz added that he would be watching bills carefully, especially those for production and creative work.

A small advertising agency in Linch, Massachusetts, had been doing the advertising for Matson. It was considered too small to handle all the advertising and promotion for the merged banks but was to be assigned the radio advertising, a minor element in the advertising plans for the combined operation. The Plinth Advertising Agency was to be assigned all the rest of the advertising and sales promotion activity.

One of the first assignments for the Plinth agency was to provide a name that would be used by the merged banks. The name was to be totally different from that used by either bank and it was not to have any territorial flavor. After many suggestions and much discussion, the name to be used was "Peoples Bank." Until the merger was officially consummated, however, each bank was to operate under its own name, although Matson decided that they would use the new name regardless of the outcome of the merger. The agency, accordingly, was asked to devise a new logotype for printed advertisements, to work up Peoples Bank letterheads and to prepare print and broadcast material employing the name.

Because the Matson Trust executives were eager to give their bank and its advertising a new look, they changed their minds after the new name had been approved and decided to use it immediately in all printed matter whether advertising, correspondence, or bank displays. Stapleton Bank & Trust Company decided, however, to retain their name until such time as the merger was finally official.

A substantial budget was assigned for the new-name introduction and the Plinth organization was told to prepare advertising immediately that would stress the new look and new spirit of what had been the Matson Trust Company. Likewise, the agency was informed that during the initial months of this campaign the bank would expect almost daily service. This was in contrast to the time when L. M. Plinth called once a month upon F. N. Belsue to present advertisements and advertising plans for the Stapleton Bank & Trust Company.

Plinth, burdened by many responsibilities, decided at this point to turn over his contact duties to Art Soares, a young but experienced account executive who was, he knew, acceptable to Belsue. Soares was to spend a major portion of his time servicing Peoples Bank, which meant that he was to be in constant contact with Tim Lantz, the bank's marketing director. There was no need to call upon Belsue since Tim Lantz had been assigned advertising responsibility for Stapleton Bank & Trust as well as Peoples Bank during the period of the merger negotiations, which seemed certain to be effected.

Trouble ensued almost immediately. On the occasions when Tim Lantz visited L. M. Plinth Advertising Agency, he left dismay in his wake. Despite his inexperience with advertising, he displayed an air of overconfidence that amounted to arrogance. He rarely listened to suggestions. As one agency executive said after one of these first meetings, "This man looks like trouble. He knows all the answers and it's obvious that there's going to be just one way to do things for Peoples Bank—*his* way."

Soares found himself losing control of the account in the face of the demands of Tim Lantz. When he demurred at the speed with which the agency was being asked to execute creative assignments, Lantz would reply that the last agency found nothing unusual in being required to provide overnight service. Soares's suggestions about creative directions (based on discussions with the agency creative staff) were rebuffed. Carefully worked-out copy and art approaches were summarily rejected. When Plinth attempted to help Soares, his ideas were brushed aside just as peremptorily as were those of the account executive.

Meanwhile, a morale problem was developing in the copy, art, and production departments. Copy and layout work was done over and over. Almost nothing was accepted. Furthermore, the rejections were not explained. The production department found that all jobs for Peoples Bank were "super-rush," to the point where much night work was being done at the agency. In addition, the production people reported that the production houses with which they did business were soon going to refuse to give the Plinth agency any more rush service. Heretofore, the agency had always been careful not to ask for rush service unless it was really warranted. Thus, the production companies doing business with the agency had usually been glad to cooperate when the agency asked for especially speedy service. After a series of rush jobs for Peoples Bank, the production companies began to remind the agency that they had other clients to serve—that they couldn't handle these "crisis" orders for Peoples Bank without sacrificing the interests of their customers.

It was typical of Lantz to expect copywriters to turn out superior advertisements in two hours and to expect the art department to provide finished layouts in the same time. He seemed honestly nonplussed when informed that good advertising was not to be expected under such conditions.

Another burden for Soares was the difference in managerial philosophy between the agency and the personnel of Peoples Bank. The latter, staffed with young, aggressive types, was systems-oriented, a result of the MBA training of most of the staff. Ambitious marketing plans were outlined, usually explained in business-school jargon. The agency was expected to provide ideas for these plans as well as personnel to carry them out. Plinth viewed most of these ideas as far too grandiose for the size of the banks.

All this extensive planning was accompanied by a flurry of rush orders for advertising in newspapers and television, along with such time-taking creative jobs as service folders and in-bank displays. Most of the advertising was turned down, and Lantz was especially critical of the agency for not devising a "bell-ringing" campaign theme. On their part, the agency personnel felt that many of the campaign ideas turned down by Lantz were excellent and would have brought good results for Peoples Bank.

With Soares and most of the agency staff in a rebellious mood, Lantz announced that he was coming to the agency for an all-day meeting. He asked that representatives of different departments be present at the meeting and that the agency should discard what they had done to that point and should present a fresh new campaign at the meeting.

Once more, the lights were burning at night in the agency, but the creative people and the production department after much back and forth discussion put together a campaign that pleased everyone from Plinth down.

Upon Lantz's arrival, the agency personnel assembled in the agency's conference room. Included were Plinth, the creative director, a copywriter who did much of the work on the new campaign, the art director, the agency president, and Soares, the account executive.

From the start, it was apparent that the meeting was not going to go well. After looking briefly at the print advertisements displayed on the corkboard walls, Lantz pronounced himself dissatisfied. All arguments voiced by agency personnel were knocked down. When reminded that little time was left before the campaign was supposed to break for Peoples Bank, Lantz replied that he was sure that the agency could devise a campaign that would be suitable if it would simply make some modifications in what had been presented.

He was told that the deadlines he was proposing could not be met, an objection that he dismissed. At the end of the meeting, apparently conscious of the tense atmosphere in the conference room, he commended the agency for its efforts and left with the assurance he was looking forward to a long and productive working relationship.

Upon the departure of the marketing director, Plinth reassembled the agency personnel who had been present at the meeting. First, he addressed the art director, a busy man who also supervised print production for the agency. He asked him directly whether he felt that the deadlines proposed by Lantz for the new campaign were "realistic." (Lantz had so described them during the meeting.)

With considerable force the art director said that not only were they not realistic but that he couldn't possibly meet them. He pointed out the unprofitability of an account that demanded so much overtime work, often for material that was not used for days, and even weeks, after it was delivered rush to the client.

Going around the room, Plinth found that everyone was discouraged by the situation and wholly critical of Lantz and the general approach of the personnel at Peoples Bank. After about a half hour of spirited discussion in which various proposals and ultimatums were voiced by the participants, Plinth ended the meeting by pointing out briefly that he would consider what was said but that they must remember that the Peoples Bank account represented a sizable billing to the agency and that a certain amount of suffering could be endured by agency people if the billing was enough to warrant the trials and tribulations imposed by client demands.

When the agency people left Plinth's office, he could hear them discussing the meeting. So far as he could tell, their mood was black and their condemnation of Lantz and the Peoples Bank account was unanimous. After reflecting for a few minutes, he phoned Jon Hulzimir, the creative director, to ask him to see him. When Hulzimir appeared, he came directly to the point:

"Jon," he said to the creative director, "I've decided that because of the way all of you feel about Peoples Bank, there's just one action I can take—to resign the account."

Continuing, he said, "Personally, I've had tough, unreasonable clients before so I'd probably hang on to Peoples Bank despite the grief. What rebellion there is around here is coming from all of you, not from me. I like those dollars we get from the account, but the attitude of everyone in the shop is so negative that I don't see how we can go on like this."

Agreeing that the step seemed necessary, the creative director pointed out how little time had been spent on the work of other agency clients since Peoples Bank had been added. He mentioned the caustic comments he had received from some of these clients whose deadlines had not been met.

Plinth nodded and then spoke quickly as if he had come to an important and final decision:

"Okay. Let's go ahead. Draft up a letter of resignation for my signature to go to Hansun with a blind copy for Soares. Don't be bitter but give them a good idea of why we're resigning. And make it final. In short, I want it clear that we're not prepared to negotiate.

"While you're doing this, I think I'll phone Hansun to tell him that I'm sending such a letter and I owe it to Belsue to let him know I'm doing this, too."

With that, the creative director hurried out of the office to begin work on the letter, which was accepted without change by Plinth about 45 minutes later. This letter and Hansun's reply are reproduced below.

Figure 56-1.

FROM L. M. Plinth Advertising Agency
983 West Gant Avenue, Hanland, Mass. 02367 Phone: 412-2773

ADVERTISING MARKETING DIVISION
October 5

Raymond R. Hansum, Jr., President
Peoples Bank
11 Plaza Center
Linch, Mass. 01529

Dear Ray:

Last Thursday, as I'm sure you're aware, Tim Lantz visited the agency for a long discussion with a number of our key people, including myself.

In that meeting, he rejected a campaign submitted by us recently and gave us some deadlines for future work. A free-wheeling discussion on his part and our part took up a good portion of the time the spent with us.

Following his departure, we held a discussion among ourselves to confirm not only what he said but the implications of what he said. Then, with meeting and the post-meeting discussion in mind, I gave the situation long and serious thought.

The result of this thinking is that I have decided that our agency should resign--effective immediately--the Peoples account.

This decision is based on what we consider to be a basic incompatibility between our agency and your organization. This incompatibility stems from a number of factors.

One of these factors is our widely divergent views on what may be considered acceptable creativity. Without attempting to list specific examples, we may simply say that the bank's view of good copy and art were seldom shared by our creative and management people.

Yet, in the L. M. Plinth Company, you have an agency with deep experience in financial advertising. We have serviced large, medium-sized and small banks with a consistent record of success. Our background in creating effective advertising for bank clients is unquestioned.

Our creative people, on the copy and art sides, have outstanding records not only in financial advertising but also in many other forms of advertising in national, regional, and local areas.

Yet, consistently, we found ourselves faced with arbitrary changes in copy and art, and a series of what we viewed as niggling, nit-picking "improvements...." We discovered that these suggestions were made as a result of exposing the advertising to a number of persons. As Leo Burnett once said, "No committee has ever written an ad."

.......2

Show copy to enough people and changes and changes will be made. Not necessarily good changes but changes, nonetheless, because people asked to criticize become instant experts to the detriment of the creative work they are assessing.

At no time do we object to a client's criticisms if our copy has departed from fact, or from a copy platform that has been agreed upon.

It is our opinion, however, that the client should not make constant changes in its agency's copy style, and modes of creative expression. If it does, agency creativity is stifled. Soon the client gets only that copy which the agency feels will be approved instead of copy the agency knows is right.

The irony, of course, is that a client normally hires the agency chiefly for its creative skill. To negate that skill by becoming an expert in the agency's area of expertise makes no business sense. There should be a mutual respect in the agency-client relationship. The agency should respect the client for his knowledge of his business. The client should respect the agency for certain skills in creative expression.

There is another aspect of the Peoples-Plinth relationship that should be considered here: Deadlines.

Since we have no novices at L. M. Plinth, we are accustomed to meeting deadlines. Because we are more self-sufficient than most agencies, we are considered very nimble by our clients in the speed with which we get work done. By "self-sufficient," I refer to our in-house printing and photographic facilities, our capacity to handle finished art in the shop, along with the setting of display type.

Still, like any organization with a pride in its creative work, we are well aware that constant deadlines and unrelenting pressure do not provide a felicitous climate for creativity. Good work needs some reflection. Ideas need a gestation period. If you want hack writing and hack art, you'll get it if creative deadlines are unrealistic.

When Tim Lantz departed last Thursday leaving behind him a series of impossible deadlines, we were depressed not just because of these deadlines. It was the future outlook that dismayed us. We could see ahead of us an endless vista of such pressure-packed deadlines.

We know very well that the creative work in which we take such pride would suffer.

And there's another more mundane but very important aspect. Our other clients would suffer. By putting an inordinate amount of copy, art, and production time in Peoples jobs, we would be taking away from other accounts who don't deserve to be short-changed.

Furthermore, profitability suffers when the entire resources of an agency are expended in behalf of one account. To this point, the Peoples account has not been profitable and, as we make projections on the basis of current experience, we see no chance that the profit picture will change, except for the worse.

Since we view the resignation of an account as a serious matter, I have tried in this letter to give you some of the thinking that preceded our decision. We have avoided the listing of specific instances that made up the whole in order to avoid any bitterness, or singling out of individuals. We'd like to part as friends.

.......3

Naturally, we'll follow through on work in progress. Too, we'll be glad to turn over appropriate materials to your new agency and to work with you and the new agency in order to effect a smooth transition.

This letter is for the record. In addition, I plan to phone you today to tell you personally of our decision.

Sincerely,

L. M. Plinth
Chairman

LMP:EG
cc: Art Soares

Agency letter explaining why the account is being resigned.

Figure 56-2.

PEOPLES BANK

                                                    Raymond R. Hansun, Jr.
                                                    President

                              October 7

Mr. L. M. Plinth, Chairman
L. M. Plinth Advertising Agency
983 West Gant Avenue
Hanland, Mass. 02367

Dear Lloyd:

Your letter of October 5, which follows on our telephone conversation
of the same date, has been received. I do regret the abrupt termination
of the relationship between your agency and our institution. As I indicated
on the telephone, I had a conversation a few hours earlier with Tim Lantz.
Tim had reported on his visit to your agency and the plans which he felt had
been made for your cooperation and assistance in pursuing our marketing objectives.
Thus it was that I found myself more than a little surprised at the gist of your
communication later the same morning.

Be that as it may, I trust that the decision will be in our mutual best interest.
Perhaps the most important concern right now is to conclude our relationship with
a minimum of confusion. Tim Lantz will be working out with you or with Art Soares
a means of concluding the work on our account which is still in your shop. Naturally
we would hope that our future plans which we have shared with you and your associates
to a considerable degree would be accorded the customary professional confidentiality.

In conclusion I thank you for your candid and direct approach to what appears to
have been a significant difference in working methodology.

                                        Sincerely yours,

                                        Raymond R. Hansun, Jr.
                                        President

RRH/TM
cc: Tim Lantz
     Michael P. Flaris
     Fin. Belsue

PEOPLES BANK   11 Plaza Center, Linch, Mass. 01529   826-1813

Client letter in response to agency letter resigning account.

QUESTIONS

1. What alternatives to resigning the Peoples Bank account might have been utilized by L. M. Plinth?
2. Which of the various factors involved in this situation provided the strongest reason for Plinth's taking the action he did?
3. What is the most important lesson to be learned from this case?

ISBN-0-88244-206